Travel Agency Operations

Travel Agency Operations

A.P. RASTOGI

Director

J.P. Institute of Hotel Management and Catering Technology

Meerut (Uttar Pradesh)

AMAN PUBLICATIONS

NEW DELHI

Published by
Rajiv Jain for Aman Publications
LG-4A, Ganpati Bhawan,
4675-B/21, Ansari Road,
Darya Ganj, Delhi - 110002
PH: 23255012, 23282127
E-mail: sshjbs@yahoo.com

First Published – 2016

ISBN–81–8204–036–1

SOLE DISTRIBUTOR
JINDAL BOOK SERVICES
LG-4A, Ganpati Bhawan,
4675-B/21, Ansari Road,
Darya Ganj, Delhi - 110002

Jacket Designed by :
S.M. Graphics

Printed by:
NCT Printers , Delhi, India

PREFACE

A travel agency is a business that sells travel related products and services to end-user customers on behalf of third party travel suppliers, such as airlines, hotels and cruise lines. Customers of travel agencies include tourists and business travellers. Some agencies also serve as general service agents for foreign travel companies in different countries.

Most travel agencies do not sell airline tickets only; their services vary, and many of them sell more cruise ship packages than airline tickets. Most travel agencies also arrange car rental deals for their customers, and many concentrate on arranging charter or group trips to different destinations. For this, they deal with regular airlines, but many times, they also hire charter airlines. Many travel agencies exclusively represent a small group of supplier airlines, cruise and car hire companies and, often, the logos of the supplier companies are displayed on the windows of the agency's office. Travel agencies also market and sell train and hotel products.

Today, many travel agencies have developed an internet presence by posting a website, with detailed travel information. Full travel booking sites are often complex, and require the assistance of outside travel consolidators. These companies can provide up to the minute, detailed data on tens of thousands of hotel vacancies. Some of the popular online travel sites allow visitors to compare hotel and flight rates with multiple companies. They often allow visitors to sort the travel packages by amenities, price, and or proximity to a city or landmark.

This book is concerned with the operational and management aspects of travel agencies. It highlights the role of travel agents as creators of tourism resources and image builders of tourist attractions. Its contents will be highly useful for students and research scholars as well as academicians interested in this newly emerging discipline.

Editor

Contents

1

Travel and Tourism

Travel is the transport of people on a trip/journey or the process or time involved in a person or object moving from one location to another. Reasons for travel include:

— Tourism—travel for recreation. This may apply to the travel itself, or the travel may just be the necessary investment to arrive at a desired location.

— Visiting friends and family

— Trade

— Commuting–going to various routine activities, such as work or meetings.

— Migration—travel to begin life somewhere else; nomadic people do this

— Pilgrimages—travel for religious reasons.

Tourism is the act of travel for the purpose of recreation and business, and the provision of services for this act. Tourists are people who are travelling to and staying in places outside their usual environment for not more than one consecutive year for leisure, business and other purposes not related to the exercise of an activity remunerated from within the place visited. The distance between these two places is of no significance.

Tourism is a service industry, comprising a number of tangible and intangible components. The tangible elements include transport systems — air, rail, road, water and now, space; hospitality services — accommodation, foods and beverages, tours, souvenirs; and related services such as banking, insurance and safety and security. The intangible elements include: rest and relaxation, culture, escape, adventure, new and different experiences.

Many countries depend heavily upon travel expenditures by foreigners as a source of taxation and as a source of income for the enterprises that sell services to these travellers. Consequently the development of tourism is often a strategy employed either by a Non-governmental organization (NGO) or a governmental agency to promote a particular region for the purpose of increasing commerce through exporting goods and services to non-locals.

People have been travelling for centuries. The first travelers were Greek and Roman traders and religious pilgrims of the Middle Ages. They moved about for work and religion unlike today's tourist in pursuit of leisure. In the19th Century, the term 'tourist' took on a new meaning when travel for pleasure experienced enormous growth. In the post-industrial revolution era, and at a time when rail and steam ships offered easier access to foreign soil, travel was no longer restricted to the British gentry.

Tourism as an industry earns more foreign exchange than any other single sector. Its multiplier effect means the influence is felt across many non-related industries. We are all tourists. A tourist can be from a nearby town or from overseas and is defined as 'a person travelling for pleasure'. The activities on offer for any visitor domestic or international - are part of the fabric of the tourism industry. People on holiday, those visiting friends or relatives (the VFR market), travelling for business or sport need a whole range of services.

- They need a way of finding out about the business e.g. pamphlets, websites.
- They need transport from where they live their 'point of origin'.
- They need transport once they have reached their destination.
- They need accommodation.
- They need food and drink.
- They need activities to entertain them.

Tourism is not a quick fix for a declining region. It is a competitive industry where the rewards are subject to seasonal highs and lows and changing fads in destinations can shrink supply of visitors.

Shocking international events such as September 11 can potentially have a dramatic effect on the numbers of overseas visitors-decreasing numbers from certain markets yet increasing interest from others. Experience has shown that these effects are not always long-lasting if a destination still holds appeal for the traveler. Despite these pitfalls, the potential for supplementing the local economy through tourism makes it worth investigating In order to cater for visitors facilities have to be provided which are also available to local population. Local businesses servicing those who service the visitor also get a boost - the multiplier effect in action.

Tourism, if successful, can leave a very large footprint on the destination. Its impact on local facilities such as transport, shops and places to eat can cause friction and resentment between people making money from tourists and those who feel their quality of life is compromised.

Volumes of people passing through a region cause wear and tear on infrastructure that is often repaired or replaced at the expense of the community as a whole. Striking a balance between attracting visitors and maintaining a quality of life for local residents is a serious challenge.

Tourism is about people caring for people. Given below are two definitions of Tourism: The sum of phenomena and relationships arising from the interaction of tourists, business suppliers, host governments, and host communities in the process of attracting and hosting these tourists and other visitors.

The Growth of the International Tourism Industry Since the Second World War, the growth of international tourism has been phenomenal. Annual tourist arrivals worldwide increased from 25 million in 1950 to 450 million in 1990. Between 1969 and 1979, the World Bank encouraged developing countries to invest in tourism as a strategy for attracting foreign investment, and the governments of developing countries began to see tourism as a means to redistribute resources from North to South.

In the words of the World Tourism Organization (WTO), tourism became "one of the most important economic, social, cultural and political phenomena of the twentieth century".

Today tourism is often described as the world's "biggest" industry on the basis of its contribution to global gross domestic product (GDP), the number of jobs it generates, and the number of clients it serves. However, these conclusions are based largely on arrivals statistics, which focus on international tourism and therefore hide the significance of domestic tourism. These statistics may also underestimate regional tourists traveling by land rather than air or sea. The WTO estimates that the ratio of domestic to international tourism is as high as 10:1- although this varies hugely from country to country. The size of the industry and its rate of growth present both opportunities and threats for bio-diversity conservation.

Statistics produced by the World Travel and Tourism Council (WTTC) indicate that tourism generates 11 percent of global GDP, it employs 200 million people, and transports nearly 700 million international travelers per year-a figure that is expected to double by 2020.

According to the World Tourism Organization, international tourism

— accounts for 36 percent of trade in commercial services in advanced economies and 66 percent in developing economies;
— constitutes 3-10 percent of GDP in advanced economies and up to 40 percent in developing economies;
— generated US$464 billion in tourism receipts in 2001;
— Is one of the top five exports for 83 percent of countries and the main source of foreign currency for at least 38 percent of countries.

Nature of Travel and Tourism Industry

The travel and tourism industry is an interrelated amalgamation of those businesses and agencies that totally or in part provide the means of transport, goods, services, and other facilities for travel outside of the home community for any purpose not related to day-to-day activity. Douglas Fretchling, professor of tourism studies at George Washington University, provides another definition that is somewhat similar but a bit clearer, and therefore the one we will adopt. Fretchling defines the travel and tourism industry as "a collection of organizations and establishments that derive all or a significant portion of their income from providing goods and services purchased on a trip to the traveler." lists businesses that make up the travel and tourism industry. The businesses under the headings "Accommodations" and

"Food and Beverage," along with institutional food service operations, constitute the hospitality industry.

Multiplier Effect

The Multiplier effect is a basic economic concept, which refers to changes in the level of activity that brings further changes in the level of other activities throughout the economy. When an injection of expenditure into an economy leads to an increase in national income more than the original injection, this is the multiplier effect. In other words, the multiplier effect is the effect from continuous respending of incomes. There are different types of multipliers, such as the sales or transaction multiplier, the output multiplier the employment multiplier, government revenue multiplier and the import multiplier. However, this paper will focus on the income multiplier in tourism. What is the multiplier? The multiplier indicates how many times that the injection of original spending circulates through a local economy.

As a result of respending, it benefits the local people. According to "Tourism: Economic, Physical and Social Impacts", "tourists expenditures in a destination creates new incomes and outputs in the region which, in turn, produce further expenditures and incomes." How to calculate the multiplier and how does it work in tourism? Some examples will be given to illustrate the economic concept of multiplier effect. The income multiplier considers three levels of impact created by the change in tourist expenditure, which includes direct spending, indirect spending and induces spending. Let us look at the illustration:

— *Direct impact:* A tourist stays in a hotel and eats at the food establishment there. The tourist pays for the hotel accommodation, food and beverages. (This is the tourist's initial spending in a hotel, which creates direct revenue to the hotel).

— *Indirect impact*: Upon receipt of the tourist dollars, the process of respending begins. The hotel makes payments to its employees, suppliers, and so on. (This is the indirect effect of the tourist's initial expenditure, which creates additional income and employment for the local economy).

— *Induced impact*: The employees receive incomes and consume on goods and services. The supplier replenishes its stock makes payments of wages to their employees etc. This is induced effect of the tourist's initial expenditure, which creates further economic activities. To calculate the income multiplier, one of the simplest ways is to add "direct, indirect and induced spending" then divide by the direct spending.

Motivations of Travel

The various reasons for why people travel can be placed into five broad categories:

1. *Recreation*. Recreation includes leisure and activities related to sports, entertainment, and rest. Beach vacations, ski vacations, and adventure travel such as white-water rafting all fall into this category. Destinations such as the Caribbean, Disney World, and national parks benefit largely from recreational travel.
2. *Culture*. People travel for cultural reasons as well-a desire to learn about things and places that interest them. These interests can be historical, ethnic, educational, or they can relate to-the arts or religion.
3. *Business*. Business travel is a significant portion of all travel. This category includes individual business travelers as well as travelers attending meetings and conventions. The trend now is to combine business and recreational travel-thus business meetings and conventions are held at resort hotels, theme parks, and

even on cruise ships, and spouses and even children often come along.

4. *Visiting Friends and Relatives (VFR).* Research has shown that much travel involves visiting friends and relatives. This is difficult to measure, however, and has little economic impact compared to recreational, cultural, or business travel.
5. *Health.* Many persons travel to visit diagnostic centers and receive treatment at clinics, hospitals, or spas such as the Mayo Clinic in Rochester, Minnesota, or the Canyon Ranch in Tucson, Arizona. This type of travel, too, has relatively little economic impact.

The U.S. Travel Data Center has done a good deal of research to determine what types of Americans travel and how many of them there are. According to the center, 150 million Americans take one or more trips away from home every year. Some groups, as we have pointed out, have a higher tendency to travel.

Demographic segmentation is widely used in almost all industries as demographics are easily measured and classified. This is segmentation based on income, race, age, nationality, religion, gender, education, etc.

Psychographic segments are based on attitudes, interests and opinions (AIO), selfconcepts and lifestyle behaviors. Usage segmentation is a broad term that applies to the purpose for which something is used, the frequency or regularity of usage, size of purchase (or expenditure), timing or seasonal consideration, and more. Several types of market segmentation exist, with demographic and geographic segmentation being the most commonly used. As marketing knowledge has advanced and competition has increased, however, the need for a more precise segmentation tool has grown. Psychographics, often referred to as lifestyle, is just the tool. Psychographics has been around for more than 30 years, but is still one of the least understood concepts in marketing research.

It seems that every scholar has his or her own definition of exactly what constitutes psychographics. Some define it simply as values or lifestyles while others have more elaborate definitions. Their definition claims that psychographics "seeks to describe the human characteristics of consumers that may have bearing on their response to products, packaging, advertising and public relations efforts. Such variables may span a spectrum from self-concept and lifestyle to attitudes, interests and opinions, as well as perceptions of product attributes" Psychographics are used to determine lifestyle characteristics and traits that can be correlated into targeted marketing programs.

Psychographics and lifestyle are often used interchangeably, but psychographics is actually the way that lifestyle is made operationally useful to marketing managers. Psychographics appraises a consumer's activities, interests, opinions, and values and correlates them with a consumer's demographics. Psychographics allow for a more complete picture of an individual, making it easier to understand how to market products to them.

One can not begin to explain psychographics without first defining the manner in which psychographic research is conducted. Psychographic research is quantitative research that attempts to place consumers based on psychological, as opposed to strictly demographic dimensions.

Psychological Motives

Just as internal and external environment factors affect the hospitality industry, internal and external psychological factors affect the guests and clients of the hospitality industry, and thus the industry as well. Research that attempt to classify people's internal motives and behavior is called psychographic research. Hospitality promoters use psychographic research data to decide which market segments to target and what kinds of amenities to offer at a location. All psychological motives can be classified as either basic or secondary. Basic motives influence everyone and include unlearned needs such as thirst, hunger, sex, fear, and avoidance of pain. Secondary motives are learned needs and include achievement, desire for power, and other specialized needs. Secondary motives usually vary from person to person.

People's basic needs from a lodging facility are a good night's rest in a comfortable and safe room. Beyond that, lodging facilities appeal to secondary motives by offering luxury suites that symbolize achievement or esteem. All foodservice establishments fulfill the basic needs for nourishment. Secondary motives are fulfilled by celebrating special moments - birthdays, wedding anniversaries, bon voyages - in social settings provided by restaurants and hotel banquet rooms. In all areas of hospitality, people expect to be safe from harm. Highly publicized attacks on tourists in Florida in 1993 influenced whether some people chose to visit the state. The desire to avoid pain influences some people to byepass sites where outbreaks of disease have occurred or where political conflicts might erupt in violence.

In psychographic research, the push/pull theory explains the combination of push and pull forces in human motivation. According to the push/pull theory, internal factors lead or "push" people to travel, while external forces "pull" them to certain destinations. The following is an example of the push/pull forces in action. It's the middle of spring semester. The gray skies and cold winds of winter have finally gives way to bright sun and warm breezes. Rachel, a sophomore at a Michigan college, has been putting in a lot of hours studying for exams, quizzes, class projects, and homework, and now she's tried of school. "I can't wait for spring break," she thinks as she watches friends tossing a Frisbee on the quad. "I just have to get away from all this work." Rachel has begun to feel the "push" to get away from college for a change of pace and for rest and relaxation.

Rachel has heard her friends' plan for spring break; traveling to a sunny beach, visiting friends, or simply going home. She has also seen spring break travel ads in the school newspapers and on the local television station. All of these things have begun to "pull" Rachel away from the college. As a result of these push and pull factors working together, Rachel decides to spend spring break in Myrtle Beach, South California, soaking up the sun and relaxing with friends.

Positive destination images, enhance the pull effect. But negative destination images may trigger the basic human motives of avoidance of pain or fear. These motives may cause some people to byepass that destination, choosing another that they perceive as safer. Other people may prefer their homes to places away regardless of image or time or money available for eating out or travel. They may fear flying or suffer motion sickness. Or they may not be comfortable dealing with change or new experiences.

The tourist psychographic profile is an important tool for marketers. Knowing what kind of person would be attracted to a particular place helps marketers develop and place advertising to attract the right personality types. For example, placing an ad for Yosemite National park (a typical U.S. psychocentric destination) in a magazine featuring mountain climbing in Nepal (a typical U.S. allocentric destination) probably would have little effect. The readers of the magazine would likely be looking for excitement in exotic locales. The ad probably would fare better in a history magazine, whose readers might be looking for a psychocentric locale for their vacation.

Marketers combine information from psychographic and demographic studies to find out what services will attract specific market segments. For example, knowing what factors motivate senior citizens to use hospitality services helps operators tailor their services to attract this growing market.

Because of their freedom to travel year-round and their increasing numbers and purchasing power, seniors will continue to be an important marketing segment of the industry. Some businesses, such as Choice Hotels, have already set up programs to target this expanding market.

Many travel and hospitality companies have programs aimed at senior citizens. Holiday Inn and other establishments offer a discount for members of the American Association of Retired Persons (AARP). Some restaurants offer special menus for seniors, usually smaller portion meals and lower-calorie menu items. Some respond with modestly priced, all-you-can-eat buffets, a feature especially attractive to this group. Psychographics helps marketers understand consumer behavior. Consumers behave unpredictably. "They demonstrate loyalties to brands (or not), blindly follow trends (or not), and buy according to their convictions and aspirations (or not). Individuals are innovators in some product categories, but not in others. What they say they do and what they really do are seldom the same". Psychographics is one way to clarify the behaviors consumers exhibit. Psychographics, like all other segmentation tools, also helps minimize risks. On the other hand, psychographics also has several limitations associated with it. Psychographic research is complex and often confusing. It can also be very costly.

Completing psychographic research usually costs upwards of $50,000. Critics also claim that the categories psychographic research places consumers in overlaps so much that it does not differentiate among consumers. Psychographic research can also be lengthy and narrow, or unable to be projected onto an entire population. Even with these limitations, however, psychographics have been used successfully innumerable times.The government of Bermuda conducted psychographic research in the United States to determine who would be most interested in going to Bermuda on vacation. In a sample of persons who were potential vacationers, three groups emerged:

— The price and sights group. These people were interested in seeing the most things for the least amount of money. They wanted tours that covered ten countries in nine days at a bargain price. The best cruises were the cheapest ones that visited the most ports, and a good hotel was one that offered budgetpriced accommodations within walking distance of everything they might want to see.

— The sun and surf group. These people sought a vacation where they could lie on a beach and get a golden tan. Value was important, but even more important was finding a destination where there was good weather, guaranteed sunshine, and a beautiful beach where they could soak up the sun and swim in clear waters.

— The quality group. The quality of the vacation experience was of paramount importance to this group. Members of this group felt they had worked hard for a vacation and now it was their turn to relax and be taken care of. This group valued destinations and accommodations that were first-class or deluxe. Service was very important-they wanted and expected lots of pampering and were willing to pay a fair price for it. They also wanted gourmet dining and sophisticated entertainment.

Agents of Travel and tourism

Travel and tourism can be thought of as a manufacturing industry. Components, e.g. hotel rooms, meals, coach or airline seats, are bought and put together by a tour operator to produce holidays. These are sold to the public by retail travel agents, with representatives of the tour operator providing the after sales service to the consumer.

Large tour operators may own the companies that produce the component, e.g. Britannia Airways are owned by Thomson Holidays, and travel agents may also sell the components separately, e.g. air rail and theatre tickets or hotel rooms. Another aspect of the travel and tourism industry is the work of the tourist authorities and boards, set up to promote the counties.

Tour Operators

Although the holidays which are 'manufactured' by tour operators are usually sold by travel agents, some companies have their own retail outlets or sell direct to the public by telephone or post. Thus the work of a large operator may encompass all the stages in the production and sale of a holiday.

The larger the company, the more specialised each employee's role becomes, e.g. there are those concerned with negotiating the various components of a holiday with carriers and hotel owners etc., those who produce the brochure or 'label' of the product, those involved with the research and development of new ideas or marketing them, and those dealing with reservations, They also have separate finance, personnel and other administrative departments.

Several of the large companies run graduate recruitment schemes and operate 'in-house' training programmes for employees.

Representatives/couriers are employed by tour operators to look after the holidaymakers and escort parties of tourists. They work very long hours and are always on call. Besides supervising arrivals, departures, excursions and answering questions, representatives have to deal with any complaints, accidents or illnesses (even deaths) that occur within their group of tourists.

Employment is usually on a seasonal basis. Most companies stipulate a minimum age of 20/21. Good conversational ability in one or more languages, besides native English, is needed. The work involves close personal contact with people and requires the ability to communicate effectively, patiently and tactfully; sometimes in very difficult circumstances.

Planning vacations or business trips to new places can be quite tiring and strenuous without the help of a travel agent. They have answers to all possible questions concerning the shortest route to the destination, travel mode, the important documents that will be required (visa, passport, vaccination certificates etc.), suitable places to stay, current exchange rates, tourist spots to visit, climate and they will plan the trip keeping in mind the clients' preferences, budgets and special needs.

A great deal of work is done on the computer where the latest information on flight schedules, departure/ arrival timings, hotel ratings etc. can be obtained. Agencies may involve themselves in special discount packages, slide/movie presentations on various places and other promotional work to attract customers.

The four departments of a travel agency are:

— Accounts (handles the billing for individuals and groups)

— Tours (deal in in-expensive packaged tours, with the accomodation, food, transport etc. all taken care of)

— Travel (provide detailed information on routes, costs)
— Cargo (covers the booking and recovery of all cargo from the destination points connected by either Air, rail or road)

The Department of Tourism in the Government does major amounts of work for the international market, in formulating policies, developing centres to attract tourists, providing adequate transport, advertising the different spots and publicising the various experiences, providing accurate information on all possible tourist areas.

Since this industry has so many areas, the requirements for each field will naturally be different. In general, most candidates enter the field through a travel agency or a tour-operating company. For the government positions, advertisements are usually given in the newspapers regarding the vacancies. Candidates for these positions are only selected after passing a written exam, interview and medical examination. Most private sector companies are flexible in their choosing - focusing more on interest, aptitude and personality rather than academic achievement.

Experience is definitely an advantage, but on-the-job training is also given to new entrants. The higher the post one seeks, the better should be the qualifications.This industry is highly competitive and finally, those with better education in the field of travel and tourism are more likely to move ahead faster. The basic needs are a school-leaving certificate (10+2) for those seeking a position, upto the tourist guide level while candidates aspiring for managerial positions, need a graduate degree, in any of the fields dealing with history, art, languages, geography etc.

A travel agency may either be one of a chain of retail outlets or a single operation. The work of the larger agencies is often divided between different divisions, e.g.

counter service, business travel and foreign exchange. In smaller concerns each member of the staff will have to handle many aspects of the agency's business. Some agencies limit their activities to arranging travel and/or holidays to a specific area, but most cater for a very much wider demand and fulfil all the functions associated with acting as intermediary between the providers of holidays, transport, accommodation etc., and the client.

Companies that deal only with business travel are called Business Travel Houses. They may also be responsible for dealing with the planning, publicity and bookings for trade fairs and conferences.

Travel agency sales clerks take bookings on behalf of tour operators, sell tickets for travel, make hotel bookings, take payments from the public and give advice, on types of holidays, methods of travel, passports, visas, travellers cheques, foreign currency etc., They need to have a good knowledge of the products and destinations offered by the tour operating and travel companies.

Managers and assistant managers are responsible for the day-to-day operation of branch offices. This includes staffing, marketing, accountancy, complaints etc. Travel managers should have professional qualifications and experience. In a small agency training will probably be on-the-job. Large companies may offer a training programme.

Tourist Boards

Tourist Boards/Authorities are public bodies which have been set up to promote tourism to the public, tour operators and travel agents, both at home and overseas, thus encouraging the development or tourism. They exist at the national level., Their main functions are marketing of an area, research/development of new ideas to attract tourists and information provision. The development of facilities is also a role at some levels.

Careers in Travel and Tourism holidays and travel are a part of life in modern society. The annual break from work, school, college or family life is an important objective - and the very thought of holiday sustains most of us throughout our daily lives. The British alone take something in the order of 21.5 million trips abroad each year and rather more than 50 million holidays, or short breaks, are taken within the confines of the United Kingdom.

Apart from the holiday business however, the travel and tourism industry also affects our lives in many other ways. Visiting friends and relatives; attending family events: travelling for business purposes; attending conferences; winning travel prizes in advertising campaigns or on television quiz shows are all part of modern living. It is not surprising, therefore, that a vast, complicated industry exists to provide the facilities that make these journeys possible, convenient and, very enjoyable.

Recent statistics indicate that in Great Britain alone, some 1.5 million people (out of a working population of some 26 million) depend on the travel arid tourism industry for their livelihoods. The number of jobs in the industry are increasing at the rate of some 50,000 a year therefore tourism is slowly becoming one of the most important industries in the world. As far as Britain's economy is concerned, did you know that after North Sea Oil, the tourism industry earns more in foreign currencies than any other industry? As our manufacturing industries have declined, our service industries are contributing more and more to the country's prosperity. These industries contribute to the economy by means of what are called invisible exports - in addition exports - in addition to tourism; insurance, commodity dealings, shopping and financial services fall into this category.

2

ROLE OF TRAVEL AGENTS

A travel agency is a business that sells travel related products and services to end-user customers on behalf of third party travel suppliers, such as airlines, hotels and cruise lines. Customers of travel agencies include tourists and business travellers. Some agencies also serve as general service agents for foreign travel companies in different countries.

Travel agencies have been organized mostly since the development of commercial aviation from the 1920s, although Thomas Cook was a notable early, pre-flight pioneer in 1841. The Portuguese company Viagens Abreu is the oldest travel organization, founded in 1840. Some operate with a chain of stores and others are one store operations. A few of the larger travel agencies sell their own products. Agencies without their own product are arguably more impartial and more likely to offer something to suit the traveller; they are known as independent agencies. there are three different types of agencies: these are Multiples, Miniples and independent agencies.

Most travel agencies do not sell airline tickets only; their services vary, and many of them sell more cruise ship packages than airline tickets. Most travel agencies also arrange car rental deals for their customers, and many concentrate on arranging charter or group trips to different destinations. For this, they deal with regular airlines, but many times, they also hire charter airlines. Many travel agencies exclusively represent a small group of supplier airlines, cruise and car hire companies and, often, the logos of the supplier companies are displayed on the windows of the agency's office.

Travel agencies also market and sell train and hotel products. Generally, their goal is to try to fit an ideal schedule onto the requirements of each specific customer.

The phrase travel agency has changed meaning since the emergence of companies like Thomson or Thomas Cook, who are now considered to be tour operators rather than travel agents. The difference is that tour operators manufacture and sell their own holidays whereas independent travel agents sell holidays from all the tour operators without limiting the range they offer to just their own product. The best travel agents deal honestly with a wide range of customers.

In the UK a group of just such travel agents formed a consortium which became known as Worldchoice. Each agency was independently owned, bonded members of ABTA and Worldchoice was the vehicle for both commercial negotiations with the tour operators and also a forum for best practise. In 2006 there were 700 agents in the Worldchoice consortium of independent travel agents

Responsibilities of Travel Agents

Customer Advocacy

The travel agents are there to act on your behalf to see that restitution is made if you have a problem with a particular part of your travel experience. ASTA, for example, is the only travel association aggressively fighting to improve the travel experience, and air transportation in particular, for all consumers, not just those with access to the Internet.

Expert Guidance

Travel agents, unlike instructions on a Web page, are experts in understanding and deciphering the myriad of travel information and codes out there. It's what they've been trained to do and they do it every day. They provide convenient one-stop shopping.

Personalised Service

Travel agents are your neighbors, not the impersonal voice thousand of miles away. They know what you want and what you value in your travel experience. They have a vested interest in making sure you have the best travel experience possible.

Professional Advice

Travel agents are there to make sure you get where you want to go, when you want to go and for the best price. They have intimate knowledge of the destinations they sell and are able to select the most appropriate travel arrangements to meet their clients needs.

Time Saving

Instead of checking a long list of travel Web pages, which only provide rates and fares for the companies that have contracted with them, why not go straight to the source? A travel agent has all the information at their fingertips, saving you a few hours in front of a computer screen.

Unbiased Information

Travel agents work for their clients (you-the consumer),

not for a travel supplier. It makes sense that a happy customer will be a repeat customer.

Dest Ideals

Travel agents are out to find the consumer the best rate available. Agents are there to save you money as well as time.

Organizations

On April 20, 1931, the American Society of Travel Agents (ASTA) was formed in New York City, to defend the rights of US travel agents over the power of the growing commercial airline systems of the day. Now headquartered in Alexandria, Virginia, ASTA still represents travel agencies and agents.

The international body for registering travel agents is the International Air Transport Association (IATA), although most travel agents are registered through national bodies such as the Australian Federation of Travel Agents.

ASFA, The Association of Special Fares Agents, Airline Consolidators, Bucketshops and Discount Travel Agents is the mother source for finding cheap fares online. ASFA was founded in 1985 as a platform for discount travel specialists, consolidators and bucketshops from all over the world. ASFA agents are registered and bonded according to the laws of the countries and states that they are operating in. Association of Special Fares Agents web site

Many agencies feared their services would no longer be needed when many airlines and other travel companies began to sell directly to passengers over the Internet. They were afraid they would be victims of what management science experts call disintermediation.

Another worry was over the fact that airlines have been cutting back the commissions paid to travel agents on each tickets sold; the airlines feel that they are perfectly capable of dealing directly with their own passengers and do not need travel agents as much as in the past to fill seats.

Since 1995, many travel agents have exited the industry, and relatively few young people have entered the field due to a collapse in salaries. However, others have abandoned the "brick and mortar" agency for a home-based business to reduce overhead, and those who remain have managed to survive by promoting other travel products like cruise lines and train excursions, or by promoting their ability to aggressively research and assemble complex travel packages on a moment's notice (essentially acting as a very advanced concierge).

Many travel agencies have developed an internet presence by posting a website, with detailed travel information. Full travel booking sites are often complex, and require the assistance of outside travel consolidators. These companies such as Sabre and others can provide up to the minute, detailed data on tens of thousands of hotel vacancies.

Some of the popular online travel sites allow visitors to compare hotel and flight rates with multiple companies. They often allow visitors to sort the travel packages by amenities, price, and or proximity to a city or landmark.

Secrets of Successful Travel agencies

Everyone is different and each of us travels his or her own road to success, but over the years we have noticed a number of qualities that make for success in the travel agency business. Here then are some observations about just a few qualities that successful agents bring to the table when they start out.

If you are not already a agent, the very fact that you are reading this web site suggests that you like to arm yourself with all the information available before making a decision.

We regularly hear from agents who signed up with the first agency that caught their eye. Now they regret it and wonder if we can point them in the right direction. We explain to them (hopefully with a certain amount of patience) that we cannot make decisions for them.

The thing many beginners (especially those with no real experience of being in business for themselves) fail to understand is that the sellers of business opportunities are just that – sellers. Just as the car dealer won't volunteer that the car you have your eye on sits at the bottom of the "Consumer Reports" safety rankings, the ads for a host agency offer won't volunteer the downsides of their offer or reveal that a better deal is being offered by someone else.

Please understand, we are not saying these people are being dishonest. They are simply putting the best face on what they have to offer. That's simply what sellers do. When you start selling travel, you'll do it too. We sure that if you are considering starting a travel agency you have visited at least several sites offering such business opportunities and we are also sure you understand what we are talking about.

Becoming a travel agent is easy. The problem is knowing what kind of travel agent to become. There are probably as many ways of being a travel agent as there are travel agents. No one does it exactly the same.

This is where a lot of people make costly mistakes. Because they don't know the full range of options available to them, they pick the first one that comes along. Or they look at two or three options and pick the wrong one.

There are two basic types of agents.

— Referral agents.

— Booking and selling agents.

Within each category there are a lot of different ways to go about it but, for now, let's consider these two basic types one at a time.

Referral Agents

Referral agents, as the name implies, do not actually book or sell travel products. Instead, they simply refer people to a travel agency. That travel agency's "inside agents" do all the work of closing the sale and making the booking. In exchange for steering the customer to the agency, the referral agent receives a percentage of the commission that the travel agency gets from the supplier (the cruise line, the airline, the hotel, or whatever). The referral agent also typically books his or her personal travel through the agency and receives a commission on that as well (a sort of "rebate" or "discount" in effect).

As a referral agent, you don't have to know a great deal about the mechanics of the travel industry. You don't have to know all the airline codes, or what's the best hotel in Hawaii, or the difference between Category C and Category D on a cruise ship. Your job is to communicate the fun and excitement of travel and get people to call the toll-free number of your agency.

So far, there's nothing new or controversial about this. It's been going on for decades in the travel industry, where referral agents have traditionally be known as "bird dogs." But in recent years, some travel agencies have made the use of referral agents the core of their business model and the practice has been getting a lot more attention. And attracting some controversy.

Referral agencies issue their referral agents a photo ID that the agent can use to receive some travel industry discounts and courtesies from some suppliers. This annoys some people in the travel industry but, the practice is perfectly legal. The agencies that accredit travel agencies have not taken any action against the travel agencies issuing these cards, nor have any travel suppliers. The federal government specifically declined to take any action, saying this was simply an alternative way of marketing travel.

The fact of the matter is, the referral agencies sell an awful lot of travel and who wants to argue with success?

Booking and Selling Agents

A lot of people, however, are attracted to the idea of becoming travel agents because they love getting involved in all the details of planning wonderful trips, across the country or around the world. Or perhaps they have developed some expertise in a particular destination or type of vacation or mode of travel and they are looking for a way to turn what they love into a source of income.

Travel agents like this clearly do a lot more than the referral agent. They work with their clients to determine what kind of travel experience the client is looking for. Then they research the available options, speaking directly with the travel supplier. Then they present the options to their client, help the client make a decision, and make the booking arrangements with the supplier. In exchange for doing all this work, they receive a much higher percentage of the commission than the referral agent. In fact, they might get it all!

The term "booking and selling agent" is something we are using here just to make clear the distinction between referral agents and all other travel agents. As far as the travel industry is concerned, an agent who does all the booking and selling is a travel agent pure and simple. If you are interested in becoming a referral agent, you will find information about that option elsewhere on this web site. For now, however, let's concentrate on how to become a full-fledged booking and selling agent.

Being a travel agent means representing and marketing travel products that are created by someone else. You are not going to start your own airline, or go out and buy a cruise ship, or build a chain of all-inclusive resorts. That's why you so often hear travel agents referred to as "outside sales representatives." "Outside" because you do not work in the office of the company whose products you represent.

Whether you deal directly with a travel supplier or through a middleman, it's important to remember that you are not an employee, either of the host agency or the ultimate travel supplier. Because you are not an employee, you do not receive a salary or any of the benefits (medical, dental, vacations, etc.) that go along with being an employee. You make your money ("get paid") through commissions on what you sell. You negotiate your commission level with either the host agency or the travel supplier. Sell a lot, make a lot. Sell a little, make a little.

Although you are independent and on your own, you are never alone as a travel agent. You must constantly work with others to provide service to your clients. Virtually every travel agent must form a relationship with a host agency. And your success hinges on your understanding of this relationship.

There are many ways to connect with a host agency. You can do it for free, or you can pay a fee. You may have to sell yourself to an agency. Or several agencies may compete in offering you the "best deal" to sign up with them. Regardless of how it happens, once you've hooked up with a host agency, a commitment has been made. If money has changed hands then a certain "investment" has been made. Even though it is possible to work with more than one host agency at the same time, it is far more convenient to work with just one, so a certain sense of loyalty tends to develop. It can be a hassle to switch host agencies, so inertia sets in.

Perhaps for these reasons, many travel agents start to think that they work for this host agency. They may know, intellectually, that this is not the case. But they behave as if it is. Because the host agency has a certain way of doing things, they start to think that this is the only way of doing things. Again, on an intellectual level, they may know this is not the case, but they behave as if it is.

They are thinking like employees. They gradually start thinking that their destiny, their success, is wrapped up with the destiny of the host agency. This is a mistake, but an easily corrected one. However, it is not the biggest mistake beginners make. No, the biggest mistake newcomers to the travel agent profession make — especially those who have had no prior experience running their own business —is that they think they are customers of the host agency. This is especially true if they paid a fee to get set up as an outside agent with that agency.

You and the host agency are two separate and independent business entities that have freely entered into a purely business relationship, because each party has independently decided that there's something in it for them. In the business-to-consumer model there is an unspoken assumption that the business is smarter and more powerful and that the customer is less knowledgeable and less powerful. Therefore, the reasoning goes, the customer's interests must be protected. In the business-to-business model there is an unspoken assumption that the parties involved are equally capable.

Modern Trends in Travel Industry

Travel agents work hard on behalf of the consumer. The role of a travel agent is to make the process of going on a trip - whether for work or pleasure - be a stressfree and memorable experience. Travel agents spend time not only booking tickets and searching for affordable prices, but also personalizing their services for individual clients.

The job of a travel agent has grown and adapted to reflect the changes within the travel industry, and to reflect the difference in the way people think about travel. Travel agents recognize that consumers today have done their homework and are more knowledgeable about what they want. Clients who turn to a travel agent desire an in-depth, personal approach and want the advice and expertise of a professional. This is why a travel agent:

- Distills product information;
- Investigates and supplies competitive information;
- Stays abreast of the most current and timely promotions;
- Analyzes the current promotions;
- Clarifies the fine print, such as cancellation penalties and restrictions;
- Makes recommendations on travel-related options;
- Simplifies the research and subsequent transaction;
- Enhances the trip with value-added benefits and amenities;
- Uses their clout to obtain the best possible arrangements in seemingly impossible situations; and
- Gets problems resolved.

The Internet has helped transform the travel industry. It helps educate the consumer by providing vast amounts of information about destinations and different travel options. Both consumers and travel professionals have benefited from the Internet, which makes the possibility of travel to exotic places more imaginable. It has helped consumers see in full color and, in some cases, real time, where they would like to visit. The Internet gives travelers the ability to do comparative shopping for attractive deals or packages. It also has helped many travel agencies, hotels, resorts and other travel-related suppliers flourish by bringing in business through Web sites.

The Internet has become such an integral part of the travel agency business that 98 percent of travel agencies currently subscribe to a consumer on-line service or an Internet access provider in order to help them better serve their clients. Gathering information increasingly involves the use of the Internet. Almost 95 percent of agents have conducted online research. Nearly 83 percent of travel agencies report they have booked directly on supplier's Web sites without using their GDS or calling the supplier in question.

The Internet can be a powerful tool. It can increase the scope and reach of a consumer's efforts and allow a person to check hundreds of options or research destinations in depth. But to make the Internet work effectively, a person has to understand where to look and what questions to ask, otherwise hours can be wasted surfing the Web and ultimately produce unsatisfactory results. This is where a travel agent can make a world of difference.

A professional travel agent is trained to guide a client through the entire process of planning a trip, whether for business or for leisure. Travel agents take classes, participate in seminars, become destination specialists and join professional associations, in order to ensure they make each client's travel experience as personalized, convenient and memorable as possible. When planning a business trip or family vacation, the Internet can be a valuable resource, but it cannot replace the expertise and guidance of a travel agent. Also, during travel crises, the Internet can't replace a human being who will persist to help a client. Travel agents, meanwhile, can offer a myriad of intermediate options.

There are some things technology cannot replicate, and personal touch is one of them. The Internet is a valuable resource, but it cannot replace the expertise, guidance and personal service of a travel agent. At a time when travelers are stressed out with hectic schedules, travel agents have all of the information at their fingertips, saving valuable hours of surfing on the Web. Agents also can offer insider tips generally based on personal experience.

The leisure travel industry has changed from being an option of the upper class to one open to all segments of society - in fact, travel has become an everyday part of life whether for a meeting across the country or a last minute trip to a nearby city. Over time it has become price driven. Many people today base a large part of their travel buying decisions on cost and convenience of travel. People are booking closer in to their travel dates. Thanks to dramatic discounting across the industry, consumers have been conditioned to wait until the last minute before booking in hopes of securing a deeply discounted package deal.

Consumers value the services and unbiased expertise offered by professional agents who represent an impartial source of information for travelers. Travel agents have and will survive in the new marketplace, because consumers know the value they provide.

While there has been contraction and consolidation of brick-and-mortar travel agencies, the number of travel agents has remained fairly steady. Some travel agencies have grown and improved their businesses through new business practices. For example, many travel agencies have focused on providing an increased value to their customers by becoming experts or specialists in certain types of travel or specific destinations. Some agencies have implemented new services that add value to client transactions, such as tracking of frequent flyer accounts or discounted upgrades.

Selecting a Travel Agent

Every travel agency is different and accordingly, some are better suited to a given consumer than others. Here are some tips on choosing a travel agent who is right for you.

— *Ask Around*: Tap friends, neighbors and relatives who use an agent they trust. You may want to visit or call several agencies to find the one that best suits your needs. Consider everything from the appearance of the office to the agent's willingness to listen and answer questions The best agents want to establish a long-term relationship with a client, not just make one sale.

— *Ask About Fees*: Good agents will notify their clients of any additional fees, including service fees, up front. Doing otherwise is pointless, as the fee will appear as a separate charge on the client's credit card bill.

— *Search the Web*: Go to a search engine and use the "Find an Agent" tool. Search for agents with expertise in destinations or specific subjects that interest you.

— *Check Credentials*: Many agents have been trained in business management, travel and tourism or geography. Others have supplemented their agency experience with extensive education and training courses. Some travel agents are Certified Travel Counselors (CTC), having completed an educational program with the Travel Institute, or Master Cruise Counselors (MCC), having completed a program with the Cruise Lines International Association (CLIA).

— *Find Out an Agency's Track Record*: Call authentic associations to see whether a member agency has had a complaint against it in the prior six months. Check with the local Better Business Bureau, while keeping in mind they will only have records of agencies that have had reports filed against them.

3

Responsibilities of Tour Operators

Tour operators are people who solely concentrates on marketing the concept of travel. They plan and `sell' trips to individuals and groups. They book tickets - for air, rail, sea or road travel, arrange hotel reservations or guest houses, hire taxis etc. Besides domestic, all travel agents undertake international bookings and special business tours or conferences. They are mostly into travel management. They organise and put together package trips and holidays. These could be for incoming tourists from abroad or outbound tours or even domestic travellers. They can offer special packages, which could include such diverse attractions as deep-sea diving, snorkelling, trekking or even camel safaris.

Working in this field means dealing with people directly on a daily basis. Helping people plan their itinerary, providing ticketing services to company executives, co-ordinating with the airlines, railways or transport company staff, arranging passports and visas, booking hotels - all these require not only a great deal of mobility but also regular contact with representatives of the various services. One must be up-to-date on rules and regulations governing foreign travel, documents required, hindrances if any; so as to correctly advise the clients. All the staff, be it in marketing, counter sales or guide services must be knowledgeable about the places their clients intend to visit - the best way to reach your destination, places to visit, facilities available etc.

Major areas of work in a travel agency include counter work, marketing and management. Counter work involves helping clients with their itineraries, chalking out travel routes, procuring tickets, arranging for passports and visas, making hotel reservations, organising cargo transport and the like. Counter clerks must be able to have easy access to timetable information and be extremely accurate with the information provided to clients. A small slip on their part could result in embarrassing or even disastrous consequences. Marketing area includes advertising and an aggressive promotion of the agency to potential customers. Procuring steady business for the company is their major job. The management staff deals with the administration of the agency. The managers co- ordinate and streamline the work of the clerks and select brochures of the various tours and packages available with them, among other things.

The major responsibilities of a tour operator are the following:

1. *Planning*: The planning of the tours is done by the tour directors or once-in-a-while by experienced counter clerks. Planning involves chalking out the tour programme, working out the cost, confirmation of accommodation and other facilities like food and entertainment, and consulting tourist officials.
2. *Sales and Reservations*: The staff has to ensure that travel brochures are on display at agencies. They also take bookings from travel agents or individuals.
3. *Representatives/guides*: These are freelancers mostly whose job involves accompanying tourists to their

destination and looking after their needs while travelling. A smattering knowledge of different languages can be useful as well as a general awareness and history of the place visited. This job can be easily done by students or even office workers and others who are interested in travelling. Tour operators or local tourism departments often employ professional guides who have a thorough knowledge of the history and cultural significance of a place. Many tour operators, nowadays specialise in areas such as adventure tourism, beach tourism, mountain holidays etc.

4. *Entry*: A basic diploma in travel and tourism management can be advantageous to a person seeking to work in this field. Advertisements appear from time to time for jobs available in travel agencies and tour operating companies or for a position in a government department or corporation. In general, the minimum requirement for entry into this industry are: (i) 10+2 and fluency in the spoken language up to tourist guide level. (ii) for higher positions, a graduate degree in any discipline with a specialisation in history and architecture or geography and archaeology can be a great asset as is the knowledge of one or more foreign languages. If one is applying for a government post, he/she has to clear a written test, a personal interview and a medical examination.

5. *Training*: With the demand for trained people increasing by the day, it is wise to gain some insights into the field through professional training. There are a number of institutions in the country which offer training courses on different aspects of the industry. There are equally good correspondence courses too.

6. *Career prospects*: A career in travel and tourism can be exciting and full of fun. Not only is it flexible, but certain jobs in the field can provide excellent travelling

opportunities. Job prospects include working in: travel agencies as tour operators, in airlines transport and cargo companies; travel consultancy services and in the government run tourism departments. With enough experience and capital, one can even start one's own travel consultancy.

Changing Role of Tour Opeartors

The tourism industry is a high-growth industry which can only expand with time, what with more and more people finding the means and the inclination to discover new places and seek new adventures. At the rate the industry is growing, it is certain to be the industry of the 21st century, providing ample job opportunities to all kinds of people at all levels. It has been expressing much concern over the five million Indian outbound tourists that are amounting to a revenue outflow of about Rs 25000 crore annually. In an endeavour to divert some of this revenue toward domestic tourism, the industry is all geared up to develop this segment further to give it a much needed thrust.

Tour operators have awakened to the fact that domestic tourism is the foundation of strong tourist inflow. With an intent to focus on inter-regional tourism promotion and to boost the potent domestic tourism segment, Indian travel agents and tour operators have for the first time joined hands to aggressively tap this lucrative sector. Until a few years back, India's domestic tourism was limited to only pilgrim tours. However, today the movement of the domestic market has increased tremendously. This is evident from the fact that even time-share, which till recently was one of the most infamous segments of the industry is now gaining popularity as an easy vacation option. To attract customers, travel agents are now exploring new territories and are sprucing up their itineraries and products. According to the latest travel surveys, there has been a phenomenal rise of ten per cent annual growth in the domestic tourism segment.

Explosion of domestic tourism is an inevitable by-product of economic development in the country. As there is an increase of disposable income, the demand for travel has grown exponentially, diverting most of the traffic toward the outbound segment., putting domestic tourism on the back burner. Where as Indian tourism has been equated with foreign visitors alone or the inbound tourism segment which has been sluggish over the last few years. It is time that India starts equating domestic tourists at par with the foreign tourists to boost its domestic tourism.

Indian tourism has no foundation and lacks projection and awareness. In addition, whenever India has tried to pep up the scenario, several uncalled for events like 9/11, attacks on the parliament and other natural calamities have become major deterrents in the movement of travellers internationally. Weighing the socio-political scenario globally and its adverse impacts on the international movement of both the business and leisure traffic it is only natural that all tour operators have turned focus on domestic tourism, which is both a profitable and feasible proposition in the given scenario.

Tour operators are now diverting outbound tourists by enticing them with attractive domestic packages. The industry is now working with various airlines and state tourism departments to work out incentives for the domestic travellers. To promote domestic tourism, the biggest hurdle has been the inadequate infrastructure. Now the Ministry of Tourism is becoming aggressive as far as infrastructure development is concerned, development of the tourism circuits is has received a big impetus by the same. While infrastructure development is a continuous process, many agents believe that it is not a burning issue.

Tourism experts observe that infrastructure development will take place automatically once there is aggressive movement of tourists. To strengthen the country's tourism, the geographical diversity can be fruitfully marketed nationally and internationally. This exercise has a lot of significance even regionally.

Initiatives like re-introduction of Leave Travel Concession (LTC) are much required to boost domestic tourism. The government's decision to restore the LTC facility to its employees with the hope that the consequential additional outgoing from the exchequer on this account, will at least benefit the tourism industry, has been a welcome decision. Two years ago, the ban on LTC came as a serious blow to the domestic travel agents, depriving them from booking travel tickets for government employees willing to go for leisure tours. LTC has been termed as a good tool to offer a fillip to the leisure travel. The withdrawal of LTC for last two years was counted as an obstacle to the growth of the domestic tourism and was criticised by prominent tour operators. The government employees with the allowance as a disposable income would now be prominent travellers.

In order to create adequate awareness, tourism practitioners point out that media can create the desired hype amongst the populace. Besides, state tourism offices should carry out extensive marketing campaigns jointly with the help of media, tour operators and travel agents, finance companies, hotels and airlines by offering attractive holiday packages to lure the consumers. Due to the lack of publicity, public is unaware of the destinations within the State and outside which are worth seeing and comes under one's budget to spend holidays. States should organise inter-state Travel Marts/Exhibitions to expose the tourism potential in their areas. Development of integrated tourist circuits as envisaged in the National Tourism Policy need to be aggressively promoted by the travel trade. This will enable the tourist to visit more than one destination at a given time while planning holidays. Indian Railways can play a major role in this regard by developing special holiday packages for domestic tourists.

Manging Package Tour

Tour operators enter into long term contracts with air carriers, hotels and other suppliers for the provision of bulk travel services. Discrete travel services are then assembled into a package tour featuring round trip transportation, seven nights accommodations, ground transportation and tours of local sites. The package tour is marketed to the general public through travel agents.

Tour operators are principals and responsible to consumers for the provision of the component travel services of each tour package. Each of these ruined vacations involve a complex marketing system which includes suppliers, both domestic and foreign, wholesalers and tour operators, travel agents and informal travel promoters. Often the negligence of a foreign supplier, i.e., hotel, para-sailing operator, horse or camel stable, tour bus company, air carrier or cruise ship, will be the primary cause of the consumer's injury.

Unfortunately such a potential defendant may be irresponsible, insolvent, uninsured or unavailable because of a lack of jurisdiction or the U.S. forum selected is deemed inconvenient. Assuming availability the potential defendant may be insulated from liability, in whole or in part, because of the application of foreign law, enforceable disclaimers and releases, the Warsaw Convention, U.S. federal and state statutes limiting the liability of cruise ships and hotels and tariffs limiting the liability of carriers. Successful travel litigation depends upon the selection of viable defendants and the application of modern liability theories.

Cooperating air carriers may function as tour operators and be subject to the same theories of liability. For example, an air carrier may own and/or control a captive tour operator. Or the air carrier may be a partner or joint venturer and help finance, organize, operate or market tours to the general public. Air carriers may, however, function as independent contractors entering into arm's length transactions with tour operators. Under these circumstances a cooperating air carrier may be held vicariously liable because of an assumed duty, breach of warranty, apparent authority or third party beneficiary theory. Lastly, the duties and obligations of both tour operators and air carriers may be governed by DOT Public Charter regulations or State travel seller regulations.

As a general rule tour operators may be able to disclaim liability, in the absence of their own negligence, for a consumer's physical injures caused, primarily, by the negligence of a foreign supplier. The traditional theory being that a principal should not be liable for the torts of independent contractors. This general rule can be circumvented by applying one or more of the following theories of liability.

A tour operator may be held liable for the consumer's physical injuries if the tour operator promised, either expressly or implicitly, that the tour would be delivered in a safe and careful manner. Brochure language such as "safe and enjoyable cycling area", "Marenco's administration and staff work together to make your stay comfortable, safe", "suitable for handicapped individuals", "perfectly safe" canoeing conditions and "safe buses" may generate liability under a breach of warranty theory. Alternatively, the tour operator may assume a duty to deliver safe travel services. Assumed duties may more readily overcome written disclaimers than a warranty.

Escorted tours feature close supervision and tour coordination provided by professional tour guides. Older consumers and the parents of students purchase escorted tours. Some sports' tours provide instructors to train and supervise the activities of the participants. In their brochures tour operators will promise that " every tour will be escorted by a qualified professional tour director...carefully selected and trained...informative, they know precisely what you will be seeing and doing...they've been there before "and their " tour escort was a professional and qualified to serve travelers in all matters". Consumers, especially the parents of students, rely upon promises of close supervision in purchasing such a tour. Consumer injuries caused by the negligence of the tour guide may support claims against the tour operator for negligent selection and supervision of tour guides and misrepresentation of their training, expertise and knowledge of the tour locale.

Tour operators and air carriers may lend their names to promotional brochures giving consumers the impression of ownership and control. When Trans World Airlines describes tours as TWA Getaway tours it is reasonable for consumers to believe that TWA owns, operates, controls and is responsible for the delivery of such tours. When hotel and rental car franchisors fail to distinguish between themselves and foreign franchisees the former may be held liable for the torts of the latter. Describing foreign bus companies, taxi services and ground service providers in possessory terms can generate liability.

Tour operators select the suppliers that will provide the component travel services which make up the package tour. Tour operators should investigate the reliability and willingness of suppliers to deliver safe travel services. Such an investigation should reveal the supplier's financial solvency, prior accident and safety history, the existence of insurance and compliance with all applicable licensing and safety regulations, both domestic and foreign.

A failure to conduct such an investigation may generate liability for the negligent selection of suppliers. Tour operators should design itineraries which maximize safety and minimize the consumer's exposure to risk. Of course, calculated exposure to risk may be a strong selling point in marketing "adventure" tours featuring challenging terrain or white water rafting.

Tour operators may be held liable for unnecessarily exposing consumers to risk or designing itineraries in a negligent manner. If tour operators hold themselves out as owning or controlling a foreign service provider then they may be estopped from denying liability for the torts of foreign air carriers, resorts, rental car companies, tour bus companies and other independent contractors. Consumers reasonably rely upon the appearance of ownership and control in purchasing the tour package.

Supply Chain Engagement

As intermediaries between tourists and tourism service providers, tour operators bring together a variety of tourism-related services to form a complete holiday package, which is then marketed to customers either directly or through travel agents. Each package generally consists of accommodation, transport both to and from the destination, ground transport within the destination, and events or activities such as excursions and social activities. Because most of the goods and services included in a holiday package are provided by a supply chain of subcontracted companies, organizations and agents, tour operators are not always in direct control of the environmental and social impacts of those products. Yet, consumers increasingly expect the companies they buy from to ensure that their products provide not just quality and value-for-money, but also safeguard environmental and social sustainability.

Companies must take responsibility for ensuring the sustainability of all the inputs that go into their products. For tour operators, who offer products comprised almost entirely of contracted goods and services, this means that effectively implementing sustainability policies requires working closely with suppliers to improve sustainability performance in all the components of a holiday - throughout the life cycle of a holiday package. "Consumers are increasingly interested in the world behind the product they buy. Life cycle thinking implies that everyone in the whole chain of a product's life cycle, from cradle to grave, has a responsibility and a role to play, taking into account all the relevant external effects." The actions presented are applicable to tour operators of any size, from the smallest to the largest.

Working with suppliers to integrate sustainability into the supply chain can benefit tour operators, suppliers, customers and destinations. From a financial standpoint, improved sustainability can lower costs through greater operating efficiency, reduced waste generation, and reduced consumption of energy and water. Sustainability practices can also lead to increased revenue and shareholder value by generating more repeat business and attracting new business from customers who value good environmental and social performance.

A strong positive reputation as a company that cares about sustainability issues, coupled with improvements to the quality of the tourism experience provided to clients, can result in increased customer satisfaction and loyalty, strengthened brand value, enhanced publicity and marketing opportunities, and better acceptance by local communities in destinations.

Good performance and a high-quality, sustainable product can also help a tour operator reduce the risk of conflict or problems with suppliers, governments, staff and local communities, and improve its status as a respected partner in destinations. This may mean enhanced access to key business resources such as capital, the ability to develop products to meet growing market demand, improved relationships with governments, and a motivated and loyal staff. The costs and benefits of integrating sustainability criteria into the supply chain will vary for each company, depending on:

— Purchasing and contracting arrangements with suppliers;

— Availability of alternate suppliers in key destinations;

— Suppliers' current levels of sustainability performance and potential for change;

— Barriers to sustainability, such as external factors;

— A company's main sustainability and operational concerns; and

— Resources available to implement and promote sustainability throughout the supply chain.

For a tour operator, effectively integrating sustainability into its supply chain will require the establishment of a coherent company policy and accompanying management system that set out clear targets and actions on economic, environmental and social performance. Building this system on already existing internal processes will help keep down the costs of implementation and promote integration within a company's overall operations. To establish this policy, a company needs to conduct a baseline assessment of its tourism service suppliers' current performance on sustainability, in order to determine priority targets and actions. The management system should include procedures for monitoring, reviewing and reporting on progress made in integrating sustainability principles into the company's supply chain. This helps to ensure transparency and allow tour operators to adapt any policies or actions that are not achieving their stated goals.

Progress can be measured against the initial baseline assessment.

Tour operators are well-placed to support suppliers in improving their economic, environmental and social performance. As tour operators interact directly with potential customers, they understand their clients' growing demands for high quality and sustainability. They also often have access to technology and information that smaller suppliers may have difficulty obtaining on their own. Because tour operators deal with a wide range of different suppliers, they can more easily gather information on a variety of best practices and facilitate the sharing of experiences amongst suppliers.

There are a number of ways that tour operators can enable their suppliers to improve their sustainability performance and meet set sustainability criteria and targets. Three of these measures - awareness raising, technical support and the provision of incentives. The appropriate mix of support measures for each company and supplier will depend on the results of the baseline assessment and the approach that the company has chosen to adopt for implementing its sustainable supply chain strategy.

Full integration of sustainability issues into a tour operator's business practices will require alterations to the way purchasing choices are made and suppliers' contracts are written. Inclusion of sustainability criteria in suppliers' contracts highlights the importance of sustainability issues to the tour operator's core business and ensures that priority issues are addressed with suppliers from the start. Sustainability criteria can be incorporated into suppliers' contracts to set both minimum performance standards that all suppliers of a particular type must meet and further optional criteria that they are encouraged to achieve. Performance against sustainability criteria will need to be monitored and assessed as part of regular reviews of suppliers.

4

HOME-BASED TRAVEL AGENTS

The twentieth century saw the rise of the travel agent. Middlemen (which is what travel agents are, in effect) became necessary for a number of reasons. Travel is a very complex product—a whole series of products, in effect. In the early days, at least, the companies that provided the products were far more adept at providing than at selling. Their customers were also very widely distributed geographically. These and other factors created an opportunity for entrepreneurs who agreed to represent the products of many different travel suppliers to a local market in exchange for a commission on the sale. That commission was traditionally ten percent, although as in all selling situations top producers were rewarded with higher commissions, called "overrides" in the travel business.

The system of distributing travel products through a network of travel agencies took hold and travel agencies themselves came to look very much alike, sharing a great many common features. They were storefront, retail businesses, located in commercial districts of town, open during normal retail business hours. In short, they were very much like the clothing shops, boutiques, grocery stores, bookstores, and other retailers with whom they shared the block. This picture is what we call the "traditional" travel agency.

The traditional travel agency looks the way it does for many reasons, but several concern us here. Mostly they have to do with the airlines. Airline tickets are written (or printed, now) on blank paper called "ticket stock." In its blank form this paper is like a blank, but valid, check. Anyone who has it can write a ticket to anywhere for any value. Hence the term, "write your own ticket." Ticket stock is extremely valuable and since it is entrusted to travel agencies the airlines had a very valid reason to ensure that their ticket stock was safe. So they developed a set of rules that would tend to ensure that they could trust the travel agents who were selling their tickets. These rules included things like:

A business location in a commercial district. In other words, the travel agency had to look and act like a "store." A system of bonding, to assure the airline that the travel agency owner was solvent and respectable and, therefore, not likely to be tempted to do anything fishy with the airline's precious ticket stock.

Another factor determining the look and feel of the traditional travel agency is the computer. Travel agencies were one of the first businesses to be extensively computerized. The complex and expensive computerized reservations systems (CRS) that made ticketing easy encouraged even more centralization and "professionalism" in the travel agent industry. In other words, if you wanted to be a travel agent you had to open a storefront agency with its high overhead and complex computer systems. This took a lot of money. Of course, you could also get trained to operate a CRS and go to work in a storefront agency, and many agency owners started out just this way.

This pattern, in turn, created another distinguishing characteristic of the traditional travel agency: it was a place to which would-be travelers came to talk to agents sitting at a desk operating a CRS. Most travel agents became "order takers." Of course, there were always exceptions to this general rule. Many travel agencies employed "outside agents" to hustle up business. These outside agents were, in effect, free ranging inside agents who returned to the agency and their CRSs to generate the airline tickets and other bookings they had made outside. Some agencies used "bird dogs" as they are called, people who sent customers into the agency location where inside agents would cater to their needs. Bird dogs performed a valuable service and were compensated with a small percentage of any commissions that resulted from their referrals. This was very much akin to the "finder's fees" paid in other industries. Nonetheless, these were exceptions that proved the rule: most travel agents were reactive order takers tied to their desks and the CRSs that sat on them. All this began to change in the 90s thanks to a number of intertwining trends.

Smart Marketing

Some clever fellow decided he could make money marketing the "romance" and "mystique" of being a travel agent, or more specifically the travel benefits that (in theory) came with the mere fact of identifying yourself as a travel agent.This notion was copied and very quickly there were any number of travel agencies working a high-powered and sophisticated twist on the old bird-dog system. "Be one of our outside independent agents," the pitch went, "and refer business to our inside agents. In return, we'll give you a small commission and, best of all, a photo ID card that proves you're a travel agent and that you can use to get all sorts of discounts and other goodies."

This marketing approach has met with varying degrees of success on its own terms. What is less in doubt is the fact that it has been extremely controversial within the travel agent community and vigorous efforts have been made to put an end to it, thus far to no avail. Although this may change in the future, the current situation appears to be that, while what these travel agencies are doing may anger other travel agents, it is not illegal. These agencies call themselves referral agencies; their critics call them card mills. Whatever terminology you prefer, they seem to here to stay.

The rise of the personal computer. Employees of travel agencies were for a long while the most computer-savvy people to be found outside academia or large corporations. When personal computers started popping up everywhere, just about anyone could do what travel agents did if they had the right software.

Improved communications. It's hard to imagine now how recent and revolutionary the introduction of the fax machine was. In retrospect, it had a profound effect on the travel distribution system with its ability to transmit bookings quickly and accurately. Now, the Internet is replacing the fax as a means to quickly send and receive data.

Commission caps and cuts. Then the airlines started cutting travel agents' commission rates and limiting the amount of commissions they paid at those rates. Airline tickets had never been something that travel agents got rich on, but they were steady and those first and business class tickets paid very healthy commissions. Now the airlines were dropping agents' pay below their costs. In other words, many agents were actually losing money on every airline ticket they wrote.

A lot of agents started asking themselves some hard-hitting questions. "Why am I carrying all this expensive overhead just to please the airlines when the airlines are driving me out of business?" A lot of smaller agencies closed, some to go out of business forever but many to reopen as home-based agencies, freed from the heavy financial burdens of a storefront agency and also free to spurn the airlines that had spurned them, free to concentrate on selling higher-priced, higher-margin products. Many agents who took this route saw a dramatic increase in their take-home pay.

As we enter a new millennium, these intertwining forces have combined to create a true revolution in how travel products are distributed. If the twentieth century was the century of the travel agent, the twenty-first will be the century of the home-based travel agent. Home-based travel agencies are opening up at an ever-increasing rate, while the number of storefront agencies has been declining every year. The home-based agent can be a seasoned storefront veteran or a newcomer, but both are in the same boat. They are entering a brave new world of travel marketing that is very different from the traditional storefront model. To succeed in this new environment requires new strategies and new skills.

Responsibilities of Home-based Travel Agents

Broadly speaking, a home-based travel agent is anyone engaged in the marketing and selling of travel products from a home office. That can cover a wide variety of different types of home-based travel agents. However, in the travel industry and more specifically in the travel distribution industry, the term "home-based travel agent" is most often used to refer to someone who works out of their home office as an outside sales representative for a bonded, accredited ARC/IATAN travel agency, usually referred to as the "host agency." The home-based travel agent finds, qualifies, and books the customer; the host agency prints the tickets (if any) and serves as the conduit between the home-based agent and the travel supplier whose product the home-based agent is selling. The home-based travel agent and the host agency share the commissions paid by travel suppliers according to a negotiated percentage split that reflects (or should reflect) the amount of work and effort expended by each party in making the booking happen.

By definition, the home-based travel agent is an independent contractor, which means that he or she has a great degree of freedom as far as determining how and with whom to do business. That means that some home-based travel agents function simply as referral agents, funneling business to a travel agency but not handling any of the booking details themselves. Some home-based travel agents bypass host agencies altogether. One way to do this is to become a "cruise-only" agency. Another way to do this is to specialize in condominium vacations, a niche that has been underserved by traditional travel agencies and which is more than happy to deal directly with home-based travel agents. Other home-based travel agents simply market a limited number of travel products and form direct relationships with individual travel suppliers whose products they represent.

Some home-based travel agents specialize in forms of travel that have developed distribution channels outside the traditional storefront travel agency distribution channel. For example, some people are very content to market educational tours that not only offer extremely attractive pricing but allow the tour organizer (the home-based travel agent) to travel free and earn a stipend (a sort of commission) as well. Organizers of student travel, many of whom are full-time students, are another example of this approach.

Home-based travel agents, of whatever description or level of sophistication, can work either full-time or part-time or only occasionally. That's because the very nature of being an independent contractor is that no one can tell you when to work, how to work, or how hard to work.

There are home-based travel agents who earn pin money, home-based travel agents who earn a tidy part-time income, home-based travel agents who bring down a substantial middle-class income, and home-based travel agents who earn six-figure incomes.

There are so many variations and combinations that it is difficult to define the "typical" home-based travel agent. This means that virtually anyone can be a home-based travel agent, on their own terms and at their own pace, creating the type of home-based travel marketing business that makes sense for them.

If you've been searching for travel agent career information, you know it's hard to get straight advice on your new travel agent career. Information can be gard to come by and everyone has their own opinion. This page gives travel agent career information for home-based travel agents. On this site you will also find information on travel agent schools.

Travel agent career information tailored to your situation. In the meantime, however, consider these good solid reasons for joining the thousands of people who are having fun and making money in their travel agent career - information you can put to use now.

Are you a traveler? If you love travel yourself, you have already mastered a major challenge for anyone in sales—you know your product. It is now a relatively simple matter to translate the knowledge and enthusiasm you already possess into powerful sales presentations that will bring you your first bookings and steady repeat business. In addition, you'll start saving money on your own travel instantly.

Are you looking for a low-investment part-time business? Look no further. You can become a part-time home-based travel agent today. And your initial investment can be absolutely zero.

Do you need a flexible schedule? Here's a business that allows you to set your own hours like few others. You can chat with folks at work or call them at home at night. Work full-time one week and scale back the next. Whatever schedule works best for you, you can design a travel business to accommodate it.

Are you a teacher? Many opportunities in the part-time travel field are aimed specifically at teachers. Moreover, teachers have more free time than many other professionals —free time that can be both a boon and a curse. As a part-time travel agent you can use your free time to sell travel and take advantage of it too!

Do you have a built-in audience? Teachers do. They can reach their students and their students' parents. But other professions also offer their practitioners access to large groups of people—ministers, accountants, salespeople, beauticians, the list goes on. All of these people come in contact with many people in the course of their work, people who are often prime prospects for any travel business.

Are you a small businessperson? If so, why not make travel an add-on to your existing product line? Everyone who comes into your shop can learn about the travel opportunities you have to offer. If you send catalogs or brochures to your customers on a regular basis you have already paid for the postage to send them a flyer about a great bargain on an upcoming tour or cruise. Or why not offer discounted travel to your employees as an extra benefit? You'll forego some or all of the commission, but the goodwill you generate will be hard to beat.

Do you travel on business? Many people who travel on business pay their own way and then get reimbursed by their employer or client. As a travel agent, you can earn a commission on every bit of that travel. If you own your own business and spend a considerable amount of money on travel, then the prospect of saving 5% to 7% on your travel expenditures should make your bottom line sit up and take notice.

Are you in sales? If you are, you've probably already thought of a dozen ways you can prosper in this sideline. Your existing sales skills will fit perfectly in a home-based travel business and you no doubt already have a large and ever-growing pool of prospects.

Are you retired? Perfect. Not only do you now have the time to devote to learning about travel, but you are an integral part of the largest and fastest growing market for leisure travel. You can make a handsome income, and enjoy some wonderful fringe benefits, just by specializing in the travel interests and needs of folks just like you.

Are you home with the kids? Here's a way to make a bit of extra money at the same time you're burping and diapering. Much of your business with customers can be conducted on the phone; your friends probably won't mind if you're bouncing junior on your knee while you talk to them. You can use baby's nap time to get on the phone and call the travel suppliers. It's a perfect scenario for the homemaker or househusband.

Are you committed to a full-time career? If you are not sure, the information on this site will show you how to test the waters for a minimal investment. If you find you love the travel business as much as you thought, great! You'll be ideally situated to maximize your income potential. If, on the other hand, you decide the travel business is not for you, you have the option of continuing on a part-time basis or getting out altogether without having spent a small fortune discovering you've made a wrong career turn.

Importance of Travel Agent License

Other than that single exception, there really is no such

thing as a travel agent license - if by license you mean having to pass some sort of state-administered test, like you do when you apply for a driver's license. However, some local governments (counties, towns, cities, etc.) might have "license" provisions for those operating a home-based business. This is more in the nature of a tax than a license (in the "driver's license" sense of the word). The local municipality uses ordinances like this to keep tabs on who's operating businesses in residential neighborhoods.

This is pretty much a formality and you shouldn't be worried that the local powers that be will tell you that you can't run your business. Their main concern is that you don't start a manufacturing business that might involve dangerous chemicals or processes, or a retail business that might bring a steady stream of cars and customers to your house, thus compromising the residential character of the neighborhood. And, of course, they get some more money for the municipal coffers.

Regulations like this are not a universal rule. There is a very good chance your local area has no such regulation. There is no such requirement in New York City, which is one of the most heavily taxed and regulated business environments in the country. If your local government has such a rule, you should abide by it. Check with your local Chamber of Commerce; they should be able to tell you all about local ordinances. And don't worry about it. Likewise, you do not have to be "certified" as a travel agent to become a home-based travel agent.

Some host agencies only want to deal with agents who have experience. So if you've just graduated from a travel school, you may have a "certificate" but no experience. Other host agencies won't deal with rank beginners but will deal with recent travel school graduates; in this case a certificate can be helpful. Many, many host agencies will sign you up pretty much no questions asked. No certificate required. No travel agent license needed.

Another thing that can seem something like a "license" or "certificate" is the "fictitious name certificate," which is called different things in different places. Essentially, it's a legal formality that allows you to cash checks written to your business name. Let's take the case of Sue Jones and her home-based travel business, called Travel With Sue. Now the bank will not deposit a check made out to "Travel With Sue" into Sue Jones' personal account. The solution? Sue registers her business name at the town hall or county court house, gets her fictitious name certificate for "Travel With Sue," takes it to the bank and opens a business account in the name "Travel With Sue."

Some states have laws that require travel agents to register. Again, these are not true licensing laws. They are a misguided form of taxation on travel agents that lets the state pretend it is protecting the interests of consumers. You don't need to pass a test to register under these laws; all the state wants is your money. Many beginners want to know what it will cost them to "get started" as a home-based travel agent. It's a somewhat tricky question to answer, because everyone is different, with different goals and different needs.

It is actually possible to start for "free." The quotation marks are there to indicate that even what's free can cost you something in time, energy, postage, phone calls, shoe leather, business fees, transportation, and any number of other miscellaneous expenditures. But the fact remains that it is possible to become an outside agent with no "upfront fee." The classic way to do that is to find an agency, usually a local agency, to take you on as an outside sales representative. No money changes hands. You agree to find clients and book their travel.

The problem with this scenario is that it can be difficult to find an agency willing to take you on. It's a little different, of course, if you are an experienced agent with an inside track record and (preferably) a following. But even experienced agents can find it hard to locate an amenable local agency. Another issue is that the commission splits offered in this situation are typically lower than the splits you can find elsewhere.

Most fledgling home-based agents, however, start out by paying a fee to a host agency that specializes, to a greater or lesser extent, in dealing with outside agents. The fee can range anywhere from a few hundred dollars to nearly $10,000. One reason for this is that many new agents don't know there's any alternative. But there are a number of very good reasons to take this route. In fact, many experienced agents and even former agency owners have chosen to start their home-based ventures in this fashion.

Why do the upfront fees vary so widely? In theory, the more you pay the more you get - in terms of training, support, and miscellaneous hand holding. That's the theory. In some cases, it seems that the host agencies are charging a given fee because they think they can get it. The host agencies, to give them their due, have a valid interest in discouraging those who will not become productive agents and a high sign up fee is a good way to do that. A productive agent will quickly amortize his or her upfront investment. In addition to any costs of signing up with a host there are an array of miscellaneous expenses that are common to starting up any business, although a home-based agent can keep those to a minimum.

Probably the must-have accessory is a business card and these are very cheap. You should also register with your local and/or state government if that is required. Surprisingly, many people don't bother. However, once you want a business checking account you will have to register with the county courthouse in your business name.

Many of these "additional" business expenses can be spread out over time so as to keep your upfront cost to a minimum. Hopefully, many of these initial outlays will be quickly recovered in commission income.

Seriously though, it is a small price to pay for knowledge that will put you on an equal footing with the host agencies and suppliers with whom you'll be dealing. The component on choosing a host agency has the potential to save you thousands of dollars in sign up fees and earn you thousands more in the form of more generous commissions.

HOST AGENCY

Most home-based travel agents work with at least one "host agency." A host agency is a bonded, accredited ARC/ IATAN agency through which the home-based agent makes bookings.Home-based travel agents are not employees of their host agency, although many home-based travel agents seem to think they are and many host agencies treat them just that way. The home-based travel agent is an independent contractor, a separate business, just like the host agency. The home-based travel agent and the host agency are two, theoretically equal, businesses that join forces to accomplish goals that neither would be able to accomplish alone.

The primary reason a home-based travel agent works with a host agency is to collect commissions that he or she otherwise would not be able to collect.The most obvious example is airline tickets. Airlines will not ticket for independent home-based agents. Only an ARC/IATAN agency can print airline tickets, and only an ARC/IATAN agency can collect commissions paid on those tickets. Consequently, the home-based travel agent needs the host agency in order to provide his or her clients with airline tickets; the host agency needs the business the home-based travel agent generates to expand its market share.

In other cases, working through a host agency makes it easier to collect commissions, since many travel suppliers have long used the ARC and/or IATAN numbers of travel agencies to track who is owed what commissions. That's changing and many home-based travel agents have direct relationships with many travel suppliers. Still, a surprising number of home-based travel agents simply funnel all their business through their host agency whether they "need to" or not.

The challenge for home-based travel agents is to balance their business between bookings that must be shared with the host agency and bookings that they can keep all to themselves. Sometimes it's not obvious. If you get a 70% split from your host agency and could get the entire commission directly from the supplier, that might seem like a no brainer. But what if the host agency has a "preferred supplier" relationship with the supplier and gets a 15% commission, while you, as an independent home-based travel agent, could only get 10%? Do the math and you'll realize that going through the host agency earns you more money in this case.

Beginners try to establish direct relationships with suppliers until they have learned the ropes —paid their dues, so to speak. But established home-based travel agents should carefully examine their business to see if they are "giving away" commissions to their host agency that they could put directly into their own pocket.

Refferral Agents

Most of the "become a travel agent today!" deals you see advertised involve becoming a "referral agent." The companies offering these deals may say you'll be an "associate agent" or and "independent agent" or something else, but you'll be a referral agent nonetheless. That means that your job is simply to refer potential customers to the sponsoring agency —get them to call a toll-free number where the agency's "inside agents" will take care of closing the sale and handle the booking details. In exchange for providing this service, you receive a portion of the commission earned by the agency.

So far, there's is nothing new or controversial in this. It's called "bird-dogging" and has been going on in the travel industry for years. What's new and controversial is the aggressive packaging and marketing of the concept that has occurred in recent years. To complicate things a bit, there are two basic types of referral agent programs.

One incorporates a multi-level marketing (MLM) component, whereby you not only receive compensation for signing up new agents but participate in the commissions generated through their activities as well. To some observers this looks uncomfortably like a pyramid scheme. Consequently, agencies in this category have been attacked on legal grounds. Some have been outlawed in several states. Others have gone out of business as a result of the legal actions taken against them, only to resurface after modifying their programs. Not surprisingly, they have been attacked vigorously by travel agents and the travel trade press. In short, they have been unstable.

Referral agencies of this sort are becoming increasingly rare. For one thing, MLM programs require hefty margins and the 10% commission on a lot of travel products is wafer thin, especially when you are trying to divvy it up for a downline.

Non-MLM Referral Agencies

Another type of referral agency has been more successful than the MLMers, at least in gaining the grudging respect of the travel industry. These agencies are multi-level to the extent that they pay a bounty or referral fee if you sign up new agents, but they don't have any of those complicated formulas that promise that you'll earn income though a "downline" of the agents you've signed up. They, too, have been controversial, although they have actually managed to some good notices from the travel trade press if not from the rank and file travel agent.

Referral agencies have remarkable similarities. It's almost as if they all worked off the same business and marketing plans. Here are some of the hallmarks of a referral agency:

— A $495 sign-up fee. Most, maybe all, referral agencies will charge you $495 to become one of their agents. If they charged $500 or more, they would trigger much stricter regulatory oversight, a fact that raises eyebrows among more cynical observers. In addition, you will probably have to pay an annual fee of $99, $149, or more.

— A photo ID card. A big part of the marketing lure is the photo ID card they issue to their agents. This card, you are told, will unlock the door to discounts and privileges available only to travel agents. This is why referral agencies are called "card mills" by many professional travel agents.

— A bounty on new agents. Referral agencies are constantly looking for more agents. They will pay you anywhere from $75 to $200 for each new one you recruit.

— "Selling" travel. Most referral agencies encourage you to talk up the joys of travel in general, talk up their agency in particular, and pass out to all and sundry a business card with their 800 number. The card contains your "PIN number," a unique identifier that assures you get your commission. One of the most attractive aspects of this deal is that once a customer has your PIN attached to his or her name, you receive a cut of all that person's travel in perpetuity.

— Fixed commissions on everything else. Most referral agencies "assume" that the commission is always 10% and pay you a portion of that commission on everything other than air. In fact, the agency may be earning a commission as high as 17% from some suppliers. In this case, the referring agent gets 5%, while the agency itself gets 12%.

— Agent-only discounts. Most referral agencies offer special in-house deals to their own agents. These are deals you purchase through the agency, as opposed to deals you request from a supplier using your ID card.

Viewed strictly as a way to make money by selling travel, the answer is probably no. First of all, you're not "selling travel" precisely. You are referring business to inside agents who do the actual selling. That's one reason why the commissions never exceed 50% of a fixed 10% commission. If you are looking to roll up your sleeves and do the same job as a "traditional" travel agent, this deal is clearly not for you. On the other hand, a five percent commission for simply referring a customer is not a bad deal at all. And that appeals to a great many people.

Figures released by the major referral agencies suggest that the average referral agent is only referring about $5,000 in business a year, so none of them would appear to be getting rich. Of course, some referral agents no doubt refer far more business and do fairly well.

Even the management of referral agencies will admit, off the record, that none of their agents is making a living doing this. The few who join wanting to be full- or even part-time travel agents no doubt soon realize their mistake and seek out the more businesslike deals available to home-based travel agents.

Most people who sign up do so for the benefits — real, imagined, or a bit of both. A salesperson for one referral agency said that "most of our members pay for the card in one weekend just with the hotel discounts."

Let's start with air fare. First of all, don't expect to wave your referral agent ID at an airline reservationist and get a discount. Travel agents do get discounts from the airlines but there's a lot of paperwork involved, a higher standard of proof, and restrictions on travel dates. Even then, the travel agent flying on a reduced fare is subject to being bumped if the flight fills up. A lot of travel agents, in fact, think these discounts are more trouble than they're worth.

What you might get from an airline with your ID card is a complimentary upgrade to first or business class on a flight for which you hold a paid-for coach ticket. You show your ID card to the gate agent and ask if there are any "courtesy upgrades" available.

Now as you might expect, this is the sort of thing that gets "real" travel agents especially hot under the collar. Because they complained so loudly, the airlines (the domestic ones at least) have been getting a lot savvier about travel agent ID cards. Most of them have declared that they will only accept the IATAN card as proof that the holder is a travel agent.

Because of the furor over this ploy, the referral agencies are very careful about how they position this benefit. Still, the anecdotal evidence is that it can be pulled off, by some people some of the time.

For some people, this ploy can raise ethical questions. Others claim that using a referral agency ID in this fashion is technically illegal, although we can't imagine an airline pressing charges. At most, you can expect to be humiliated when a knowledgeable gate agent turns you down and gives you a piece of his or her mind. Still, a business class seat can be mighty tempting. This potential benefit lures a lot of referral agents.

Also, the end of base commissions on airline tickets for travel agencies has made the referral agencies less attractive. Time was when you could book your air travel through a referral agency and get a modest discount. If you flew a lot, those discounts could add up. No more.

You can get discounts on hotel rates and rental cars by flashing your referral agent ID, but these discounts are not really "travel agent discounts" like the ones extended to holders of the IATAN card. Rather, they are similar in nature to discounts given to travel club members. In some case, however, the hotel discounts are real and very attractive. You have to know the "going rate" to know how good a particular discount actually is.

The "for our agents only" deals on cruises, hotel packages, and the like are something else again. Some of these can be quite attractive. Typically they are for mid-market products in destinations most popular with the masses of tourists. You are unlikely to find any deals on luxury properties or niche products. You are more likely to find cruise deals on Carnival than on Seabourne.

One of the major problems with referral agencies is that their infrastructure sometimes has trouble keeping up with their marketing. In other words, they sign up so many agents that they have trouble answering the flood of phone calls that results. This can be particularly embarrassing when you have handed out a business card to a friend who calls you a week later to complain that "that number you gave me is always busy." Long waits on hold and unmet promises to return calls are other problems.

The agencies are aware of these problems and seem to make a good faith effort to solve them. Once you get through to the agency, the inside agents all seem to be well-trained, efficient, and reasonably accomplished at searching out the best fare. If you have a straightforward ticketing request, you are likely to get good service.

It must be said that for some people there is the thrill that they are "beating the system" even if, in their heart of hearts, they know they're not really. Clearly these deals appeal to a great many people. Becoming a referral agent will make the most sense if:

— You travel a lot. Those hotel discounts do add up, although it may take you more than a weekend to recoup your investment.

— You are an upscale traveler. If you are used to staying in $300-a-night hotels, the discounts may be attractive —if and when you get them. And if you regularly travel overseas in coach class, getting an upgrade on a single trip could make this deal worthwhile to you.

— You are willing to sign up a few new agents. If this is the sort of thing you're good at, you can actually make some money. Just be prepared for some negative blow-back when people to whom you have sold a card find that they get less than they anticipated.

— You are bold enough to try for the free upgrade every time you fly. If you are successful, you may find your investment paying for itself very quickly.

Travel Agent Fams

There is a great deal of misinformation floating about on the subject of travel agent fams. Some people think that all they have to do is pay for a travel agent ID card to instantly join a never-ending gravy train of free vacations under the guise of travel agent fams. Alas, that's simply not true.

Travel agent fams exist and they can be very, very economical, even free. Travel agent fams (or "familiarization trips" as they are more formally known) exist because travel suppliers understand that travel agents do a better job of selling travel products and destinations when they have experienced them for themselves. Travel agent fams, then, are designed to give the travel agent product knowledge he or she wouldn't have otherwise.

It should be fairly obvious, even from that brief description, that travel suppliers want something in return for sponsoring travel agent fams. They want the travel agents who go on these travel agent fams to send them customers. Lots of customers.

That being the case, the travel supplier has a vested interest in making sure that the people invited on travel agent fams really are travel agents. And not just travel agents but productive travel agents. Increasingly, those travel agent ID cards just don't cut it, because travel suppliers are wising up to the fact that most of the people holding them don't really sell all that much travel.

Because travel suppliers spend a great deal of money when they offer travel agent fams, they want a return on their investment. That's why they keep travel agents busy on these fams. Yes, there is free time, but it is limited. Most travel agent fams are a relentless schedule of site visits and hotel inspections. At each stop, someone bombards you with facts and figures about their attraction or property. This is vital information for serious travel agents, but a living hell for those who go on travel agent fams thinking they are getting a low-cost vacation.

It is possible for newly-minted home-baseed travel agent to take advantage of travel agent fams. The secret is to sign up for seminars offered by suppliers who understand the value of home-based agents and are eager to tap this growing market. The cost can be surprisingly modestand the best part is you get world-class professional training into the bargain. How to profit from this perk is explained in our home-based travel agent training course.

5

Retail Travel Services

The Retail Travel Services Industry is labor intensive. Thousads of people are employed within the industry's retail outlets, administrative support locations and head offices. However, since 1990, the Retail Travel Services Industry (RTSI) has been under great pressure to operate with less revenue from the airline industry because of the lowering, capping and ultimate elimination of commissions. Profit margins have traditionally been small within the industry hindering investment in staff training and new technologies among SMEs - requirements for remaining competitive in the retail travel business.

A majority of travel retailers have introduced service fees to make up for a portion of the lost revenues. But retailers will have to develop new products and services to generate additional revenues and add value to their businesses. As well, the RTSI must become less dependent on the airlines and computer reservation systems (CRSs) as traditional distribution channels as these stakeholders adjust their business models in the e-travel landscape. In addition, e-commerce, the Internet and other technologies are revolutionizing the industry and traditional roles within it.

Travel agents face disintermediation - the threat of being squeezed out of their role as intermediaries in the industry. Airlines have become more aggressive competitors through their online marketing initiatives. These front-end web portals have been important catalysts for the industry to rapidly adapt to this changing environment. Mitigating this dilemma means reevaluating the existing business model and its value proposition to the consumer, suppliers and other stakeholders. Any transformation must take into consideration factors such as the development of new business relationships, re - deployment of human resources, technology, training and the development of new products and services focusing on sectors of the travel industry, which are forecast to have a speedier recovery, at least in the short-term.

Transformations and Emerging IT Strategies

Business-to-business (B2B) and businessto- consumer (B2C) applications are driving industry efforts to reduce costs through the use of online business tools and the increased use of automation. After investing and then offsetting their costs of development, travel suppliers have increasingly adopted a business strategy that encourages B2B and B2C sales. Brochures, catalogues, e-procurement and other ordering mechanisms are readily available on the Internet by most of the tourism supply chain. New technologies have allowed many suppliers to achieve economies of scale by eliminating redundancies within their organizations such as the rationalization of reservation and purchasing staff. Increasingly, suppliers are focused on minimizing their distribution costs for products and services.

The methods and mechanisms used to access these travel products and services often determine the manner in which sales can be closed and the data stored and mined for future e-marketing initiatives. These new business systems are becoming increasingly sophisticated in managing both B2B and B2C relationships. This trend to gain control over relationship management and their costs will continue for the near future. This is particularly relevant since 9/11/01 shocks to the Retail Travel Services Industry, which required all stakeholders to reduce expenses while trying to improve sales opportunities.

As well, many larger companies in the tour operator and Retail Travel Services Industry have vertically integrated.They have found a need to own, command and control the distribution of their products and services within a hierarchical or linear value chain. In the fourth quarter of 2001, Expedia, a leader in online travel reservations, overtook Travelocity.com as the Web's top travel agency. Forrester Research forecasts these "Web agencies will integrate vertically and across channels, eventually dictating pricing and terms to suppliers who will lose control over retail pricing and marketing."However, these strategies are not an all - purpose solution for a complex industry.

Small and medium - sized travel service retailers can also find competitive opportunities by forming alliances, strategic partnerships, or informal/formal methods of collaboration to create a competitive advantage. Those firms which partner successfully and focus on their core competencies aimed at retaining customer loyalty, are often more successful in their abilities to compete effectively and efficiently. Direct contact between buyer and seller helps ensure that customer needs are fulfilled with professional customer service. Customer loyalty remains one of the pillars of success within the Retail Travel Services Industry. However, new technologies are empowering customers and changing their buying habits. Customer loyalty may be a purchase - by - purchase experience remaining only as long as service meets or exceeds expectations.

A recent trend in the Internet technology arena is the ability of organizations to deliver and manage applications through remote centers to multiple clients. These are known as Application Service Providers (ASP). The development and emergence of the hosted applications model has been targeted at the small and medium-sized enterprises (SMEs). ASP firms can deploy, manage and remotely host software applications now packaged in "suite" applications. This is done through central servers, which are contracted by lease or rental agreements for the services they provide. This model ideally suits the majority of the RTSI, which is primarily composed of SMEs. This allows more time for the travel retailer to focus on their customers while leaving the technical know-how to the ASP.

The ability to offer personal service and customization has been a key to the success of the off-line Retail Travel Services Industry. But online travel sites are emulating this business style. Customer loyalty in the e-commerce environment means replacing human interaction by giving online users inter-active options to explore and express their travel preferences and ensuring easier and faster access to the information each time they log on.

Most on-line travel agent sites offer customization. It is easily performed (by allowing users to register and using cookies to recognize them on each of their visits) and offers many benefits, such as the ability to gain a better knowledge of the preferences and traveling habits of customers and to target offers and products more effectively. The "clicks and bricks" retail travel agency combining e-commerce sales tools and the ability to have personal contact (either face - to - face or via traditional communications), is becoming an important sales link to convert a sale comfortably.

Another popular trend has been the development of niche products and services. Offering products targeted at a specific segment of the market allows an online travel company to differentiate itself from its competitors, as well as developing a strong customer base loyal to the brand as it offers products and services few competitors can match. These strategies can be complementary to - or departures from - their core businesses. The RTSI was quick to adopt the simplest forms of technology as supplied by the CRS vendors. However, most suppliers have outpaced the RTSI in adopting Web strategies focused on B2C transactions. They are often moving from their core competencies into new e-business ventures.

Many of the primary suppliers of the Retail Travel Services Industry are experimenting with these new business opportunities. Others have moved aggressively in this direction. The airline industries are developing an e-commerce direct sales approach for their air seats and merchandise. The accommodations industry has found new opportunities in retailing. many hotels doubles as a home furnishings store online. Whotels is an example of one company's efforts to think and market "outside - the - box" developing a successful new business from a distinctive look to its room furnishings originally designed to meet the expectations of upscale travelers. At the end of 1999, the hotelier initiated "Heavenly Beds." These specially - designed rooms are furnished with upgraded products including fine bedding, duvets and especially comfortable pillows offering new and unique hotel living experiences.

While some have ventured into uncharted marketplaces, the Retail Travel Services Industry remains linked to the Computer Reservation Systems (CRS) and the Global Distribution Systems (GDS) as their main source of access and supply to the travel industry supply chain. Many retail travel agents are re-positioning their businesses through the strategic use of the Internet as an information-marketing tool for a range of products and services. However, many others have not changed the primary use of the CRS as their reservations tool. Their accounting systems are tied to the electronic data transactions generated by the CRS each time a sale is made. The data must be routed through the CRS to create the necessary financial reporting and accounting needs.

Suppliers hope to cut costs with direct connect, to boost cross - selling and win travel agency allegiance. Therefore, an emerging trend with suppliers will be a transition to integrated direct connect (IDC) systems which bypass the CRS/GDS. The CRS/GDS with more than $1.5 billion of booking fees at risk, must expand their hosting clients.To remain competitive and relevant to the industry, the CRS/GDS must offer a wider range of products and services. There has been a flurry of activity in this sector to gain competitive advantage.Sabre, a dominant CRS player recently took control of Travelocity, making it possible for them to offer web - based solutions and other Internet strategies to the RTSI to maintain their competitive advantage.

Human Resource Matters

While these trends gather momentum, the RTSI has been required to reduce costs, rationalize staff and operate within new economies of scale. The challenge for remaining employees in the RTSI has been to maintain a customer - centric service focus for their clients. Travel agency staffs are being asked to do more for the same - or less - in order to remain employed.

The British arm of Thomas Cook, a global retail travel business, has demonstrated this worldwide trend. The company announced redundancies and pay cuts in 2002. They also scrutinized their benefits package and their true cost of pensions versus wages. Career progression within the company will not mean earning more each year in the same job, but doing different things in the organization thereby enhancing employee skills sets and offering rewards based on their adaptability.

The potential to generate revenues is also declining. In February 2002, British Airways announced the airline will cut its global distribution costs to generate £100 million of savings, including reducing payments to travel agents in the UK for short haul bookings.In March 2002, the American carriers and Air Canada cut commissions to the RTSI. In April 2002, at least two major car rental companies announced they too would no longer pay commission on corporate rates to the RTSI signalling the possibility of further commission cuts in the future. The RTSI must find new sources and techniques for revenue generation in order to provide job stability, opportunities for advancement and meaningful compensation for its employees.

Ironically, the need to restructure has arrived at a time when the intellectual capital and dollars to effect change are extremely limited. However, the cornerstones for success - retaining customer loyalty through enhanced customer service, personalization of products and services and improved communication through the Internet and other traditional vehicles remain important factors. These core competencies are an important platform for the RTSI to evolve their customer (managed) relationships using e-commerce and the Web to retain customers and strengthen supplier relationships at a time when it is needed most.

As well, the industry seasonally sells similar products or services making it difficult to differentiate one company from another. Branding is often the only way to differentiate firms from their competitors. Europe's second largest travel firm, Thomas Cook AG, owned by airline Lufthansa and retail group KarstadtQuelle, will adopt the Thomas Cook logo to boost their customer base and focus on the higher end travel market.Affiliated air carriers will adopt the Thomas Cook brand on all their aircraft reinforcing the retail sector. This reflects one firm's belief in the importance of brand recognition for their retail "bricks and mortar" business component.

Equity in Customer Relationships

Like many other industries, the RTSI must find and create new markets for its services and products, streamline operations through new technologies, identify and work within new economies of scale and re - define their business model. Yet within this complex and ever-changing business landscape, there are industry pillars to build on the traditional role of the retail travel agent.

Consumers continue to be attracted - and faithful to - high levels of personal service. They want value, a composite of quality, price and convenience in the products and services that they purchase. The value of the retail travel agent is a function of location, ease of access and availability. Customers continue to value longstanding, trusted relationships with agents and brands. But in the e-commerce world, consumers have more choices in selecting travel products and customer loyalty is a more fragile commodity.

It is important for the industry to find new ways to retain their value to consumers and in this way preserve their long-term profitability. Re-shaping the business of the Retail Travel Services Industry needs to consider the lifetime value of customers. The industry has to make choices - investing in training for staff, adopting new technologies and creating new products and services such as expanding sales through inbound travel and other valued -added or complementary businesses. Finally, the industry must identify new measurements for success.

Customer value includes both current and future profitability. This supports the notion that "each customer is an investment and determining how much to invest is based on expected returns".Understanding costs is a prerequisite to understanding profitability.

New technologies such as Customer Relationship Management (CRM) allows organizations such as the RTSI to monitor their interaction with customers and determine costs on a customer - by - customer and transaction - by - transaction basis. Recent surveys "clearly point to high levels of trust and loyalty in established travel brands and a very strong interest in recommendation tools serving up professional travel advice on the best getaways and vacation products for each customer.

An overwhelming majority of online vacation package buyers view personalized destination, product content and advice as very valuable. Over 75% share high levels of interest in personal tour recommendations, while over 85% demand personalized emails tailored to their individual needs and travel preferences. Moreover, over 80% of customers firmly support the idea of receiving tailored vacation information and specials, which are constructed to uniquely fit their lifestyle."

How can retail travel agents maintain continuing relationships with customers in a world of well-informed consumers making full use of Internet research tools? While brand equity (the customer's subjective assessment of the brand beyond its objectively perceived value) and value equity (the consumer's assessment of the benefits of a brand) of products are important, they may not retain customers. Companies must make extra efforts to cement their relationships with consumers through retention initiatives insulating their best customers from competitive offers.

For example, a firm can create benefits that would make it more costly to switch to another firm. Discounts, recognition through non-monetary rewards (such as travel points rewarding both the distance and the duration of the travel experience) and special treatment (such as Consumer Appreciation Nights) are just a few ways in which companies can further their relationship with customers. This is referred to as retention equity (the customer's tendency to stick with the brand above and beyond objective and subjective assessments of the brand).

There is a technological aspect involved in retaining customers and enhancing customer loyalty through Web sites. Many companies are developing techniques to attract and encourage customers to stay longer on their sites. These sites have a "stickiness" or "adhesive" content that engages visitor interest. The longer the visitor stays at a site and the more pages that are viewed, the greater the opportunity to generate revenues through advertising sales or online purchases. The challenge lies in understanding customers and providing enriched web site content that convinces them to stay with your site and product.

Business Model of Retail Travel Services

The traditional business model of the Retail Travel Services Industry largely focuses on out bound travel. Statistics reflect that most people buy travel packages during the winter months to travel to southern destinations. During the summer season, The RTSI has segmented with some firms specializing in managed or corporate travel, conference planning, leisure and group travel or niche and incentive travel planning. In recent years, many corporate agencies have become travel management companies for various corporations. In this business model, the travel firms assist in the management of travel budgets and corporate policy of their clients on a contractual fee for service basis. Often, the advantage to the corporate client, is discounted rates in exchange for established volumes of business. As a result, SMEs marketing both corporate and leisure travel are examining new marketplaces outside the competitive domain of managed travel businesses. All stakeholders are examining ways to maximize their business opportunities in the domestic travel market - a market perceived by travelers as a safe destination. Can new strategies, the Internet and technologies such as CRM be catalytic in developing new products and services for the RTSI? Let's examine some facts.

The World Tourism Organization, which keeps statistics on the travel industry around the globe, summed up the 2001 tourism picture noting that the trends were positive until the fall of that year. The organization believes that three types of destinations suffered most from the resulting uncertainty of the travel marketplace. They were "countries that are highly dependent on U.S. outbound travel; destinations that are a long distance from their main generating markets, and countries of the Moslem world."

The World Tourism Organization (WTO) also noted other changing trends in travel including the substitution of domestic trips for international ones and the choice of trips by car or rail rather than air.Although this may not be a long-term development, this is important market intelligence for destination marketing organizations (DMOs) such as the Canadian Tourism Commission (CTC), provincial government destination marketing organizations (PMOs) and visitors and convention bureau's (VCBs) demonstrating the resilience and potential of inbound tourism. This information cannot be taken in isolation of the growing trend in the use of the Internet for shopping. This is particularly important in understanding the opportunities of expanding sales. The Internet is the vehicle for attracting new business opportunities. The Ontario Government recently announced a $16.2 million dollar infusion to enhance the online tourist trade. The Ontario Minister of Tourism indicated that tourism contributes $17.5 billion dollars to the Ontario economy and that the Internet is the first place tourists look for travel.The Ontario site engine will follow emerging trends in e-commerce and allow customization. It will perform searches based on the customer's preferences allowing for maximum flexibility of products and services. This is an ideal opportunity for retail travel services in Ontario to become part of an emerging IT emarketing opportunity. This continues to be one of the most crical challenges facing the RTSI — to adapt to the new ecommerce economy and to participate with important players in online travel sales including the DMOs.

Similar activities are being undertaken by the CVBs, another significant partner for the RTSI with links to local accommodations, attractions and events. The challenge for CVBs is part of a North American trend to find new ways to attract the tourists and to fill hotels.

The RTSI leisure travel model has focused on outbound travel to southern destinations during the winter season and international travel during the summer season. The RTSI has largely depended on attracting a type of traffic tied to factors beyond the control of the industry. Fluctuations in the dollar, shrinkage in commission revenues, the competitive invasion of dot-com suppliers and innovators in other industries such as transportation and accommodation, have shaped consumer spending habits. All stakeholders are searching to identify niche markets and other products or services, which will provide resiliency, stability and a means to remain competitive.

estination Marketing Organizations (DMOs) such as the Canadian Tourism Commission (CTC), provincial tourism agencies (PMOs) and Convention and Visitors Bureaus (CVBs) are unique and untapped resources able to help the RTSI sell Canada smarter. They have a mandate and responsibility to sell Canada to suppliers and the travel trade. Often, they market directly to Canadian and international consumers. They employ a number of different models and partnerships designed to encourage and promote product development and marketing opportunities. One such partnership is the Ontario Tourism Marketing Partnership (OTMP), a partnership that includes the participation of Visitors and Convention Bureaus.

The RTSI has the potential of building and expanding marketing and sales opportunities by partnering with these agencies to expand tourism opportunities. Their marketing strategies are directed at improving sales opportunities within three sectors of the travel industry - retail, wholesale and inbound receptor services.

While there will always be room for small and medium-sized companies, they will be under the greatest stress in the next few years. Some will be purchased by the larger players or be consolidated by like-sized companies with greater capital resources at their disposal. The pace of this process will depend on market conditions and the ability of larger players to begin acquisitions. The hospitality industry has always been tied to the economy at large. In the longterm, the industry will demonstrate confidence, growth, stability and prosperity. However, the road ahead is laden with challenges. The RTSI in Canada has an opportunity to adjust to the long - range viability of their businesses by focusing on short and mid - term strategies.

Developing a Tactical Advantage

Those businesses which recognize the advantage of having an inbound program must move methodically and incrementally to develop a viable product. There is an opportunity to develop new products which feature and market local events, attractions and accommodations. Communities across the world would welcome new partners such as the RTSI, to stimulate tourism. Market entry can be achieved by creating a new product.

The most successful method of launching a new service is through direct marketing to an existing clientele. Most successful retail travel agents have a nucleus of loyal clients, which they may be able to draw upon. By partnering with others who have the same business goals, travel retailers can shorten the start-up period for market entry by sharing skills, knowledge and duties.

Another way of entry is through acquisition or share trade of an existing business (es). Whatever choice is made, shifting the business model to take the first step to competitiveness is often the most difficult. SMEs often fear the time spent away from what they do best has opportunity cost. However, there are new technologies designed to save time and enhance existing and new customer relationships.

Consumers are increasingly looking to the travel retailer to provide what they are searching for, whenever and however they are able to offer it - on the Web, in the store, or on the telephone. The Retail Travel Services Industry has worked hard to present itself as customer - centric and able to fulfill this expectation. Developing a strategy to maintain the loyalty of repeat customers will be critical for the financial viability of the RTSI. The RTSI needs to take on the challenge of Customer Relationship Management (CRM).

Customer Relationship Management (CRM) is a leading-edge topic in contemporary marketing research. It embraces a wide range of different strategies to achieve a systematic process for effectively managing the relationships between companies and their customers. CRM is a business strategy to select and manage the most valuable customer relationships, identifying a business philosophy and culture, which supports effective marketing, sales and service processes. Successful CRM translates into faster service, higher customer satisfaction, customer retention, customer acquisition, repeat purchases, lower cost and profitability.

These technologies can help to reduce the dependency on manual labour, the principal cost to travel retailers while expanding market reach. CRM systems present a product to the customer at the beginning or the end of the customer's purchasing cycle. CRMs allow businesses to know when the customer is likely to buy again and then puts products in front of that customer tailored to meet their known needs and preferences. This helps to prevent the customer from looking elsewhere to purchase a product or service.

As companies acquire more precise knowledge of their clients, they are able to reward their most promising customers (or most profitable) by offering promotions, reduced prices and special incentives based on an evaluation of their individual needs. Usually the firm's top customers constitute a disproportionate value within the company's total client base. The knowledge and ability to focus on profitable customers, while spending less time with less lucrative clients, is a measurable advantage to most firms.

These are traditional tools currently used by the Retail Travel Services Industry in a non- CRM environment. The present method to qualify customers is primarily done by the individual travel agent. Telephone or faceto- face interview techniques are the most common strategy although email is an increasingly important method of communication. It's time-consuming and sometimes discouraging work as external shocks, trends, seasonal peaks and valleys and the competitive nature of the Internet have complicated this process. The relentless pursuit of information from a rich network of sources on the Web has created an information overload.

Increasingly, consumers are testing the number of choices available against the knowledge and technologies available to the retail travel agent. The importance of correctly qualifying the purchaser can either reinforce or erode the client - agent relationship. CRM can assist in the aggregation of data allowing travel retailers to market more effectively to their target audiences. CRM should lead to increased customer satisfaction enhancing greater overall business performance. Although CRM applications for the SME are at an early stage of implementation for the RTSI, preliminary research indicates the potential benefit to the industry.

Some of the benefits of CRM include:

— *Customer Retention*: CRM enables a company to retain loyal and profitable customers and channel members. According to the International Data Corporation, it costs online merchants from $0.90 to $2.67 to get a visitor to their website for the first time. These companies must find a way to achieve repeat business in order to justify their initial acquisition expenditures. CRM through its extensive data warehousing solutions could help companies attract and retain customers.

— *Customer Acquisition:* Based on known or learned client characteristics, CRM may assist companies in acquiring the right customer through effective targeting and segmentation.

— *Lower Cost*: The automation process minimizes paper work and manual labour.

— *Customer Loyalty and Satisfaction*: One of the prominent features of CRM is its ability to create the opportunity of mass customization. Increasingly, today's traveler wants customized products. When the service is personalized and tailored to meet the preference and choice of the customer, client satisfaction can be expected to increase. Customer satisfaction, over time, builds allegiance.

— *Profitability*: All of the factors listed above translate into profitability. Annual customer profits increase over time as the client - agency relationship expands. CRM can offer additional items to the companies that provide new profitability curves.

Pros and Cons for Change

The travel industry is poised for change. However, there is a tendency during periods of recovery to ignore trends and the bigger picture. Below are some considerations, which indicate the direction of change in the traditional business model of the RTSI.

The Retail Travel Services Industry:

— It is important to demonstrate progress and efforts made to revitalize the business to financial institutions.

— It is the right time for the RTSI to examine the products and services delivered to customers and their revenue opportunities.

— New revenue streams can supplement lost opportunity due to external shocks beyond the control of the RTSI.

— Loyalty, trust and personal service are an excellent foundation to build upon.

— The RTSI has difficulty in characterizing itself as stable industry where there is opportunity for advancement, benefits and adequate remuneration and the ability to reward employees properly.

— Retention of staff and recruiting will become more difficult until the trade is stabilized.

— The size of the RTSI is declining with increased pressure for many to consolidate.

— There is a place for small niche players and regional companies that command customer loyalty through consistent delivery.

The destination marketing organisations:

— The CTC, PMOs and CVBs are valuable resources for information and marketing expertise for the travel industry.

— Each has a wide range of ongoing marketing activities complementary to the RTSI.

— Intra - Canadian tourism and the inbound business from the U.S. is so significant, they are powerful business drivers for the RTSI to establish a beachhead in this market sector.

Markets:

— Dramatic world events can impact on the travel market. In times of uncertainty, consumers may prefer short haul travel to destinations they perceive to be safe.

— Business travel is often a barometer of the economy declining sharply during slower economic activity and increasing during periods of recovery.

— The accommodations industry experienced lower than normal occupancy rates in 2001 mirroring the cyclical nature of the business and a slower Canadian economy.

— Leisure travel is resilient.

Pricing factors:

The following pricing factors are influencing the current state of the travel marketplace:

— The strength of the US dollar and its purchasing power in US and abroad.

— Hoteliers in the in US have lowered their rates to attract travelers. As pricing tends to move in tandem with hotel occupancy, real profitability in the hotel industry remains uncertain.

— Steadily rising fuel surcharges, new taxes and service fees have affected the price stability of airfares.

Yield Management and the Air Careers: Air carriers are also adjusting to a changing marketplace.

— Airlines continue to suffer staggering losses due to fluctuating customer demand particularly on the long haul domestic and international routes, competitiveness globally in the airline industry, higher cost structures of established carriers, the economy and security and safety concerns.

— New discount air carriers are entering the market place, which has established three new competing discount airlines.

— Declining remuneration from the airline industry to the RTSI is forcing the industry to generate new revenues through fee for services and new products.

— Fee for services are in themselves a motivator to redefine customer service.

— Consumers are comparing and evaluating agency services with the introduction of fees to compensate for reduced airline commissions.

E-commerce:

— Travel is one of the preferred products, which consumers shop and purchase through the Internet.

— Privacy and security of data are important factors in handling personal and financial information.

— The Government is developing a uniform standard in the "e-protection" of information on the Net.

— E-commerce applications have the ability to embody personalization through CRM applications.

— The RTSI must use e-commerce and the Internet for competitive advantage combining bricks and mortar to increase their value proposition to the online shopper.

— Application service providers (ASPs) have made CRM and other software applications affordable. For example, Sabre, a CRS provider, has included CRM applications in their suite of new business tools for the RTSI.

Product and Service Standards:

— The RTSI can provide personal and unbiased information.

— Because service fees are becoming increasingly prevalent, the consumer expects improved service and product differentiation.

— It is an excellent time to provide a high level of service as service standards from most air carriers and some hoteliers have languished.

— Consumers want customization of individual trips and holiday packages.

— Partnering with suppliers to develop new products is a means of weathering uncertain times.

— Branding, the packaging of niche products and service, are core competencies of the RTSI. This is an important foundation for new initiatives.

— Brands can provide a sense of security and stability when supported by solid marketing and distribution infrastructures.

The need for the development of a portfolio within the RTSI has arrived. As well, the RTSI should consider new and complementary business opportunities.

Revenue opportunities in RTSI

The RTSI has presented itself as an integral and value added component for providing unbiased service to consumers. The traditional method of securing reservations and distribution of this product has been through the CRS/GDS network, a costly vehicle for the air carriers. Because of the continued pressure to reduce distribution costs, the airlines have moved to a zero commission policy for the RTSI. In addition, they are endeavouring to shift the buying habits of the consumer and the RTSI through sophisticated, airline - owned and operated online reservations systems. In response, the RTSI has introduced transaction or service fees to the sale of each ticket in order to cover their costs of distribution. These fees for services replace commissions. The price of fees varies across Canada because of differences in overhead costs. However, there are common areas of products and services for which fees are chargeable.

Currency Exchange

Another business, which compliments the business activities of the RTSI, is currency exchange. Currency exchanges are highly visible businesses located at airports around the world. Every passenger traveling to the U.S. or overseas considers their needs for local currency either prior to departure or most certainly, when they arrive. Foreign exchange is an essential element of international business and travel in general. There is a high incidence of outbound travel, as well as opportunities to foster the growth for inbound travel.

Currency exchange is an everyday customer need unexploited by travel retailers. It is important to examine the manner in which currency can be purchased online and eventually become an integrated component of doing business as well as a new revenue stream. Partner relationships are the best vehicles for integrating these products to a web site. The products are the purchase of foreign currency, travelers cheques and stored value cards.

There are several business advantages for implementing a currency exchange portal into a website. Generally, it is possible to implement quickly and easily and can be done in a secure integration into any web environment. It can generate immediate revenues, has no operational impact and has limited initial installation cost. As well, it provides improved customer service and provides a flexible product mix and a customized interface that preserves the individual branding keeping the customer on the travel agent's website.

The advantage for consumers is that they can obtain rates and order more than 70 currencies at any time. Multiple products can be combined and purchased in a single order. They can access real-time quotes based on current rates. It is a simple ordering process with home delivery - often done overnight. There is toll free customer support and a 100% satisfaction guarantee.

Currency Business

The landscape of foreign currency exchange, particularly in the online internet environment, is dominated by only a few major players. Travelex, Custom House and the International Currency Exchange (ICE) are the most prominent in the business of foreign exchange and online transactions. In addition, the major banks are the largest distributors of U.S. currency.

Travelex is the largest provider of foreign exchange to the private sector in North America. Travelex, the trading name of parent holding company, Travelers Exchange Corporation Limited, is a diversified worldwide money business offering retail, corporate and commercial currency services to consumers, corporations and institutions throughout the world. They provide the foreign exchange services in North America, the UK, Ireland and Australia. Their clients include many of the major banks such as the Barclays Bank and the Bank of Montreal. Travelex has mastered the ability of online ordering through their "pick and pack" fulfillment engine, which can fill a customer order within twenty-four hours delivered to their door. They dot the landscape at airports as the only location for exchanging or purchasing foreign currency. Revenues derived from foreign currency providers at airports are nearly the third largest revenue generator for airport authorities worldwide.These types of transactions should not be confused with Paypal and Western Union whose main business is sending money or requesting money to be sent to third parties. Travelex has recognized the logical nature of the RTSI as a valuable distribution channel to drive their product. It is service, which can be provided outside the airport to the consumer. This is of strategic importance to Travelex since airport fees know as minimum annual guarantees (MAG's) and the lease costs, are factored into their administrative and contract costs, which can affect the exchange rate.

Travelex has started a partner program, originally established through Thomas Cook International, which has now spread to the U.S. and into Canada in September of 2001. As a partner, the RTSI can earn a minimum of 1% of the sale in amount of the currency purchased through their web site. Orbitz, competitor in online travel selling, has already implemented this program in their web site.

Market Entry

There are no barriers to entry other than the requirement to have a working web site, which can accommodate the addition of the Travelex linkages. This product is viewable at mytravelwallet. It should be noted that more information and an application process would be required to establish a true foreign exchange dispensary within a bricks and mortar location.

Insurance

The RTSI already sells travel insurance in every province. British Columbia is the only province, which requires retail travel agents to be licensed to sell this type of insurance. But the traditional means of selling travel insurance through face-to-face meetings is being impacted by e-commerce. Consumers have the ability to shop and buy travel insurance online from a wide array of providers. The Royal Bank of Canada (RBC), as an example, is the largest provider of travel insurance. It has fully developed e-business tools, which include a range of insurance products. Globetrek Travel Insurance is another entrant into the Canadian travel marketplace. Some travel companies are beginning to partner with RBC Insurance in online travel sales. Although some conditions apply, a working website is the main criteria for establishing an online link to the RBC insurance engine. A demonstration of this product can be viewed at a special RBC demo site. This site permits a 24/7 capability for clients to purchase travel insurance. Revenues earned through online sales are similar to those issued from bricks and mortar travel offices. This product would harmonize well with the development of web-based products and services.

In addition to travel insurance, RBC has other products, which can be purchased online such as property, auto, life, health and business insurance. These can be viewed at RBC Insurance. Some travel retailers such as the Canadian Automobile Association have also entered this crowded marketplace. They have a very developed insurance component, which they offer as a service to their members. Expanding horizontally into online insurance is a logical step in diversifying the products sold by the RTSI. In order to sell insurance other than travel, an insurance license would be required and would be governed by the insurance regulations of each province. There would be a need to reeducate agents to assist in the sales process.

6

WEB TECHNOLOGY FOR TRAVEL AGENTS

Both the travel and tourism industry and Web based electronic commerce are changing rapidly. The global gross output of travel and tourism was estimated at US$3.4 trillion and is expected to double by 2005. The World Wide Web (WWW) is also growing at a rapid rate. Latest estimates of Internet users range around the 120 million mark.

Organisations are becoming increasingly aware of the business potential of engaging in electronic commerce over the WWW. The WWW supports electronic commerce in four major tasks.

- Attracting new customers via marketing and advertising.
- Serving existing customers via customer service and support functions.
- Developing new markets and distribution channels for existing products.
- Developing new information based products.

IT for Travel Agents

The travel industry is an intensive user of information technology (IT) for reservation, accounting and inventory management functions. Raymond and Bergeron refer to the types of systems used by travel agents as:

i) global distribution systems (GDS) such as Galileo, Sabre and Amadeus which are used for reservations, information search, client management and reporting.

ii) organisational information systems (OIS) which are used for accounting, reporting, record management and billing.

IT has helped in reducing costs and improving service to customers. Travel and tourism is an industry sector that is highly dependent on up-to-date, accurate information. There are potential problems associated with travel agents having multiple software systems that are not interconnected. For example, data may become difficult to transfer from one system to another.

It is proposed by Raymond and Bergeron that travel agents should choose the GDS as the basic system infrastructure, rather than the OIS, since it provides the most critical information to the business. When selecting a GDS they should look for user-friendly systems having the potential to interconnect with their OIS. However, their study did not consider the WWW, and how it could be integrated with the GDS and OIS.

The Internet has tremendous potential for creating business opportunities for travel agents. There are various aspects of electronic commerce that can be exploited by travel agents. Some of these are listed below.

1) Using the Internet to build customer relationships—by having customers interact directly with the web site;

2) Gathering information from customers and potential customers to create customer profiles which can be used in marketing and product development;
3) Information partnerships—cooperation between organisations to provide a better service to the customer;
4) Transactions—reservations and bookins;
5) Specialised information provision according to the profile of the user;
6) Information and products that can be down-loaded by the user.

The opportunities provided by the WWW, coupled with business process re-engineering, have the potential to radically change the nature of the travel industry. Figure 1 shows the major link in the travel distribution chain is between retail travel agent and consumer.

Figure 2 shows that the WWW has the potential to open up the travel distribution network by creating an electronic market place. Airline companies have already started to market their products directly to the consumer via the WWW, in some cases allowing bids to be made for spare seats.

Some believe that as many as 20% of travel agents will go out of business within the next three to four years, due to the growth of large on-line travel agents, and the customers' ability to transact directly with airlines, hotels and the larger tour operators. Given the potential of the WWW in travel agencies, it is proposed that they should take an enterprise wide approach in their utilisation of Web technology focussing on the potential of business process re-engineering. Although traditional retail travel agents are facing greater competition through on-line travel agents, the WWW provides an alternative to using the travel wholesaler.

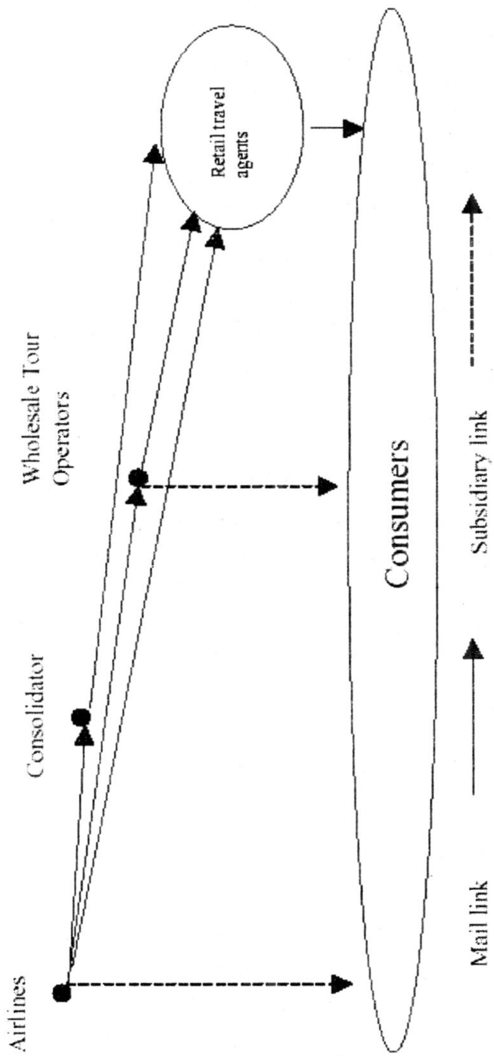

Figure 1. Participants in the Travel Distribution Network

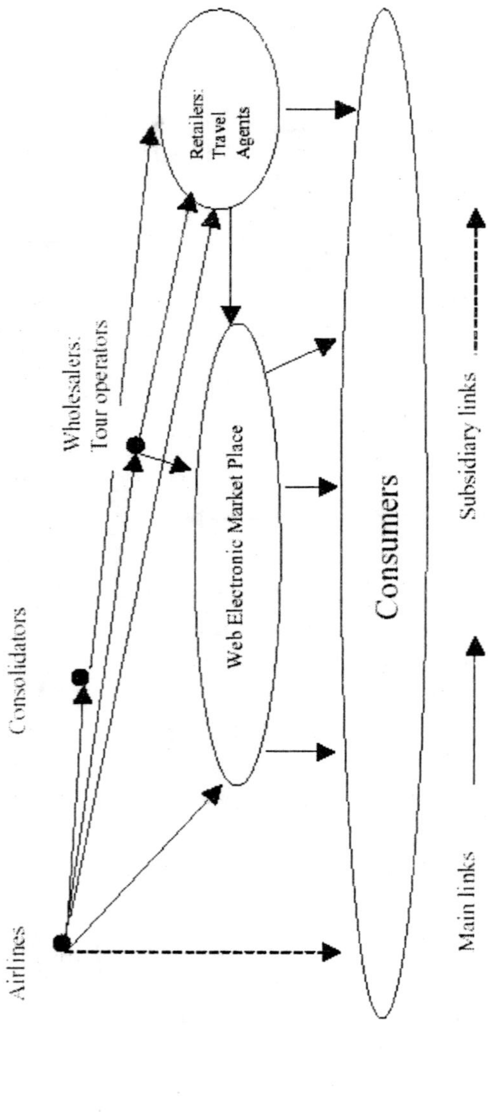

Figure 2. The Influence of the WWW on Travel Distribution Chain

The agent, if he or she wishes to do so, is now able to source travel and accommodation information, amongst other things, via the WWW. Customers of the travel agents also have the potential to interact with the agency in a more flexible way by accessing their web site at a time of their choice.

Reinders and Baker suggest there are few, if any obstacles, to extending the electronic market in travel and tourism products. The technical communications infrastructure from customers' homes provides an electronic market place. However, according to a survey by Reinders and Baker one element of confusion for consumers is the alternative platforms for electronic commerce, such as interactive television. They conclude that many consumers will wait and see which will be the market leader before making a decision on technology platform.

Travel agents are typically classified as small businesses. In Western Australia, two thirds of small businesses use a computer in their day-to-day operations and thirty percent of these are connected to the Internet. In a survey conducted by the Institute for Small Business research the uses of the Internet were: email 81%, accessing information 79%, and marketing 32%. Research by Dutta, Kwan and Segev, found that many small businesses had an Internet presence, but few took full advantage of the various forms of electronic commerce. For example, few organisations customised information according to the type of user, performed online tracking of customer behaviour, and provided online forums for customers. It seems as though even many of those that have implemented Web technology are not making the most of it.

The influences on executive decisions related to technology adoption in small businesses have been studied by Harrison, Mykytun, Riemenschneider. They found that an executive's decision to adopt IT to help his/her firm compete is a function of attitude (perceived positive and negative consequences for the firm), subjective norm (social expectations), and perceived control (resources to overcome obstacles). Additional variables such as firm and individual executive characteristics had no unique effect on adoption decisions.

Although there is general concensus that senior management support is important in IT adoption and implementation in small businesses, a study found that it may not be as critical as external IS expertise. While top management support is essential for IS effectiveness, high quality external IS expertise, in the form of consultants and vendors, is even more critical for small businesses operating in an environment of resource poverty.

Diffusion of Web Technology

The research into the diffusion of Web technologies within organisations is still in its early stages. Jarvenpaa and Ives put forward five propositions as a result of their studies of Web diffusion in two organisations in the USA. The five propositions are described below.

1) The introduction of Web technology is likely to occur with only peripheral involvement of the information technology function.
2) The introduction of Web technology is likely to occur with minimal if any involvement by top management.
3) The introduction of Web technology is likely to be accomplished by an ad-hoc, cross-functional group that has no formal organisational responsibility.
4) A performance crisis can be used to stimulate the introduction of Web technologies to an organisation, but it is not essential for this change to occur.
5) The introduction of Web technologies to an organisation can be triggered or supported by staged

events, some of which could be deliberately manufactured.

Romm and Wong's study of an Australian university found that the Web technologies project was strongly led by the information technology unit, with a high degree of involvement by top management. Also, the introduction of Web technology was not triggered by a performance crisis, and it was not driven by event based crises manufactured by the project team. The differences in the findings of the two research projects are explained by two main factors. Firstly, the American study examined two private computing companies whilst the Australian study examined a public university. Hence, the industry sector was put forward as one of the reasons for the differences. The second reason put forward was the differences in national culture; Australian organisations being more likely to be risk averters and valuing participative decision making more than American organisations.

Business Process Re-engineering (BPR)

Business Process Re-engineering (BPR) looks at enterprise processes, those that cut across business units. The information systems built for specific functions or units have often become out-dated because new processes transcend what was often seen as a compartmentalised set of functions. BPR is about identifying, and modelling business processes and changing existing systems to support those processes. There are many facets to re-engineering, although one trend is towards using newer technologies to support new ways of working.

The need for business process redesign comes about because of the following:

— rapidly changing technologies;

— shorter product life-cycles;

— increased competitive pressures and the increased demand for quality products and services;

— inefficient use of organisational resources due to organisational change, or lack of change.

For travel agents, the changing technology and increased pressures and demand for quality service would appear especially apposite.

Despite the potential of BPR, there are some that are rather wary about it as an organisational strategy. Martinson and Revenaugh for example, are of the opinion that whilst BPR has been an important concept in the nineties it has been commonly associated with negative connotations such as corporate downsizing and inflated consultancy fees. They go on to say that BPR has commonly been associated with slashing staff numbers, and while this may be a short-term fix, they suggest it is not a long-term strategy for success.

Travel Agents and Use of WWW

This section examines a range of issues related to travel agents and their use of the WWW. The areas being examined can be classified according to three broad areas.

1) The take-up rates of Web technology in travel agencies.

2) A model of Web technology diffusion is tested on the travel agencies used in the survey.

3) The type of strategy that the agents used for the decisions relating to the adoption of the WWW.

Let us examine the approaches used by travel agents according to the following characteristics of BPR identified by Hall, Rosenthal and Wade.

— BPR involves a radical level of change.

— A clean slate approach should be adopted as a starting point.

— BPR involves a great amount of time.

— Top down participation is needed for re-engineering success.

— BPR involves a great amount of risk.

— The major driver of change in BPR is information technology.

— The change brought about by BPR involves both cultural and structural change.

A recent study identified the major obstacles and perceptions that have prevented some agents from tapping into web-based electronic commerce. The various forms of web based electronic commerce that agents use are also examined. Since the travel industry and web technology are changing rapidly, the emphasis has been put on the strategy of technology adoption in the study. In this context there are a number of additional questions that are worthwhile examining. These areas or questions relate to broader issues such as: "Do small businesses plan their technology adoption?" and "Is re-engineering unlikely to be carried out in small organisations?"

The research was based upon useable responses from seventy-one travel agents in the Perth Metropolitan area in Western Australia. The questionnaires were completed by the senior managers or owner managers. Although over 50 per cent use electronic mail, almost 60 per cent do not use the WWW to search for information or provide a Web site for their customers and have no immediate plans to do so. Those that use the WWW typically use it to retrieve information on hotels, locations, fare and timetable. Few perform transactions at other sites such as bookings or payments. Those agents that have a Web site use the site primarily to provide information to the customers or potential customers.

Although some agents have established formal and informal links to other sites, their sites rarely allow customers to perform bookings and other transactions, down load brochures and gather information about customers. In this respect a restricted set of electronic commerce features are implemented. As many as 44% of agents in the survey have never considered using the WWW. Only 8 per cent classed their approach as an enterprise wide examination of the business processes. The other 48 per cent took either a modular approach or have done very little planning at all. The lack of planning is confirmed by the absence of strategic plans which incorporate the WWW and the lack of cost benefit analyses on the benefits of the WWW. It appears that there is a significant number that are unconvinced by the benefits that can be derived by using the WWW.

In nearly all cases the driving force behind the adoption of the WWW was the owner manager of the travel agency. Only one agency took on new staff to deal with the transition of working with the WWW. Lack of adequate training was the most frequently stated problem in relation to using the WWW. Others included perceived operating costs, integration of WWW with other applications and a need for the re-engineering of business processes in total conducted any sort of feasibility study including a cost benefit analysis on the potential benefits of web technology.

A Radical Level of Change

Process innovation and redesign involves making radical changes to process methods and tasks. Very few of the agents viewed the adoption of the WWW as a radical amount of change. This can be seen by the small percentage that actually performed enterprise wide planning.

A clean slate approach should be adopted as a starting point

Only 8 per cent of agents actually took this perspective. They chose to view the potential adoption of the Web technology as an ad-on to their existing systems rather than something that required a radical re-think of the organisational processes.

Re-engineering involves a great amount of time

Time was never given as one of the obstacles to implementing the Web technology. Indeed, it appeared that travel agents viewed the adoption of the technology as something that was relatively quick to perform since they did not adequately take into account the time for planning and developing a strategy.

Top down participation is needed for success

For all those that have investigated the adoption of the WWW (whether or not they decided to proceed with it) the initial idea came from top management.

Re-engineering involves a great amount of risk

Risk was not put forward as a major deterrent or obstacle for the adoption of web technology.

The major enabler of change is information technology

Clearly, the key enabler for re-engineering is information technology based.

The change involves both cultural and structural change

Only two percent of agencies employed extra staff as part of the process of Web adoption. None of the agencies gave any additional incentives to staff, such as extra pay, in cases where the WWW was being used. Very few of those that used the WWW had undergone a systematic training programme on how to use it effectively.

Very few travel agents do a form of planning that could be considered to be BPR, even though as suggested earlier in the paper, the context has all the ingredients that would make BPR a very plausible option. In some cases the shift to using the WWW is done in a bottom-up fashion by the travel agency. That is, the PC is purchased, the Internet service provider is decided upon, the browser is chosen. This is done independently of any planning that may, and more usually may not, happen in the organisation. It is little wonder that those that do use the WWW realise only a small part of the electronic commerce possibilities that are available.

In a sense, the introduction of WWW facilities into travel agents has many parallels to the widespread introduction of microcomputers in business (small and large) in the early eighties. It was often done without proper planning and resulted in under use, and subsequent poor rates of return on the investment. Suppliers of travel and tourism related products and services, such as Atlas Travel Technologies (ATT) and Galileo, are set to launch Internet booking engines that travel agent subscribers can add to their Web sites, enabling consumers to make on-line bookings and have them queued to the agent.

These types of facilities are an option to the travel agent to help them take a greater portion of on-line business. The problem is that they are tied again to a supplier, which would typically restrict the options available. The other major problem is that customers with Internet access will soon have more choice in booking their flights, hotels, and packages directly with the vendors, thereby by-passing the travel agents.

Reinders and Baker provide some optimism for agencies with staff who can navigate better through the electronic market place and find better deals on flights and hotels for example, than the do-it-yourself netsurfer. They believe this type of agency will still attract customers. This may be so, but their monopoly is coming to an end.

Diffusion of Web Technology in Travel Agencies

The introduction of web technology is likely to occur with only peripheral involvement of the information technology function. This proposition is not really applicable to travel agencies as they typically do not have a dedicated IT function or people responsible for IT. It occur with minimal if any involvement by top management. This is not true for travel agents, all cases involved a great deal of support from top managers.

The introduction of web technology is likely to be accomplished by an ad-hoc, cross-functional group that has no formal organisational responsibility. This is not true for travel agents. The introduction of Web technology was not led by informal champions.

A performance crisis can be used to stimulate the introduction of Web technologies to an organisation, but it is not essential for this change to occur. Travel agents on the whole were not stimulated into adopting Web technology because of crises within the organisation. The technology was seen more of an enhancement to the business rather than a tool or strategy to fight off a crisis.The introduction of Web technologies to an organisation can be triggered or supported by staged events, some of which could be deliberately manufactured.

Industry sector is not significant since the travel agencies were all privately owned. A small business typically relies greatly on the owner manager for ideas and drive. Many small businesses do not have a dedicated

IT section. Because of the small number of employees in each travel agency there may not be scope for political groups to develop on the same scale as in large organisations.

Web technology has the potential to transform how agencies do business with their customers and suppliers. They certainly have enough threats as a business sector to take both the technology and the planning of its introduction seriously. The actual results of the survey are perhaps very surprising when viewed in this light. Travel agents have not whole-heartedly embraced the WWW. This can be seen from the Web adoption rates, uses of the Web, and perceived levels of benefits. Travel agents appear to be doing little planning in relation to the WWW and very little of what could be classed as BPR. The reasons for this are partly due to the fact that most agencies are small businesses run by an owner manager. The impetus for any sort of BPR would have to come from this person. Web technology diffusion in travel agencies can be summarised by being owner/manager led, not instigated because of any perceived crisis, or the implementation driven by staged crises.

Apart from being top manager led, the processes used in Web technology adoption appear to have a limited sphere of scope. Web technology is often portrayed to consumers as a bottom-up technology, which will compliment current operations. The marketing strategy of many Internet service providers has parallels with the introduction of micro-computers. The only thing we can learn from history is that we never learn from history. If this is true for travel agents then many of the potential benefits of electronic commerce will not be realised first time round. The danger is that many travel agencies will not get a second chance to re-engineer as large on-line agents become more established and more customers become web wise and prefer to by-pass the agents.

Electronic Markets in Travel Industry

The travel industry, one of the largest and fastest growing industries in the world, appears particularly interesting in terms of the possibilities offered by electronic commerce. It is one of the industries where business is conducted successfully on the Internet already today, and where the importance of electronic commerce is likely to grow. It is also expected that the travel industry will be one of the first industries to be transformed by technology and to experience Internet disintermediation as Internet-based purchase and sales models arise.

Theoretically, the presumed suitability of the travel industry for electronic commerce can be explained by the qualities of the travel services and the tourist product. The tourist product is highly information-intensive, offering potential for value-adding informational services. As an almost totally informational service, all transactions and arrangements can be made online. The only nonvirtualizable part is the actual travel, the physical passenger traffic. According to Byerley and Ewers, the tourism sector appears to have a very large potential as a generator of usage of networks and value-added services. Typically, the products need to be viewed and booked at a distance and the products are natural candidates for multimedia descriptions.

Electronic markets are not a new phenomenon in the travel and tourism industry. It has been possible for travel agencies to book flights and hotel rooms online since the mid-1970s through the so called computerized reservation systems (CRS), also known as global distribution systems (GDS). Using the global CRSs, travel agencies can make reservations directly from their terminal with any airline and on all continents without having to go through coordination processes or contract negotiations. The global CRSs, nearly all of which are airline-owned, provide the basic functions for the reservation process such as product presentation, reservation, fare quote and ticketing and additional services. Traditionally, CRSs have had at least two major practical limitations:

First, small and medium-sized tourism enterprises remain under-represented in most CRSs, effectively (SMTEs) endangering their competitiveness and market share. Considering the fact that the vast majority of tourism enterprises around the globe can be classified as SMTEs, this limitation of the CRSs put not only the SMTEs at issue at a disadvantage, but also the prospective tourists, whose choice of service providers is more restricted as a result. In addition, the fact that many SMTEs are not connected to CRSs has had a negative effect on the rapidity of the booking process.

Second, the customers themselves have not had direct access to these proprietary computerized reservation systems, meaning that the travel industry currently relies on an outdated distribution network, essentially relying on third-parties, and hence is faced with a need to change. As a result of the opportunities offered by the Internet, a great number of suppliers can, and will, be connected over a common - and open - computer network. The Internet serves as the medium providing online access to travel industry actors at destinations worldwide. Through this network consumer access to CRSs or similar systems, for instance independent, proprietary systems developed by travel agencies in cooperation with IT companies, is now possible.

An almost unlimited amount of tourist service providers - including small ones - can be reached directly or through travel agencies online, meaning that the tourists are offered a considerably greater choice of suppliers. A possible implication is that we will be moving from what was primarily straightforward reservation systems to consumer-friendly networks including trip planning, video clips and virtual tours, maps, weather forecasts, chat rooms, and personal services, as well as direct payment facilities in addition to the direct booking opportunities. As the consumer is directly connected to a real-time system, the tour operators, airlines, hotels and the prospective tourists all can benefit from the greater opportunities to make last minute reservations.

Disintermediation

In the travel and tourism industry, as in most other industries these days, the impact of electronic commerce is an issue of great interest and concern for industry players as well as researchers. Although most of the different electronic age scenarios that have been put forward contain some elements that intuitively may appear realistic, it seems to be the case that the scenarios suggesting an industry reformation of some kind, especially the threatened intermediaries hypothesis, have attracted by far the greatest attention by business representatives as well as researchers.

The logic of the threatened intermediaries hypothesis is that the firm's value system is in an ongoing state of flux in part due to advancements in information technology. IT, and especially the direct business-toconsumer communication possibilities offered by the Internet, allows manufacturers to internalize activities that have been traditionally performed by intermediaries which, as has been shown by Benjamin and Wigand, add significant costs to the value chain. Hence, intermediaries may be by-passed in the distribution chain, resulting in a redistribution of profits along the value system, which may benefit both manufacturers and consumers.

Besides such obvious advantages of electronic commerce as greater convenience and a wider selection of items and information, the consumer may also experience price reductions as a direct result of the the redistribution of profits resulting from the disintermediation effect and more suppliers being able to compete in an electronically open marketplace. The threatened intermediaries hypothesis was presented by Malone et al., who used the term 'electronic brokerage effect' for the phenomenon. Their forecasts were based on a conceptual analysis rather than on empirical studies, but according to the authors, a dramatic example of the shift toward electronic markets had already occurred in the airline industry by the time the study was made.

Opposed Views on the Threatened Intermediaries Hypothesis

The case for the elimination of intermediaries as a result of electronic commerce is based on questionable assumptions, concluding that more, rather than fewer intermediaries will be involved in electronic markets. Their assumptions are backed up by the results of an exploratory study by Bailey and Bakos, suggesting that the need for intermediaries is not likely to be eliminated in the near future, although some of the traditional roles of intermediaries may become less important as a results of advances in IT.

Bakos argue that electronic marketplaces will more than compensate for this disintermediation by promoting the growth of new types of electronic intermediaries. Likewise, Girishankar argues that Internet-based selling is creating a breed of virtual intermediaries and new versions of traditional middlemen and product distribution channels. Chircu and Kauffman go a step further to propose an 'IDR cycle', a recurring pattern of intermediation, disintermediation and reintermediation, arguing that traditional non-technological middlemen will be able to reintermediate in the long run as EC-able intermediaries.

Travel and Tourism Industry Disintermediation

Traditionally, the travel distribution chain has been heavily dependent on intermediaries, i.e. travel agencies, whose business concept is to tie travelers and tourist service providers, mainly airlines and hotels, together. This is illustrated as alternatives (i) and (iii) in figure 3. Tourists, especially from an international point of view, have varying holiday preferences and, hence, a demand for a great choice of resorts and service providers, highlighting the importance of establishing extensive distribution networks of different tourism industry actors.

As we speak of a disintermediation effect in the travel industry, it should be noted that the discussions on the precarious existence of the travel agencies by no means are new or exclusively connected to the emergence of the Internet. As a matter of fact, the travel agency has been pointed out as the one actor in the travel distribution chain under severe pressure for quite a long time.

According to Mayhew, it is seen as the last of the litter, a sector condemned to an early death. The threat of disintermediation in the travel industry began already when advance booking started to become less necessary for many kinds of travel, and tour operators and service providers (hotels and airlines) began to suspect that the travel agent was an unnecessary overhead in the sale of their package holidays starting to possess physical retail outlets and to sell their products directly to the travelers in order to cut out the profit margin of the travel agencies. This is illustrated as alternatives (ii) and (iv) in figure 3.

Recently, the issue of disintermediation has been brought up again as a result of the fact that electronic markets are emerging on the Internet, a global medium through which the prospective travelers can manage all their arrangements by themselves as direct online bookings or through e-intermediaries (illustrated as (v) in figure 3).

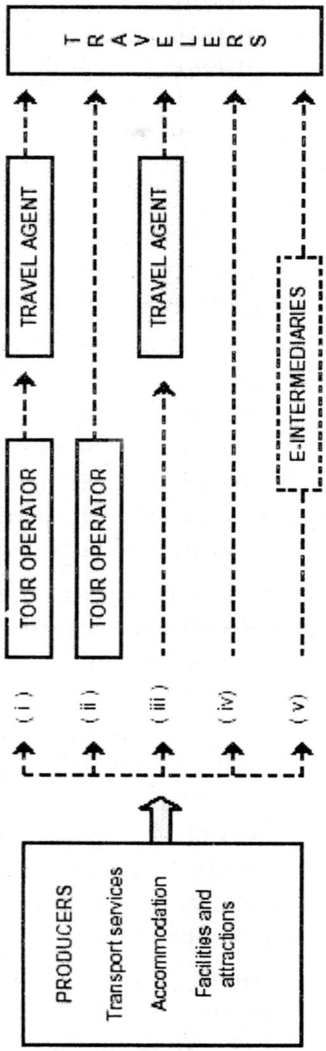

Figure 1. Alternative chains of distribution in the travel and tourism industry.

However, visions on different methods for consumer self-bookings through IT developments - and their possible disintermediational implications - have been presented in the travel and tourism literature long before the commercial possibilities offered by the Internet became widely known.

With the commercial potentials offered by the Internet today being a matter of common knowledge, many statements on the trying conditions facing travel agencies in the electronic age have been made in academic works, the popular press, at organizational levels, and by travel industry representatives, denoting that their threat of being squeezed out of business is real. The concerns do not necessarily always originate from a direct disintermediation threat, but from the indirect effects of by-pass opportunities offered on electronic markets, namely (i) the necessity to refocus and reinvent as new roles emerge for travel agencies as a result of the changing business models ; and (ii) heavy commission cuts. Most larger airlines have already lowered the commission rates to travel agencies as a result of high distribution costs and the potential for launching their own reservation services on the Internet. In online bookings, the commissions are particularly tiny, and will probably continue to be cut since the work involved is less demanding.

However, a common and intuitively reasonable view is that travel agencies themselves can gain some control over the design and implementation of IT and act creatively on the opportunities e-commerce can give them. As has been pointed out by Bloch et al., competitiveness in today's tourist economy is increasingly determined by the ability to develop and assimilate innovative ways to respond to the dynamic environment and its new paradigms in the production process of valueadding tourist services.

It should be noted that the threat of being by-passed in the travel distribution chain in some works has been extended to concern not only travel agents, but tour operators as well. However, as Burkart and Medlik and Goodall and Bergsma correctly point out, the retail travel agent must be carefully distinguished from the tour operator, as the retail travel agent is just a retailer, while the tour operator is without doubt a manufacturer of a particular travel product. The inclusive tour offered by the tour operator is not something the individual customer himself can put together by contacting online travel sites. It is a tourist product in itself.

Consumer Problems in Internet Bookings

Determining how the Internet will transform markets begins with an understanding of how consumers accomplish their interests - i.e. consumer behavior. Although the threat of disintermediation may be real as a result of the customer opportunities offered by ecommerce, intuitively there seem to be, however, several potential hindrances to a mass-market adoption of direct consumer-to-producer electronic shopping solutions. This goes not only for the travel industry, but also for most - if not all - other industries as well. Potential consumer barriers to e-commerce arise from several issues, but here our aim is merely to look into different industry- and product-specific problems and practical limitations associated with electronic travel bookings by individual customers.

Well-known barriers to e-commerce such as cost of entry, and security and privacy issues are excluded from this work. The issues investigated are presented in a model (figure 4) showing the potential problem areas, how they are interrelated, and the stages at which they may arise. As no research to our knowledge has been made on the practical problems facing a self-booking prospective traveler, the arguments presented are based on theoretical assumptions as well as experiences and thoughts presented in the popular press.

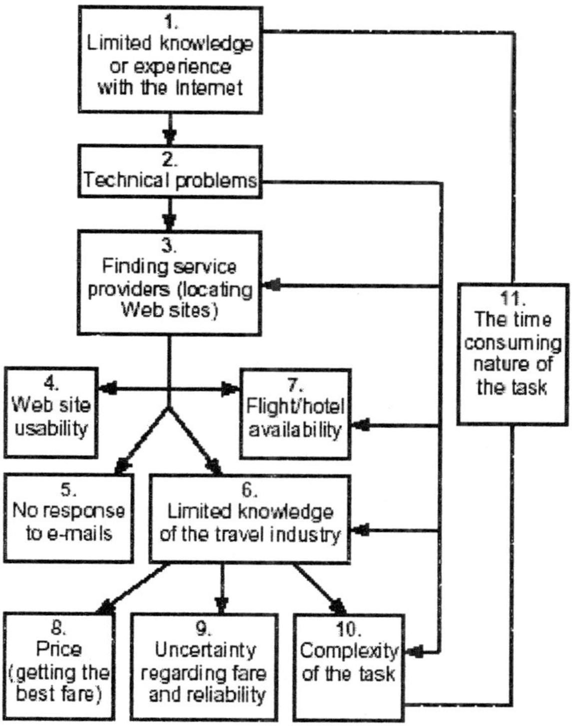

Figure 2. Potential problem areas in Internet bookings

A prerequisite for a consumer making his own travel arrangements on the Web is that he has some degree of proficiency with the Internet. Consequently, a lack of knowledge or experience with the Internet can constitute a serious barrier to consumer-to-business electronic commerce not only in the travel industry, but in any industry sector. Beside, or in addition to the limitations of the user, technical problems or systems limitations, as well as the poor usability of the service providers' Web sites (the term usability including, as has been suggested by Rajani and Rosenberg, aspects as color, sound, navigation and placement) may obstruct Internet bookings.

The first non-technical problem is about finding the right service providers, i.e. locating the Web sites offering the services needed. A typical problem regarding the Internet has been the immense supply of information, and the subsequent difficulty of finding the information you are looking for - at least to find it quickly enough. Accessing the many sources of information requires knowledge (to know where the servers are located), time and perseverance, as it is often not possible to book travel directly on-line and certainly not possible to buy the separate parts of a trip through the same supplier.

Having found the right service providers, the issue of availability remains. In most cases, there will be some available flight to the destination, but not necessarily the cheapest alternative or by the desired airline. Naturally, the same goes for the accommodation reservations. In a situation like this, is it possible to find cheaper and more suitable flights through other travel sites connected to another, competing CRS (or an equivalent system)? As we speak of the problem of finding service providers and the availability issue, one should bear in mind that the greatest customer convenience is achieved when all the reservations and gathering of travel information can be made from the one and the same source.

Another related problem concerns the rich supply of service providers, and the uncertainty that can result in, especially if the consumer's knowledge and experiences of the travel industry leave a great deal to be desired. How is the potential traveler to know if the service providers found are the most inexpensive and reliable? Although price comparisons can be made among the service providers, they cannot be made for service providers whose sites the customer has not found. The feeling that "there may still be cheaper travel sites, but I can't seem to find them" can be an impediment to shopping on the Web. According to Harris, special fares with restrictions are not always advertised (on the online travel sites). His view is that it is worth calling the local travel agent to see if he or she can beat the fare you have found. If your agent succeeds, you know you have got a good agent; if not, you got the best deal possible.

For many travelers the price of the journey may be the primary priority. However, getting the lowest possible fare is likely to be very hard - if not impossible - if you don't have some basic knowledge about the pricing principles of the travel industry and follow the strategies your travel agent uses to get you a low fare. The basic guidelines include : Stay over on a Saturday night; avoid traveling on Mondays, Fridays or holidays; purchase your ticket more than 21 days in advance; use the same carrier for all legs of your journey; depart mid-morning or late evening.

Not only is knowing the low-price booking strategies necessary for making a non-expensive and well-planned booking. A journey consists of many problematic elements that an inexperienced traveler may not consider. For instance, what is the minimum time needed to pass in transit at different international airports? Travel is a complicated industry with a lot of rules, meaning that many people want to interface with humans. Consumer online reservation systems (where the consumer himself is responsible for planning the trip and making the arrangements) may prove to be impractical for all but the most sophisticated users due to regulatory obstacles, currency fluctuations, and the complexity of international flights and CRS systems.

As many tourists - at least today - lack the possibility, knowledge, or courage to shop electronically, it seems reasonable to assume that they want familiar, reliable travel agencies, who, according to Wilson, still offer knowledge and intuition that cannot be found in an online service, to administer their travels. This also holds for travel arrangements made over the Internet. In addition, it has been pointed out that the price offered by online travel sites is often considerably higher than the price offered by the travel agencies, partly owing to the fact that the customer's knowledge of the pricing principles in the tourism industry usually is very limited.

The issue of price comparison was briefly mentioned above. Although the potential for making price comparisons often has been mentioned as a great consumer benefit of electronic commerce, it is no doubt a time demanding task. Naturally, this goes only for travel sites offering online bookings, since identical price inquiries easily can be sent to several Web-based travel agencies.

As a result of any, some, or all of these potential problems, the whole process of making travel arrangements on one's own can be extremely time consuming. In practice, this can be expected to be the greatest barrier for potential travelers to make their travel arrangements over the Internet.

To investigate the opportunities offered as well as the problems facing any consumer trying to make his own travel reservations over the Internet today, a study was conducted among 24 students attending an intermediary level course on Electronic Commerce at the Åbo Akademi University in Turku, Finland. The study was divided into two parts, consisting of (i) a quotation competition in which the students were to act as travel agents, submitting an offer for a journey according to some given specifications; and (ii) a questionnaire, in which the students who submitted offers were asked to report on their booking experiences, especially the problems they encountered during the task.

Nearly all of the 24 students (17 males, 7 females) making up the sample considered themselves proficient Internet users as the task was announced. Hence, the sample was not representative for the average consumer as the students' knowledge of and experience with the Internet by far exceeded that of the average consumer.

The students were instructed to submit an offer of a round-trip from Turku, Finland to Maui, Hawaii for two persons. No student or regular customer discounts were allowed. The point of departure was Turku, Finland. According to the instructions given, the travelers were to set out on the journey on January 2nd in the early morning (local time). The students were allowed to use their own judgement when planning the route. However, a booking comprising more than 8 intermediate landings during the journey (there and back) was considered unacceptable. An additional requirement was that none of the intermediate landings would last longer than 5 hours - with one exception: The travelers wanted to rest by putting up at a hotel for one night on both routes.

All accommodation facilities (two single rooms) during the journey were to be high-class (the students were given detailed instructions). During the visit, the travelers also wanted to make a day's journey to the island of Kauai. The students were instructed to submit an offer on this excursion as well. The travelers wanted to be back in Turku on January 15th in the morning (local time).

The students were given 14 days to complete the task under clear instructions that all bookings were to be made over the Internet. Hence, they were not allowed to pay a visit to a travel agency, nor to contact one by phone or fax. However, sending e-mails to Web-based travel agencies was fully acceptable, but this possbility was deliberately not emphasized when the students received their instructions, as an interesting aspect of the task was to see which approach the students would consider and choose.

The task was announced as a competition; the student offering the lowest price would be awarded a prize. However, the students were unaware of the fact that they would be competing against a real (and accepted) offer made by a local office of a large international travel agency chain. The travel agency was given exactly the same task as the students. According to the clerk at the travel agency, making all the reservations took her no more than 30 minutes.

All the submitted offers are a sum of the two travelers' total travel arrangements and are stated in US dollars.

The task was completed by 23 students, however with very varying results: The price difference between the highest ($ 19.587) and the lowest ($ 5810) offer was as much as $ 13.777, or 337,1 %. Despite the clear and unequivocal instructions as many as 14 of the 23 bookings were not made strictly according to the given instructions. Hence, comparing the offers is neither easy nor quite correct, especially considering the great variations in the price level of the chosen hotels.

Some students felt that a high-class accommodation was not necessary, thereby acting as poor travel agents by not taking the wishes of the travelers fully into consideration. However, some other students performed the task with great care. Several students, on their own, rented a car for the entire stay when no hotel rooms were available in the proximity to the conference area. Consequently, a total of 4 students managed to submit an offer lower than the one made by the travel agency ($ 7364). However, only one of the students managed to undercut the price offered by the travel agency as far as the flights were concerned (the lowest student offer for flights only was $ 3093 whereas the total costs of the flights as offered by the travel agency amounted to $ 3216). The students' average offer for the flights only amounted to $ 6921, the highest offer being $ 14.760, i.e. 458,8 % higher than the price offered by the travel agency.

A summary of the offers made by the students as well as the one made by the travel agency can be seen in table 1. In some cases it was necessary to correct the initial offered prices somewhat, since the students had left out some specific component of the travel (or booked it incorrectly), making the offer incomplete. The price was corrected by adding a sum roughly equivalent to the average offered price for the specific component to the total price.

Table 1. Summary of quotations made by students and the travel agency (stated in USD)

Students	Flights	Hotel	Total
Mean	6921	4308	11381
Std. Deviation	4118	1440	4610
Minimum	3093	2394	5810
Maximum	14760	7339	19587
Travel agency	3216	4148	7364

Only 2 students chose to submit an offer partly or totally made by a travel agency operating on the Web. In these cases, the clerks of the travel agencies were contacted by e-mail, meaning that the booking-process involved a person-to-person contact. The average result for these two students was $ 6835 (total price) / $ 3258 (flights only). One of these students was the winner of the price competition with an offered total price of $ 5810. It is worth noting that the student in question did not make all the reservations through the Web-based travel agency, but booked the hotel rooms through an online travel site. All students except these two made all reservations through online travel sites with an average result of $ 11.814 / $ 7287 (flights only). The lowest submitted online-offer was $ 6074 (total price) / $ 3679 (flights only).

Table 2. Price comparisons

t-values	*df*	*Sig. (2-tailed)*
Flights	4.219	21 0.000
Hotels	0.511	21 0.614
Total	4.179	22 0.000

We conducted a one-sample t-test with the travel agency's prices as test values. the difference in price is significant in total price, and for flights, but not in hotel prices, which may reflect the fact that some of the students did not follow the instructions.

Booking Experiences

In order to investigate the problems encountered when completing the task, the students were asked to fill in a questionnaire. The questions covered the potential problem areas mentioned in the previous chapter and the chosen approach to solving the task. In addition, the questionnaire included some questions on the workload of the task and the students' satisfaction with their performance. All but one student returned the questionnaire. In the questionnaire, the suggested impediments to smooth Internet-bookings were investigated by presenting some statements to which the respondents were to express the magnitude of their agreement (1 = strongly disagree, 5 = strongly agree). The results of this part of the questionnaire are presented in table 3.

Table 3. Perceived problems with self-booking in travel

	N	Median	Mean Score	Std. Deviation
Time consuming task	23	4.00	4.13	1.01
Proficiency with the Internet	23	4.00	3.83	0.94
Making price comparisons	23	3.00	3.57	1.27
Limited industry knowledge	23	4.00	3.52	1.16
Usability of Web sites	22	3.50	3.32	1.13
Finding Web sites	23	4.00	3.09	1.44
Finding available hotel rooms	23	3.00	2.78	1.20
Technical problems	23	2.00	2.57	1.44
Finding available flights	23	2.00	2.35	1.11

A lack of knowledge or experience with the Internet can constitute a potential barrier to consumer-to-business electronic commerce. This was certainly not the case in the study. 17 of the 23 students (73.9 %) who returned the questionnaire considered themselves very proficient or proficient Internet users at the beginning of the study. Most respondents (95.7 %) reported that they visit the Internet every day or several times a week. Accordingly, the majority (60.9 %) of the respondents disagreed or disagreed strongly to having encountered technical problems.

The investigation revealed that the students' experiences were quite differing; some had perceived certain elements as problematic whereas others felt they were relatively unproblematic. As the greatest impediments to the bookings were cited:

(i) the task being time-consuming. The average time spent on the task was 6.4 hours, the median value being 5 hours. One student reported that he needed only one hour to make all the reservations, whereas another spent 24 hours on the task;

(ii) the students' limited knowledge of the (pricing principles) of the travel industry. Although there was a large block of respondents who chose a neutral position in responding to the statement, an examination of the submitted quotations, however, suggests that this proposed impediment to self-made bookings might have been considerably more problematic than the students stated: As was already mentioned, a large number of the bookings were incomplete (lacking some specific component of the journey) or were booked incorrectly. Many proposed itineraries were highly inconvenient, reflecting the inexperience of the students as travel counselors and indicating a lack of knowledge on certain fundamental issues in the travel and tourism industry;

(iii) the usability of the service providers' Web sites. The suggestion that potential problems can arise from flights and hotel rooms not being available during the desired time period was not supported by the respondents. Finding available hotel rooms was considered considerably harder than finding available flights, but this result may partly be due to the fact that many students tried to make reservations at the preferred hotel of the travelers (specified in the detailed instructions given to the students), which turned out to be fully booked at the time when most students tried to make the reservations. As the task was announced as a price competition, it might have been expected that most students would engage in price comparisons. Whether this was the case or not did not emerge from the questionnaire, but the fact that the students on an average contacted 6 service providers indicates that price comparisons were made.

Table 4. Activities undertaken during the selfbooking process

	N	Median	Mean Score	Std. Deviation
Hours spent on the assignment	23	5	6.43	4.74

Number of service providers contacted	22	4	6.36	5.41
Number of e-mails sent	8	1.5	4.00	4.10
Number of service providers offering online-booking	21	3	3.85	1.87
Number of e-mails received	6	1	2.00	2.00

The preferred approach to solving the task was to look up a service provider offering online-services. Of all the contacted service providers, 53 % offered online services. Only 2 students chose to submit an offer partly or totally made by a travel agency operating on the Web. This fact might be explained by the poor customer service offered by most of the contacted Web-based travel agencies: Emails were sent out to travel agencies by 8 of the 23 students (34.8 %). On an average, each of these 8 students sent 4 e-mails, 57 % of which were answered. The average response time was 87 hours! On an average, the students contacted 6 service providers. One student contacted as many as 23 different actors, wheras two students felt that contacting only one service provider was sufficient. Paradoxically, the offered price was more or less the same in these three cases.

The students were also asked if they thought that they could have been offered a better price by contacting a player in the physical marketplace. An interesting result, and one confirming the fact that the students' knowledge of the travel and tourism industry was limited, was that most respondents did not have a view of the matter: 65.2 % of the students responded not sure. As to the rest, the optimism was almost non-existent: 34.8 % of the students responded yes, definitely or yes.

The students were asked to report on their satisfaction with their performance in the task. 39.1 % of the students were either extremely satisfied or satisfied, whereas 30.4 % were dissatisfied or extremely dissatisfied with their performance. When asked if they intended to make their travel reservations over the Internet in the future, it seemed to be the case that most students had not formed a strong opinion based on the experiences of the assignment: 3 students responded yes, 5 no, 15 perhaps. Those who answered yes or perhaps were aditionally asked whether they would make the reservations themselves by using online travel sites. Notable is that none of the students responded no whereas 9 responded yes and 9 perhaps. Not even the (in most cases) high quotations could deter the students from considering to make use of online booking possibilities in the future. This indicates a strong belief in more advanced reservation systems and improved consumer terms in the future.

Limitations

The study was conducted is an exploratory study on the efficacy of self-booking in travel. Due to the fact that students are among the most eager users of the Internet, we decided to use a sample of students. There are both pros and cons in the approach. The study team was aware about much of the study's possible external validity was sacrificed as students probably differ from the general population in many ways, they are for example minimally experienced travelers. Other limitations are that we were not able to control the actual search process, and that students' own preferences influenced the results as well as the relatively small sample size.

In the study, the results of the quotation competition were far more interesting than the results of the booking experiences. Especially the great range of variation in price was surprising. One of the generally stated consumer benefits of electronic commerce - and one arguing in favor of the vision of disintermediation - is the promise of lower consumer prices. The results of the study, however, not support this assumption, as the submitted offers on average were considerably more expensive than the ones made through Web-based travel agencies. The high average price, the time needed to complete the task, and the great many student bookings that were incorrect, incomplete or inconvenient, certainly gave some indications that some assistance certainly would have been needed during the booking process. Reasonably, this assistance would have been given by physical or virtual travel agencies, as simplifiers of the often complex travel decision process.

An unbundling of intermediary functions suggests that the role of the intermediaries is multifaceted, and all functions are not easily assumed by producers. However, in many cases, including the travel industry, the issue is rather whether we will see a further development of the online reservation systems in the future, eliminating the travel agencies' current advantages in speed, knowledge and intuition. At least, the questionnaires indicated a strong belief in more advanced reservation systems and improved consumer terms, as the students reported that they were not deterred from considering making use of online booking possibilities in the future.

7

SEMANTICS OF TRAVEL SERVICES

Today, travel information services are dominantly provided by Global Distribution Systems (GDS). A GDS gives its subscribers pricing and availability information for multiple travel products. Travel agents, corporate travel departments, and even Internet travel services, subscribe to one or more GDSs to check, for example, flight availability and prices for their customers. The GDSs get their revenue from the booking fees that these organizations pay. In addition to supplying information, a GDS typically provides hardware, software and technical support to its customers, including printers that allow agencies to print airline tickets. The leading GDSs today are Sabre, Galileo, Amadeus and Worldspan. All the airlines, many hotel chains and car rental companies list their inventory with major GDSs. Yet GDSs are legacy systems and suffer from the following problems:

— Mostly they rely on their own private networks although there are recent efforts to make these systems available through the Internet.

— GDSs are mainly for human use. They have difficult to use cryptic languages (with the exception of specialized APIs some GDSs are developing for the eCommerce sites). A request to the system usually involves more than one interaction with the person on the terminal in contrast to the current trend which is the automation of services over the Internet. Furthermore, GDSs have limited speed and search capabilities.

— Being legacy systems, it is difficult to interoperate them with other systems and data sources both inside the company as well as with external resources. For example, a travel agency may wish to integrate its Customer Relationship Management (CRM) system with the GDS to better serve its customers.

There are several advantages to be gained from using Web service technology in travel information systems:

— Interoperability among very many heterogeneous systems such as light reservation and hotel booking systems of individual companies will be facilitated. Furthermore, it will become possible to integrate the back end systems of the travel companies.

— Among the millions of travel agents, only about 10% to 20% of all travel agents are in connection with the GDS companies. Most travel agencies and travel organization companies choose to manage travel services by themselves, due to reasons which may be technical or economical, e.g. due to high commission rates and yearly subscription fees issued by the GDS company. Web service technology will enable such companies both to obtain the travel products they need from the Internet as well as to offer their products over the Internet.

— Also travel agencies generally choose to communicate with travel service providers directly bypassing GDSs, for better pricing than GDS listings and to obtain specialized services. Nevertheless, extra effort is required for traditional communication and necessity for establishing partnerships, whereas Web service technology provides a solution for all companies, generally small-to-medium level enterprises in the travel industry, for easily publishing and selling their tourism services as well as providing large selection options from a rich service pool.

— GDS companies do not support every type of travel product in the industry, but only the major ones; airline ticketing, hotel reservation and car rental. However, there are other types of specialized services, especially different types of tour and transportation based travel products. These services generally do not have a common, uniform structure as found in airline, hotel and car-rental services hence it is difficult to develop a common interface for such kinds of services to be provided by GDSs. On the other hand, Web service technology is an ideal for publishing such services by facilitating their discovery through the Web service registries as well.

— GDSs provide hotel booking only for major hotel chains. There are millions of hotels that cannot sell their rooms through GDSs. These hotels will benefit from the Web service technology.

— A variety of business opportunities for the companies in the travel industry will be enabled by using the communication medium as ubiquitous as Internet. The travel agencies and service providers will collaborate with each other on a new level. The companies will no longer need to make pre-agreements with respective suppliers; the service alternatives will be found on the fly through Web service discovery. It will be a possibility to construct package services which are comprised of services provided locally by the initiator company and services discovered within the network. Negotiation on the service that will be purchased as well as customization of service properties on the fly are other possible types of enhancements in the e-business for the travel domain.

A few early adopters in the travel domain have started to develop Web services. Sabre and Datalex are among the first companies to develop Web services. Sabre Web Services provide all the functionality needed to sell travel (air, car rental, hotel, passenger name record). It is especially convenient for agencies with no Sabre system format expertise. Galileo also provides a Web service based solution and claims to have cut down the development time by 80%. Another travel company which benefited from the Web service technology is the Continental Airlines in USA. To gain a competitive edge, Continental decided to provide real-time data of light status in multiple contexts, such as interactive devices and customer service agent consoles. By wrapping the data it already has in its legacy flight operations management system as Web services, the information became accessible from devices such as cellular phones or PDAs.

However to be able to exploit Web services to their full potential, it is necessary to introduce semantics to Web services. Without semantics, it is difficult for Web Services to succeed because if we cannot describe the Web service we are looking for, we cannot find it in an automated way and if we cannot describe the service we have, the probability that people will find it in an automated way is low. Furthermore, to make semantics machine-processable and interoperable, we need to define semantics through standard ontology languages. Web Ontology Language (OWL) by W3C is a good candidate. In fact, OWL-S consortium has specified an upper ontology to define the semantics of Web services. OWL-S specification, although very useful, is generic and applicable to all services. There is a need for domain specific (such as travel or healthcare domain) ontologies to be able to associate semantics with Web services. For travel domain, there are some promising efforts for developing travel domain ontologies such as the Harmonise project. The Harmonise project allows participating organisations to keep their proprietary data format and use ontology mediation while exchanging information. For this purpose, they have defined the Interoperability Minimum Harmonization Ontology (IMHO) and an interchange format for tourism industry. The Mapping FRAmework (MAFRA) tool is used for ontology mediation which supports semantic mapping definitions and the reconciliation engine.

Another important initiative for describing travel domain knowledge is the XML Schema specifications defined by the Open Travel Alliance (OTA). OTA includes majority of the key players in the industry covering airlines, hotels, car rental, rail, and tour companies and Global Distribution Systems. It has produced XML schemas of the message specifications to be exchanged between the trading partners. These messages include availability checking, booking, rental, reservation, reservation cancelling and modifying, query services for service details and quality, insurance quote request for all of the hotel, airline, vehicle sectors as well as the commission exchange services, and the statistical information services. We believe that OTA specifications can prove very useful for defining travel Web service ontologies. If such ontologies become available for the travel domain, the interoperability of all sorts of Web services can be better addressed at the semantic level through ontology mapping.

Today, the main mechanism for service discovery is service registries. However Web service registries themselves are also in need of discovery. Providing a mechanism to facilitate the automated discovery of Web service registries is also needed and we propose a peer-to-peer mechanism for the discovery of Web service registries.

Open Travel Alliance Specifications

Open Travel Alliance Specifications (OTA) exposes considerable amount of domain knowledge which can be used in describing the semantics of travel Web services. In this section, we briefy describe the functionality provided by OTA. OTA XML message schema specifications can be investigated in the following groups:

— Generic messages: Although many messages are specific to a particular travel subdomain such as Air, some messages are generally applicable and may be used more broadly. Such messages include cancel (OTA CancelRQ.xsd), and delete (OTA DeleteRQ.xsd) messages.

— Air message specifications address the structure and elements of requests and responses for airline flight related information and contain extensive set of messages like air availability request (OTA AirAvailRQ.xsd), air availability response, (OTA AirAvailRS.xsd), and low airfare search request (OTA AirLowFareSearchRQ.xsd).

— Car message specifications include all sorts of messages related with vehicles such as vehicle availability request (OTA VehAvailRateRQ.xsd) and vehicle location details (OTA VehLocDetailRQ.xsd).

— Hotel message specifications provide ability to search and obtain all related information about hotel products such as search for a hotel (OTA HotelSearchRQ.xsd), and to get a list of rooms (OTA HotelRoomListRQ.xsd).

— Golf Tee Times provides three separate request/ response pairs of messages to request data from another system to find a golf course, to inquire availability and to book a tee time.

— Insurance message specifications contain XML schemas for insurance related messages such as insurance plan search and insurance quote request (OTA InsuranceQuoteRQ.xsd).

— Package Tours/Holiday Bookings: A package holiday usually consists of a single "pre-defined" offering with or without a choice of a number of bookings. A booking can contain any number of itinerary elements, such as transport, accommodation, car rental, extra products or services, special services, extras, etc. Some example schemas from this group include package availability request (OTA PkgAvailRQ.xsd) and package booking request (OTA PkgBookRQ.xsd).

— Travel Itinerary messages are widely used to integrate, manage and service travel content and include the industry segments "Air", "Car", "Hotels", "Rail" and "Tour&Cruise". Travel itinerary read request (OTA TravelItineraryReadRQ.xsd) and response are used to get this information.

— Rail information messages contain three request/response pairs to check rail availability (OTA RailAvailRQ.xsd), rail booking (OTA RailBookRQ.xsd) and (OTA RailRetrieve-RQ.xsd) to retrieve a previously booked itinerary.

— Loyalty message specifications: Many companies in the travel industry offer loyalty programs. In the past, companies managed their own loyalty programs but now there are specialized companies to manage them. This standard message set allows the travel industry to communicate with loyalty industry. Some example messages include creating loyalty account (OTA LoyaltyAccountCreateRQ.xsd), and creating loyalty certificates (OTA Loyalty Certi.cateCreateNotifRQ.xsd).

— Profile: The Profile messages define the detailed business content of a customer profile from a travel industry perspective. This specification provides a set of common messages for transmitting customer profile data that customers provide to travel services, and for the exchange of profile information between travel services within the industry. An example message schema is "OTA Pro.leCreateRQ.xsd" These message schemas use several common types defined by OTA. Certain common types contain more basic common types.

Semantics of Web Services

WSDL (Web Service Description Language) specifies only the technical interface of the Web services. Web services, like their real life counterparts, may have many properties. Some of these properties such as the methods of charging and payment, the channels by which the service is requested and provided, constraints on temporal and spatial availability, service quality, security, trust and rights attached to a service can be generic. And such generic service semantics can be defined through DAML-S (later OWL-S) upper ontology. Service discovery and composition through DAML-S have been addressed in the literature. However some other properties of the services depend on the application domain. For example, in the travel domain the properties of an "air reservation service" include the origin and destination cities. The domain specific semantics is necessary for the Web services in the following respects:

First, in order to facilitate the discovery of the Web services, there is a need for an ontology to describe what the service does; that is, service functionality semantics in the domain. For example, in the travel domain, when a user is looking for a service to reserve a flight, he should be able to locate such a service through its meaning, independent of what the service is called and in which language, and who the business provider is. As previously noted, WSDL does not provide this semantic information.

Service functionality semantics may suffice only when all the Web services use the same message standard like OTA in the travel domain. It is not realistic to assume all the travel Web services to be OTA compliant. Then, there is a need to transform one message format into another. Although using XML transformers like XSLT may be an option for transforming one XML message into another, this approach has the following weaknesses when compared to ontology mapping:

With the XSLT approach, there is a need for a hard coded mapping between two XML schemas. Ontology mapping, on the other hand, can be performed in a more generic way since it is aided by the meaning associated with the ontology languages. More specifically, ontology languages like RDFS , or OWL express many of the important semantic information through universally accepted constructs: For example, the "subClassOf" relationship has a well defined meaning being a natural part of an ontology language. So as the "property" definition. Such definitions capture the semantic information in an application domain and prove to be useful in mapping different schemas. Although these constructs are expressed through XML eventually; in XML, they do not have this well-defined meaning.

Web Service Functionality

We note that OTA specifications also reveal considerable domain knowledge and offer significant value in developing service functionality and service message ontologies. The OTA request/response pairs can be arranged into a class hierarchy, as shown in Figure 1 to define operation semantics of travel Web services.

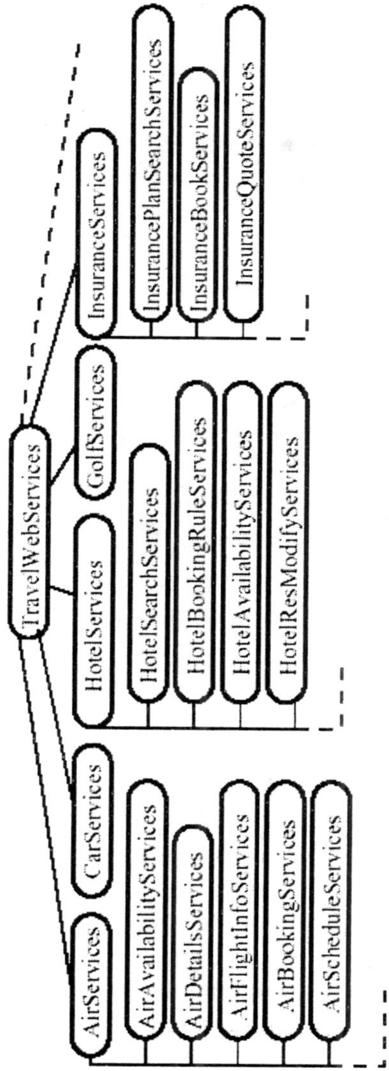

Figure 1: An OTA Compliant Service Functionality Ontology

The advantage of having such a functionality ontology is twofold:

— All sorts of Web services can be classified by using the nodes of such an ontology to make their meaning clear. For example, a Web service instance "THY Ucak Rezervasyonu" can be classified with the "AirBookingService" node of the ontology to imply that it is an air reservation service.

— Web service instance discovery is facilitated. All the services classified through a node in the ontology can be retrieved from service registries.

It is also necessary to define the semantics of the messages exchanged so that the party receiving the message can interpret it. When ontologies are used to describe the messages, since the messages can refer to ontology concepts, it becomes possible to map one message instance into another through ontology mapping although they may be defined through different ontologies.

An example input message ontology for the "AirAvailability" generic Web service is shown in Figure 2. This message ontology is based on OTA. It should be noted that our aim is not to propose ontologies but to show how such ontologies, once developed, can be used for semantic mapping. Figure 3 demonstrates a part of the ontology mapping. MAFRA uses a meta-ontology called Semantic Bridge Ontology (SBO) that defines the relations and transformations between ontologies. Semantic Bridges in SBO encapsulate the required information to translate one source entity (concept, relation, property) to a target entity. MAFRA has two primitive semantic bridges: Concept Bridge, and Property Bridge. A Concept Bridge defines the semantic equivalence between two ontology classes. At execution step, an instance concept of the target ontology is created for each source concept when the two concepts are related via a concept bridge. In the same way

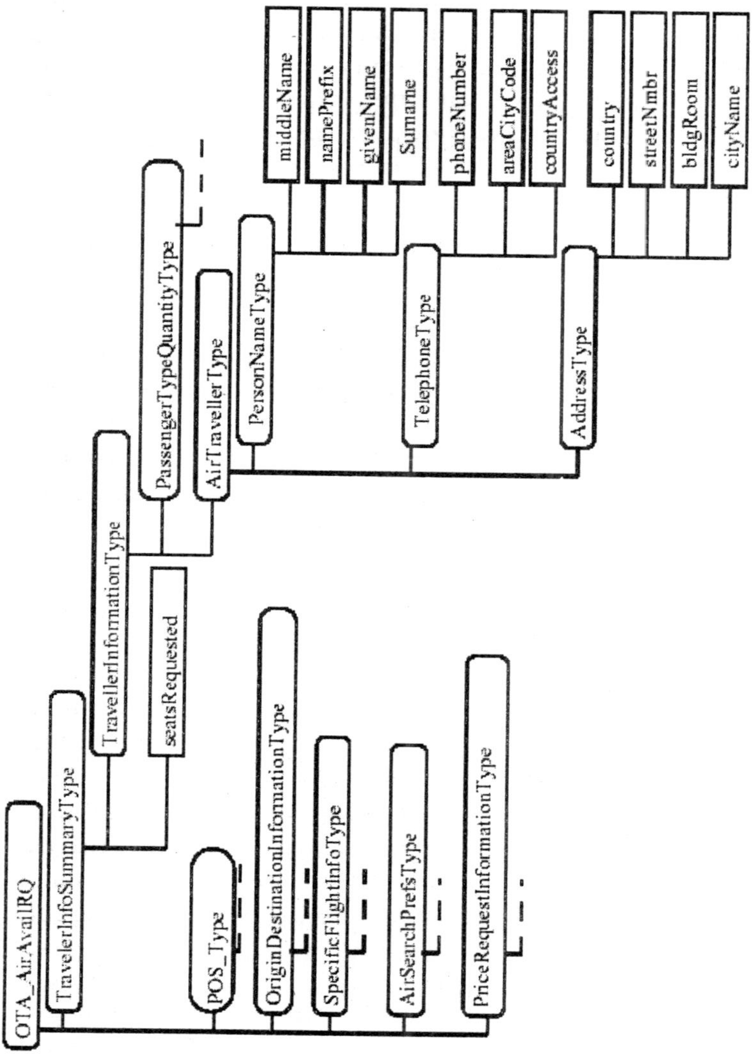

Figure 2: An Example OTA Compliant Service Message Ontology for Air Availability Request

a Property Bridge defines the equivalence between source and target properties.

To clarify the issues involved, we provide an example: In Figure 3, a mapping fragment which constructs the "Address" attribute of the "Contact" concept using the "BldgRoom", "CityName", "Country" and "StreetNmbr" attributes of the "AddressType" concept is given.

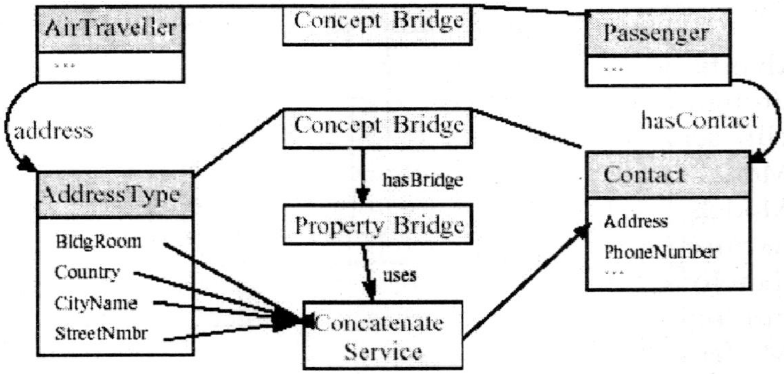

Figure 3. An Example Ontology Mapping through MAFRA

The "AddressType" and the "Contact" concepts are bound via a concept bridge which represents a semantic relation between them. The aim of the design is to concatenate the four attributes of "AddressType" into a single string and make this string the value of the "Address" attribute of "Contact". This is accomplished by defining a property bridge that uses "Concatenate Service". "Concatenate Service" takes the four attributes as input, and sets the "Address" attribute with the desired single string output.

Message Ontologies

In relating the semantics with the services advertised in service registries, there are two key issues: the first one is where to store the ontologies. UDDI does not provide a mechanism to store an ontology internal to the registry. ebXML , on the other hand, through its classification hierarchy mechanism allows domain specific ontologies to be stored in the registries. Note that for UDDI registries, domain specific ontologies can be stored by the standard bodies who define them and the server, where the service is defined, can host the semantic description of the service instance.

The second key issue is how to relate the services advertised in the registry with the semantics described through an ontology. The mechanism to relate semantics with services advertised in the UDDI registries are the tModel keys and the category bags of registry entries. tModels provide the ability to describe compliance with taxonomies, ontologies or controlled vocabularies. Therefore if tModel keys are assigned to the nodes of the ontologies and if the services put the corresponding tModel keys in their category bags, it is possible to locate services conforming to the semantic given in a particular node of this ontology. This issue is elaborated in.

An ebXML registry, on the other hand, allows to define semantics basically through two mechanisms:first, it allows properties of registry objects to be defined through "slots" and, secondly, metadata can be stored in the registry through a "Classi.cationScheme". Furthermore, "Classification" objects explicitly link the services advertised with the nodes of a "Classi.cationScheme". This information can then be used to discover the services by exploiting the ebXML query mechanisms which is detailed in. How to store ontologies in ebXML registries is described in.

Currently, the main mechanism to discover the Web services is searching the service registries. Therefore the consumer should first know where the related service registries are located.

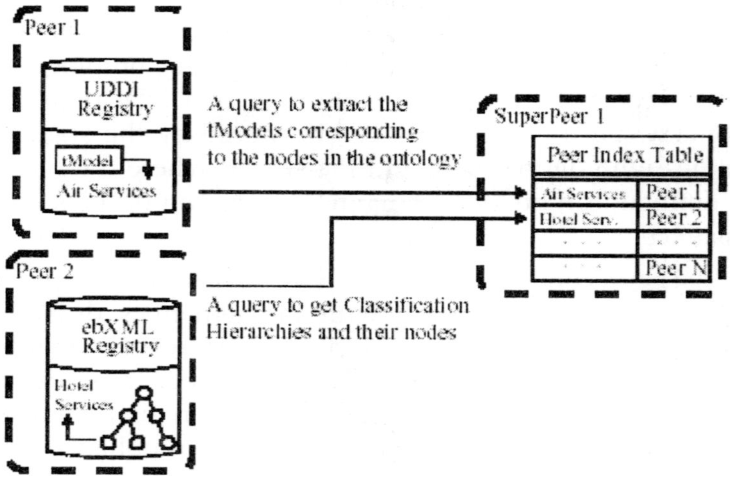

Figure 4. ExportingWeb service Registry Semantics as Super Peer Indexes

We believe that the automation of the service discovery should be extended to include the discovery of service registries themselves automatically. For this purpose, we propose to expose the semantic of Web service registries and connect the service registries through a peer-to-peer (P2P) network. With the semantics of service registries, we mean the semantics of Web services stored in these registries.

In UDDI registries, the tModel keys are used to associate semantic with Web services. To be able to associate the semantics of the proposed travel ontologies to Web service instances, we first obtain a tModel key for each node of an ontology from a UDDI registry. Then, Web service instances are advertised by putting the tModel keys of related ontology nodes in their category bags.

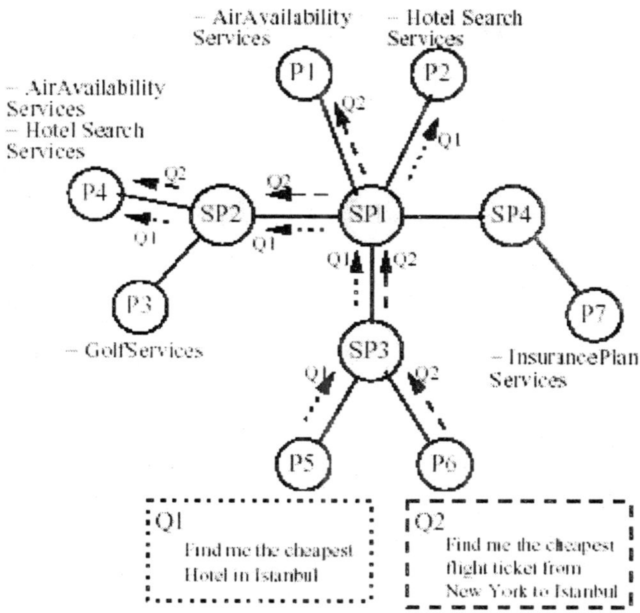

Figure 5. An Example Query Routing Based on Semantics

In ebXML registries, the semantic is associated with Web services through the "ClassificationSchemes". In other words, by relating a Web service with a node in the classification hierarchy, we make the service an explicit member of this node and the service inherits the well-defined meaning associated with this node as well as the generic properties defined for this node. These class hierarchies are then exposed as the semantic information of Web service registries.

The next step is to use this semantic information for discovering the service registries through peer-to-peer networks. Discovering peers based on the semantic information has already been addressed in the literature, mainly within the scope of the Edutella project. In

Edutella, each peer registers the metadata of the resources it stores, i.e. the schema and attributes that are used to describe the stored content, to its super-peer. These constitute the superpeer/ peer (SP/P) indices. Edutella also introduces superpeer/ super-peer routing indices (SP/SP) to forward queries among the super-peers. These SP/SP indices are essentially extracts and summaries from all super-peer local SP/P indices. Based on these indices, queries are first routed in the super-peer backbone, and then super-peers distribute them to the peers connected to them.

We use the same approach to facilitate the semantic discovery of service registries. That is, each peer registers the semantic information obtained from the service registries it owns as to its super peers as shown in Figure 4. The queries previously mentioned are used in extracting the semantic information from the registry. Besides service registries, individual peers can also advertise the semantics of the Web services they are hosting to their super peers. This facilitates P2P discovery of the web services that are not registered to any service registry. Once the semantics of the Web services both in service registries and individual peers are collected in the routing indices, this information is then used for semantic routing of the queries requesting a Web service given its semantics as shown in Figure 5. In this figure, P1 and P2 correspond to the UDDI and ebXML registry peer examples given in Figure 5. The figure shows the semantic category of the services it is hosting in reference to the nodes of the functionality ontology presented in Figure 1. Based on this information, the first query is routed to P4 and P2 by the super-peers, while the second query, which seeks flight availability information, is routed to P1 and P4.

8

Travel Distribution Technologies

As they prepare to enter the next century the small island states of the South Pacific face a number of major challenges with respect to future tourism development. In particular these isolated nations must attempt to fine tune product development and marketing strategies to meet the changing needs of the consumer, while at the same time creating a more sustainable industry that will maximise economic benefits while reducing socio-cultural and environment costs for current and future generations. Sustainable development is, of course, a complex concept to operationalise. The UN has distinguished three types of 'sustainability'.

(1) Economically sustainable development. This addresses the question of maintaining output of welfare-creating goods and services whose production depends on a limited supply of natural resource inputs.

(2) Environmentally sound and economically sustainable development. In addition to maintaining output as above this includes maintaining the stock of natural resources for the benefit of future generations.

(3) Equitable, environmentally sound and economically sustainable development.

While the final of these options is clearly the ideal outcome of any effort to develop a more sustainable form of tourism it is also the most difficult to achieve. While researchers have made significant progress in identifying the various parameters that must underlie attempts to understand and develop more sustainable forms of tourism significant gaps remain to be filled. In particular, while there is considerable lip-service paid to the importance of the equity dimension there have been relatively few attempts to provide a detailed understanding of the underlying processes that can lead to the creation of more or less equitable outcomes from tourism development.

In an attempt to shed some light on these issues this chapter focuses on the important but largely overlooked role that travel distribution technologies, especially computer reservation systems (CRS), can play in influencing the ability of small island states to achieve higher levels of local ownership and control in their tourism industries. An analysis is also presented of the role that evolving travel distribution technologies play in directing tourist flows to certain destinations in the South Pacific.

The degree to which local people are able to directly participate in tourism development is seen to be one of the most important factors determining the cultural deterioration and levels of local antagonism often ascribed to the industry. It has also been argued that increased local participation will improve levels of environmental awareness and stewardship, maximise local economic linkages and provide an important 'role model' for budding local entrepreneurs. The important role ascribed to local ownership is also reflected in long term tourism development plans that have emerged throughout much of the region.

The chapter begins with an overview of some of the key features that characterise South Pacific tourism. A brief review of past attempts to understand the causal mechanisms that underlie the equity-related outcomes associated with tourism's development in the region is then provided. The focus then shifts to the ways in which travel distribution technologies are affecting visitor flows to the South Pacific. Attention is drawn to the vital role played by computer reservation systems (CRS) and a number of hypotheses are generated about the influence that such systems can exert over the ability of small island states to reach tourism markets and maximise levels of local ownership and participation in the industry.

In an attempt to test these hypotheses the findings of two surveys are reported (one carried out among South Pacific tourism operations in the late 1980s and the other among Montreal travel agents in the summer of 1995). The findings reveal that the bias inherent in CRS is privileging some island destinations over others while at the same time tending to prevent smaller, often locally owned, niche operations from reaching the market place. This, in turn, has significant implications for the ability of microstates to promote more sustainable forms of tourism.

The island nations of the South Pacific represent some of the smallest and most isolated players in the global economic system. Their distance from major markets, limited natural resource bases and fragile environments have long posed a seemingly insurmountable hurdle to those wishing to stimulate economic growth. The continued inability of 'traditional' export-led or import substitution based strategies to overcome these constraints has led many governments in the region to adopt development approaches that place an emphasis on tourism.

Much of the literature from the South Pacific and elsewhere suggests that island microstates striving for more sustainable forms of tourism development should adopt 'new' or 'alternative' strategies rather than pursuing the 'old' or 'traditional' forms of mass tourism that have endured sustained criticism over the past 20 years due to the negative socio-cultural and environmental impacts ascribed to them and the relatively limited economic benefits they bring to local populations.

Unfortunately attempts to dichotomise tourism development strategies into 'old' and 'new' components do not match the reality of the South Pacific situation, or, for that matter, developing regions elsewhere around the world . Most of the microstates in the South Pacific are characterised by a mix of mass and alternative tourism types and are unlikely to be willing, or able, to shift away from traditional markets.

Despite its undoubted problems, mass tourism remains a vital economic tool for island governments who are attempting to maintain their citizens' relatively high living standards that are often a legacy of past colonial structures and modern-day aid and remittance payments. Indeed it can be argued that mass tourism 'subsidises' the development of alternative forms of travel to the region. Thus, without mass travel, many islands would not have sufficient tourists to justify existing flight connections. At the same time the development of mass travel has been vital for the infrastructural development that is required for the success of any form of tourism.

It should also be noted that these nations are not simply meek recipients of tourism development processes handed down by MNCs and metropolitan governments. Despite their low GDP per capita, substantial trade deficits, and limited private sector employment opportunities none of these nations exhibit the extreme levels of economic instability and poverty that would lead them to adopt a tourism 'at any cost' strategy. Put simply, local governments are not forced to adopt tourism out of an overwhelming sense of economic desperation and appear to be well aware of the negative consequences of compromising broader development goals in the hope of attracting large scale foreign investment and mass forms of tourism development.

As a result, while most of the microstates in the region have adopted elements of 'traditional' tourism, few have emerged as hard-core 'mass tourism' destinations, despite considerable growth during the past decade. Indeed many of the nations in the region have a long standing tradition of placing sustainable development objectives at the centre of their industry development plans. Even nations such as Vanuatu, which exhibit relatively high levels of foreign ownership, have placed national development objectives at the centre of tourism strategies—stressing the need to foster small, locally owned tourism businesses while at the same time controlling future development in an environmentally and culturally sustainable fashion.

Thus, not only is it hard to talk of a potential old/new dichotomy in tourism development, it is also difficult to argue that sustainable tourism initiatives are wholly new to the region. It seems clear that the main task ahead is not to simply promote alternative forms of tourism per se but to make conventional tourism, which is indispensable, more sustainable. Travel Distribution and Tourism Development in the Pacific Relatively few detailed analyses of the travel distribution system and its influence on the nature of tourism development in the South Pacific have been undertaken since the mid-1980s—with Britton's seminal contributions continuing to dominate the literature.

Drawing heavily on dependency theory, Britton focused on the influence that metropolitan based corporations exert over the nature of tourism development in small Pacific island nations. Microstates are seen to be enmeshed in a global tourism system over which they have little or no influence. The advertising strategies of metropolitan corporations shape tourist expectations—leading visitors to seek the types of experiences and facilities associated with mass tourism. Island governments are forced, in turn, to use multinational companies to provide the necessary capital to finance large scale international style hotels and provide trained staff.

The ability of these larger operations to offer higher commissions to overseas tour operators also enables them to gain control over various sectors of microstate tourist industries. Overseas concerns and local elites receive the bulk of tourist revenue flows—with profits often being drained from the island nations. Small scale, locally owned enterprises are either relegated to activities which lie beyond the immediate interests of larger companies, or find roles as sub-contractors. The final outcome is a form of tourism that primarily satisfies the commercial interests of overseas concerns and only partially meets local development needs.

Much of the work that has been conducted on the links between travel distribution and the nature of tourism development in the South Pacific has focused on the vital airline sector. Britton & Kissling stress the fact that Pacific microstates rely heavily on large overseas airlines to bring visitors to their shores and have little control over the routing and scheduling decisions of these companies. All of these nations are dependent on a small number of foreign carriers with only a handful boasting their own small international/regional airlines. The fickle nature of international routing has hurt several tourist industries. For example, Air New Zealand's decision to cut back services to the Cook Islands in the early 1980s led to a significant reduction in tourist flows, while a pilot's strike at Air Nauru in mid-1988 cut the only commercial air service between the Niue and New Zealand.

Despite the fact that international air transportation has evolved considerably since the mid-1980's Britton's concerns about the uncertainty of transportation links to the region still hold true. While continued deregulation of the international airline industry may have opened up new markets and provided the customer with cheaper prices, ownership concentration has also grown -with small and mid-sized carriers giving way to international mega-carriers. Deregulation also means that less profitable routes are very often no longer in operation.

ROLE OF TRAVEL DISTRIBUTION TECHNOLOGIES

Somewhat surprisingly the literature on tourism development in the region has largely ignored an important feature of the evolving airline industry—the increasing importance of airline computer reservations systems (sometimes called global distribution systems). The computer reservation system is a central database connected to a network of terminals (usually housed in travel agencies) from which bookings and reservations are made. The global distribution system, or airline CRS, caters to airline schedule and rate management but has grown to include schedules and rates for a range of other tourism products.

During the late 1960's CRS were developed as reservation and accounting systems for internal use by airlines and hotels. Reduced costs and improvements to computer networking encouraged the extension of CRS and they evolved to provide reservation and distribution links between travel service providers (airlines, hotels, tours, car rentals) and the consumer, with travel agents usually acting as the intermediaries. According to a survey conducted by Travel Weekly, US travel agents use CRS to book 92% of domestic airline flights, 80% of international flights, 68% of car rentals, 53% of hotel nights, 51% of rail travel, 10% of tours and 6% of cruises. Over 95% of North American travel agencies are hooked up to one or more reservation systems. SABRE, the largest CRS, (operated by American Airlines) handles 500,000 reservations a day and has over 45 million prices in its data bank representing 650 airlines, 21,000 hotels, 52 rental car companies and 8 railroads. As Collier notes:

This is not an airline booking system, or a marketing system but a huge travel distribution network.

There have been relatively few attempts by tourism researchers to ascertain the impacts of these developments on small, tourism-oriented, island states. Much of what has been written has come from the Caribbean—with the work of Poon dominating. Poon adopts a relatively positive perspective on the various impacts associated with the tourism industry's evolving use of CRS technology. She argues that CRS allow firms to move into new, interrelated activities, generating synergies, systems gains and economies of scope.

As a result it often becomes more profitable (and just as cost effective) to produce clusters of interrelated services rather than single, unrelated items. Poon maintains that new technologies and diagonal integration are making it possible to produce flexible and segmented vacations that are cost-competitive with 'traditional' mass, standardised holidays. In her recent book she notes that such information technology facilitates the production of new, flexible and high-quality travel and tourism services that are cost competitive with mass, standardised and rigidly packaged options. IT helps to engineer the transformation of travel and tourism from its mass, standardised and rigidly packaged nature into a more flexible, individual-oriented, sustainable and diagonally integrated industry.

Poon argues that the greater array of tourist products available through CRS will facilitate the access of niche products to the travel consumer—either as stand-alone entities or as components of more flexible package structures. In simple terms this 'product deepening' may translate into greater opportunities for small locally controlled businesses to gain access to a consumer that is seeking more flexible travel products. While Poon's work is thought provoking and has opened up several important dimensions in small island tourism research it can be argued that she does have a tendency to overstate the positive impacts of CRS. While Poon acknowledges that small industry players and peripheral destinations may lose market share by not participating in these systems she counters by arguing that small firm networking and public sector intervention can overcome these hurdles. In simple terms the world of CRS and alternative tourism is seen to offer significant opportunities for small destinations to develop more flexible and sustainable tourism products.

This rather optimistic vision may not mesh with the realities of the South Pacific. The costs of joining computer reservation systems and the skilled labour required to operate them may place them out of the hands of smaller, locally owned enterprises. For example a typical CRS subscription will involve a 'join-up' fee and charge per booking made. The latter may be a percentage of the cost of the product sold—10% is a common figure—or a fixed flat rate.

If a destination is characterised by only a small number of multi-national operations, its presence on global distribution systems is likely to be relatively limited—putting it at a disadvantage vis-à-vis larger more established destinations. It can be argued that Poon has a tendency to over-emphasise the 'flexibility' of these systems. While it is indeed possible to display a range of different products and create new synergies through CRS, a number of rigidities remain. It is no coincidence, for example, that tour operators and their products are the least represented components of the travel industry on CRS. Those tours that are represented tend to be all-inclusive and relatively standardised in nature such as cruises and all-inclusive hotel stays.

The rigidities of CRS display protocol also make it difficult for niche tour and travel operations to market themselves effectively. Several studies have shown that travel agents are highly likely to draw information from the first page of CRS information that appears on their terminal screen. It is clearly in the interest of the GDS owner to present their own airline/business information on the opening page. Despite attempts to regulate this type of bias it is clear that those controlling a system can support their own products by a number of means.

An underlying hypothesis for the discussion that follows is that the high cost of CRS membership and the relatively rigid structure of the information that can be displayed will tend to lead to the exclusion of many smaller, locally owned South Pacific operations from these powerful distribution systems. It is also hypothesised that larger, often foreign owned, concerns are likely to reap the competitive rewards of being able to join these networks. The corporate level implications of gaining access to these powerful distribution systems are considerable. Pohlmann & Milne and Gill & Milne have shown that accommodation and attraction operations in Montreal and Toronto reap a number of rewards from CRS access (Table 1).

The most important benefits lie in gaining a competitive edge—primarily through achieving a greater corporate profile in the market place. Interestingly the impact on revenues appears to be more minimal—a consequence of the various membership fees and commissions charged. This latter point also reveals the important role that economies of scale can play in the decision to enter a CRS. Perhaps most significantly companies appear to have seen little increased fee-setting flexibility or networking opportunities stemming from CRS membership. This leads one to question the assumption that CRS automatically enables the creation of deeper and more flexible tourism products.

Table 1. Corporate impacts associated with inclusion on some form of CRS

Area of Impact	Impact
Competitiveness	Good
Bookings	Good
Market exposure	Good
Revenues	Acceptable
Labour productivity	Disappointing
Alliance formation	No impact
Rate flexibility	No impact

CRS related biases in tourist distribution will have a number of significant impacts on the ability of microstates to achieve more sustainable forms of tourism development:

— Several studieshave shown that largescale foreign concerns in the region exhibit higher economic leakages than their smaller, locally owned counterparts. If tourist flows are directed to large operations there may well be a commensurate increase in economic leakages. Larger operations also tend to be relatively less intensive in their use of local labour resources.

— While larger operations have been shown to generate proportionately more government revenue than their smaller counterparts it must also be remembered that they often require extensive infrastructure and may also be the recipient of government incentives and loans designed to attract initial investment.

— If tourist flows are directed to a handful of larger concerns there is every likelihood that local 'downstream' tourism businesses will be excluded.

— CRS technology is not particularly flexible in the array of tour activities and information that can be presented in a cost-effective fashion. This works against smaller operations who develop unique 'niche' products in an attempt to capture some of the tourist market.

— A lack of local participation in the industry may also have undesirable cultural and environmental consequences. The concentration of flows created by travel distribution, with high levels of expatriate ownership and management, may tend to alienate locals. At the same time local owners may be more likely to exhibit improved stewardship of natural resources, and may also exhibit greater sensitivity toward the conflicting land use issues that sometimes follow in tourism's wake.

The discussion of CRS inclusion is based on 1988 surveys and in-depth interviews conducted for the UNDP. While this work is rather dated and focused primarily on economic linkage issues, the fact that the aim of the survey instrument and interviews was to analyse corporate cost structures enabled an analysis of the number of tourism operations that are linked to some form of CRS. Due to the small scale of the countries' tourism industries and the interest of the participants it was possible to obtain excellent survey coverage. In Niue and Kiribati all relevant businesses participated in the survey while in Tonga, Papua New Guinea and Vanuatu the majority of tourist facilities were surveyed. Travel flow biases were analysed through a 'shadow shopping' survey of Montreal travel agents conducted between May and July 1995. By marketing and selling the products and services of tour operators and airlines, travel agents play a key role in influencing a traveller's choice of destination. Research has shown that as many as 40% of Canadian vacation customers only have a general idea of where to go and require an agent's assistance to identify their exact travel destination.

By suggesting airlines, cruises, tour operators or hotels, the agent can limit (or expand) the range of options available to a potential client. In fact 50% of Canadian customers seek the advice of travel agents on the choice of airline, while 66% of those seeking tour packages are strongly influenced by travel agent recommendations. Similar figures exist for customers making inquiries about car rentals or hotel accommodation. Eighty agents (randomly chosen from the Montreal Yellow Pages) were asked a 'general' question: 'I would like travel to New Zealand, and as part of the trip I would like to visit an island in the South Pacific. I'm looking for an island that is less developed, off the beaten track, not like Hawaii. Can you suggest an island?'. The stopover option was chosen because of the long-haul nature of the Montreal market for South Pacific travel. While no accurate statistics exist it is assumed that the majority of Montrealers travelling to the region are taking a multi-destination holiday—often involving Australia, New Zealand and one or more Pacific islands. This assumption was checked by asking a non-stopover general question for a short period—several agents refused to take the inquiry seriously.

In addition to flight information, the agents were asked to provide information on hotels, activities, and general background information on the island(s) they suggested. Twenty further agencies were visited in person to determine whether responses would differ with an in-person approach. These agents were asked the same 'general' question. The methodology used is consistent with other travel agency 'shadow shopping' exercises that have been conducted in recent years.

In the second component of the survey an additional 75 agents (25 per destination) were asked a more refined question: 'I would like to take a vacation in the South Pacific for three weeks. Some friends of mine recommended an island called ¼ Vanuatu, Tonga, Cook Islands. Could you provide me with some additional information'. The agents were then asked to provide as much information as possible about the island, including: hotels, activities, local weather, suggestions for visits to adjacent islands, and basic information on flights.

The results of the 1988 survey support the hypotheses presented in Table 2. In the accommodation sector, large, overseas chain-owned, hotels were well represented on both hotel and airline reservation systems. Large independent operations, some of which were under management contract to chains, were also relatively well represented—with a tendency to be part of either a voluntary hotel reservation consortia or hotel chain CRS.

Table 2. CRS Inclusion of various microstate tourism operations — 19881

Type of tourism operation	Included on CRS (%)
Accommodation	
Small/medium independent	0
Large independent	35
Chain affiliate	75
Large/medium chain member	95
Tour Operations	
Small/medium independent	0
Large independent (local)	5
Large (overseas)	25

Without exception small and medium sized operations were excluded from CRS's, with most citing costs and skills as being the major barrier to entry. This clearly places smaller operators at a competitive disadvantage in the market place. Small and medium sized operators in the tour sector were also under-represented compared to their larger counterparts.

While these results are dated it is interesting to note that they are consistent with more recent studies of differential CRS inclusion. For example Pohlmann & Milne found that 90% of small and 62% of medium sized independent hotels surveyed in Montreal were not listed on CRS's. By contrast hotels either affiliated to, or part of, chains had 100% representation.

Gill & Milne found similar variations in CRS adoption among Toronto hotels. A more recent survey of hotel CRS use in the South Pacific backs up these findings to some extent but differs in other important ways. The TCSP study is based on a postal survey of the hotel sector in several islands throughout the region. Somewhat surprising, however, is the fact that the large hotels surveyed show similar levels of CRS use to their smaller counterparts.

One reason for the divergence in this set of findings may lie in the type of CRS links that were distinguished by the two surveys, with the bulk of the CRS users in 1988 having fax-based rather than on-line connections. The results of the travel agent survey also support the hypotheses regarding the impacts of CRS on the distribution of tourist flows.

The responses of the agents to the 'general question' substantiated the view that certain South Pacific destinations are favoured over others. Fiji and French Polynesia dominated initial suggestions while further research saw an increasing profile for the Cook Islands. 'Other' islands such as Vanuatu or Tonga, were rarely mentioned (Table 3).

Further details provided by agents were generally limited to information on flights: with the three major airlines flying in the South Pacific from Canada (Canadian,

Qantas, Air New Zealand) dominating (Table 4). Air Pacific was only mentioned twice by agents—who advised a return side trip from Auckland to an island destination.

Table 3. Pacifc island destinations suggested by travel agents (n = 80)

Destination	Initial Suggestion	Suggested After Research
Fiji	19	25
French Polynesia (Papeete, Tahiti)	12	15
Cook Islands	7	15
New Caledonia	4	1
Hawaii	4	7
Tonga	3	9
Vanuatu	1	1
Western Samoa	1	5
Other1	7	11
No suggestion	21	-

Table 4 Airlines suggested by travel agents (n = 80)

Airline	Number of Times Suggested
Air Fiji (Air Pacific)	2
Canadian Airlines	16
Qantas	17
Air New Zealand	25

Half of the agents suggested a stopover on route to New Zealand, generally in Nadi, Papeete or Honolulu. This is usually cheaper than making a routing to New Zealand and then travelling out again to the islands. Five agents looked up fare information to New Zealand and suggested that the caller buy a vacation package in New Zealand. These agents stated that it would be less expensive and that the caller would have a greater variety of destinations to choose from. It is clear that if an airline does not make a stopover at a smaller island on route, those destinations tend to be neglected by the travel agents. All of the major carriers flying from North America to Australia or New Zealand make scheduled stops at either Hawaii, Fiji or Tahiti. When the agent looks up flight information on the CRS one of these destinations is sure to appear as part of a traveller's potential flight itinerary.

From the standpoint of the smaller islands, this is unfortunate, since travellers that would willingly visit more 'remote' nations are being channelled to the 'mainstream' South Pacific destinations. In spite of the CRS and airline imposed bias, smaller islands could tap into this 'stopover' market with relative ease. Air New Zealand, the most commonly suggested airline, has cooperative marketing agreements with Air Vanuatu, Air Pacific, Solomon Airlines and Air Caledonia, all of which provide service to destinations that can be included as stopovers en route to New Zealand for little additional cost. Generally, the least expensive tickets are only valid for a month and allow no stopovers on route. For only an additional $100-200 dollars, however, the traveller may stay three months and is allowed one stopover. Additional stopovers on these three month fares are allowed for only $150 per destination. Stopovers can be made at numerous South Pacific destinations: Air New Zealand offers Fiji, Tahiti, Tonga, Western Samoa, and the Cook Islands. Qantas and Canadian Airlines' stopovers options are limited to Los Angeles, Papeete, Hawaii and Hawaii and Fiji respectively. Although 25 agents mentioned Air New Zealand as a carrier, only nine agents suggested the possibility of such multiple stopovers.

Hotel information was provided by only four agents from the 'general' grouping. These agents only gave a price range and suggested making arrangements once at the destination. From the information provided it seems likely that these hotel prices were obtained from brochures in the travel agency. Ten agencies either mailed brochures or prepared packages for the researcher to pick up—stating that this was the best way to get information on the destinations.

Several responses revealed that agents have only limited awareness of the South Pacific region beyond what is available on their CRS terminals. One agent did not think any South Pacific packages were available from Canada. A few agents stated that it would not be possible to inexpensively combine New Zealand and the South Pacific in one trip and suggested buying two separate tickets. One agent began by mistakenly stating that New Zealand was a destination in Australia. A further seven suggested Hawaii in spite of being asked for a destination 'not like Hawaii'. One of these agents mentioned that only the main island of Hawaii was developed and that outlying islands were pretty much untouched. Rarotonga, the main island of the Cooks group, was introduced by one travel agent as being a beautiful destination in Tahiti!

These findings are supported by recent TCSP research on the perceptions of South Pacific travel destinations held by North American travel agents. This phone survey/focus group research found that while Fiji and Tahiti generated awareness levels of between 65 and 70% among agents, the next most popular island—the Cook Islands—had a score of only 15%. Vanuatu, Tonga and Western Samoa all exhibit figures below 10%. The clear majority of agents surveyed felt uncomfortable about dealing with travel inquiries relating to the smaller destinations in the region and listed lack of information as the major stumbling block.

While the agents that were visited in person tended to limit their research to looking for flight details, they often provided additional information in the form of brochures on Australia, New Zealand and the South Pacific. Twenty three different brochures were collected describing South Pacific packages—with Fiji and Tahiti appearing in every one. The Cook Islands is listed in only five brochures while Tonga is only briefly mentioned in one. A content analysis of the brochures revealed two key points. First, the smaller South Pacific airlines receive little or no mention in the brochures.

Air New Zealand dominates, with Qantas only appearing in 4 pamphlets. Air Pacific is the only regional carrier listed in the brochures, and even then it is only mentioned as a partner to Qantas. Second, niche, or small scale tour operators tend to be excluded. The Fiji and Tahiti pamphlets present resort holidays aimed at the 'three S's' market. All involve staying at larger hotels or resorts. If smaller hotels are listed they are, in every case, deluxe 'boutique' operations. If only those brochures listing Tonga or the Cook Islands are considered, a similar pattern holds true—wholesalers limit themselves to a very small number of large resort hotels.

Suggestions for activities are generally limited to water sports, sunbathing and shopping excursions and as a result a myriad of interesting niche products (emphasising culture, nature, wildlife) are left out. One wholesaler's brochure includes the following description of the Cook Islands: 'There is very little to do except soak up the sun, surf and sand', while another company, calling itself 'Cultural Tours' offers a three day stopover in Rarotonga to 'bask in the sunshine ¼ hire a jeep ¼ or discover exotic flowers'. Nowhere is there mention of any interaction with Cook Island Maori culture, nor is there any detailed description of the Cook Islands themselves. Faced with such limited information, it should be no surprise that agents feel unable to provide detailed information on alternative tourism products in the region.

Early into the 'specific' question section of the research it was noted that almost all of the responses for each destination were identical. In fact, a single wholesaler dominates the South Pacific travel market in Montreal. In the case of Tonga and the Cook Islands, the wholesaler was sending the agents a photocopy of a few pages from an Air New Zealand package brochure and the information was then passed on to the caller. These pages had brief descriptions of the islands and a listing of 3-5 hotels available as part of a package deal.

Questions related to Vanuatu were met with a similar response, although it was impossible to determine the source of the information. In the few cases where agents did not call a wholesaler, responses were limited to providing flight information only. It is clear from the responses to the 'specific' questions that Montreal travel agents knew little or nothing about destinations such as the Cook Islands, Tonga or Vanuatu.

Alternatives to CRS

Smaller or independent companies can overcome some of the disadvantages associated with their limited size by forming networks—which allow for the pooling of marketing resources, or enable joint access to essential technologies such as CRS. Indeed government and aid donor assistance in the establishment and running of such networks may be one of the most effective ways to foster small enterprise development in the South Pacific tourism industry.

There are already several examples of small adventure oriented operators setting up alliances in North America and elsewhere in order to gain access to elusive consumers, while small accommodation complexes have a long tradition of pooling resources to maximise market profiles. While research on similar themes in the South Pacific is non-existent there are already examples in destinations such as the Cook Islands and Vanuatu, of locally owned or small scale accommodation operations joining forces to improve market place and lobbying profiles.

It should be noted, of course, that networks of any sort rely on patterns of trust and reciprocity: for this reason it is not always an easy task to establish or maintain such groupings. Networking is also vital in the regional airline sector. Attempts to form regional airlines to escape the dependence on larger carriers have been fraught with difficulties.

For example, Air Pacific was initially established by Qantas and Air New Zealand to create a regional feeder network for the major airlines. While Air Pacific was supposed to increase microstates' access to the international airline network, disagreements over routes and frequencies of service led Tonga, Western Samoa and other islands to establish their own national airlines.

The emerging trend in the South Pacific, as elsewhere, is towards inter-airline cooperation characterised by bilateral agreements and sub-regional partnerships. As an example, Air Pacific and Royal Tongan Airlines recently jointly leased a B737, with the aircraft being shared between the two carriers. Although a few of the smaller South Pacific carriers have made some strides towards profitability, the future remains uncertain.

Carriers such as Royal Tongan and Polynesian Airlines cannot compete with Air New Zealand's larger aircraft and well established 'Coral Route' network through Polynesia. As a result, several airlines such as Air Vanuatu and Air Pacific have allied themselves with the larger carriers through code sharing agreements or joint marketing initiatives.

The regions' suppliers could also benefit from the establishment of Destination Information Systems (DIS) or databases—electronic information technology accessed via videotext, CD-Rom, and personal computers. The DIS can provide pre-trip information about a destination's accommodation, transportation, tours, and attractions to the travelling public either directly through home computers, or through travel agents or national/regional tourist offices. There is also potential for connecting the DIS with CRSs which would link the respective suppliers to travel agents around the world.

Such systems can be developed on a national or regional basis; examples of the latter exist in the Scottish Highlands, the Tyrolean region of Austria. In market regions 'characterised by small independent businesses and individualistic holidays', centralisation of information can increase visibility as well as ease of reservation. Indeed government and aid donor assistance in the establishment and running of such networks may be one of the most effective ways to foster small enterprise development in the South Pacific tourism industry. It is fair to say, however, that such systems are expensive to establish, rely on trust and reciprocity among participants and must also pay fees to allow them to 'switch' into CRSs. It seems unlikely that they can provide a cost effective answer to microstate marketing needs.

Perhaps the greatest prospects lie, however, in the emergence of new travel distribution systems—especially the internet and World Wide Web (WWW). Rapid improvements in information technologies are changing the relationship between consumers and travel suppliers and may offer new opportunities for small, niche-oriented products to reach potential markets. Airlines and hotel chains are hoping to cash in by providing easy to use reservation systems over the internet, with Holiday Inn recently becoming the first major hotel chain to offer such a service. American Airlines' Easy-Sabre, already available through Compuserve, will soon be available via the World Wide Web and other CRS's are sure to follow. Estimates suggest that up to 10% of travel arrangements in the United States are now made through such networks and this figure is expected to rise rapidly. More importantly the WWW may actually begin to eat into the dominance of CRS's as travel distribution networks. Web sites offer the possibility to break out of some of the rigidities associated with CRS's while the increased use of home computers and growing accessibility of computer networks such as Compuserve may play a role in the demise of traditional non-specialised travel agencie.

As a complement to the main body of the CRS research a search of the internet for the same three destinations that were the basis of the 'specific' agency question was undertaken. This research has since been broadened to include Western Samoa and Fiji. The search included keyword searches of the WWW (using web crawler, yahoo and other search mechanisms), and Gopherspace.

The information found on the internet can be broken down into four categories:

(1) General information including CIA Word Fact Sheets on various countries. The information is usually limited to basic geographical, political and economic data and resembles that found in encyclopedias. Information was found on all of the case study nations although it is of very limited use to potential tourists seeking details on travel and accommodation.

(2) Private, special interest sites. These are sites established by private individuals with a highly focused interest. The Tonga search brought up a site located in Berlin, Germany. The site includes numerous photos, descriptions of the archipelago, and limited travel information. Vanuatu is promoted through a similar site, located in Massachusetts. Here, internet 'surfers' can view photos of various parts of the islands, listen to an excerpt from a local radio broadcast, and see an excellent bibliography of books and travel guides about the country.

(3) Commercial sites. The search for information on the microstates also brought up several travel agencies, wholesalers and airlines operating in the region. To date, the use of the internet for commercial purposes has been frowned upon, but this is changing as large and small businesses discover its wide reaching advertising potential. One travel agency, based in Australia, sells various packages to the South Pacific destinations included in this study and its web pages include airfares, numerous hotel listings as well as descriptions of activities, climate and limited information on various island cultures. The Web pages gave more information about the islands than could be obtained from the bulk of Montreal travel agents. The company maintaining the Web site operates as a full service travel agency in Australia and is only using the internet as an extension of their regular services. A representative of the agency claimed to receive 10 to 20 inquiries per day in response to the internet ads: about 10% of these are converted into sales. Numerous airlines are also jumping into the internet fray. Of the South Pacific carriers, only Qantas and Ansett Australian Airlines had operating Web pages at the time of the search but others are likely to follow. Several wholesalers also have web sites—focusing on packages to established destinations such as Fiji, Tahiti and Hawaii.

(4) Government sponsored travel information. Several of the nations studied here were in the process of establishing tourism related web sites. Western Samoa's site allows the prospective tourist to find background information on the islands, how to get there, hotel listings and information on tour operators. There is also a listing of upcoming events. The Western Samoa site lists more than a dozen local tour operators, most of which offer small scale eco-tours

> or cultural visits, and an extensive listing of accommodation operations—many of them small scale in nature. These are exactly the types of operations that find it difficult to access CRS systems. Fiji has recently introduced a sophisticated web page and the country's Visitors Bureau is actively marketing its benefits to industry representatives. This latter point is important as a web site can only work if individual companies and operators can be convinced of its value.

The potential of the internet to assist smaller destinations seeking to develop tourism industries characterised by higher levels of local ownership is clearly enormous. With the popularity of the net constantly growing, destinations seeking to develop niche markets can promote themselves at a relatively low cost to an expanding, high income/ well educated market. Smaller operators can bypass the traditional tourist distribution network and access customers directly.

One must, however, be wary of over stating the current potential of the WWW to act as an effective marketing tool for Pacific microstates. Telecommunication services on many islands are of poor quality and computer literacy and hardware availability is limited. The onus will clearly be on governments, aid donors and prospective internet service providers to solve these problems. It is interesting to note that Western Samoa's home page was created on that island's behalf by a company based in San Francisco—showing that infrastructural problems on the islands can be circumvented.

The cost of a professional web site designer to help in the preparation of web pages can vary from $1000 to $10,000 depending on the complexity of the material. It is also important to note that credit card payments cannot yet be made securely over the internet, although VISA, Mastercard and Microsoft will soon be introducing effective encryption technology. As a result companies must still rely on customers to telephone, fax or mail an order. Despite these provisos it is clear that the internet provides small companies and peripheral nations with the potential to gain access to an international clientele that has largely evaded them in the past and at a price far below the costs of joining a CRS or attempting to use mainstream advertising media.

The growing sophistication and power of new technologies, together with increased international competition and ownership concentration, appear likely to lead to the further strengthening of large enterprises, especially multi-national chains. Mid-sized or non-specialised firms are likely to be squeezed out of the market while small firms will have to become either increasingly specialised or contract out their services to larger firms. These biases in travel flows will, it is argued, also tend to facilitate against the achievement of higher levels of local ownership and the creation of more sustainable forms of tourism development in Pacific Island microstates.

It is clear that the smaller travel destinations in the region have largely failed to make an impression (either positive or negative) with the bulk of the Montreal travel agents surveyed. This is in large part a consequence of the limited amount of information available about these destinations on computer reservation systems. While it may be argued that agents are not important sources of information for certain types of niche tourist markets this is hardly surprising given the limited amount of accurate travel data that the former are able to impart to travellers. The question remains as to how the use of travel agents by potential visitors would change if the former were able to provide accurate details about the region.

Tourists who contact agents for information on South Pacific microstate tourism products are likely to be pushed toward more established destinations such as Fiji, and toward larger, often foreign owned, accommodation operations. Perhaps most importantly the inaccuracy of much of the information provided can create problems for tourists arriving in the region. Any dissatisfaction that results may lead to negative feed back about the region being passed on to friends and relatives.

Nevertheless small islands do have some potential strategies to assist them in overcoming these barriers. Government can play an effective role by aiding the coordination of private sector efforts and by evaluating current competitive strategies in light of the processes of change identified above. The use of networking and strategic alliances will become increasingly important competitive tools for firms of all sizes.

9

Computer Reservation Systems

In the 1930s, the air services have sold tickets through third-parties almost from the beginning of commercial service. At first, the relationship with third-parties was unofficial. Frequently these representatives were not even professional advisers, but bellhops, taxi drivers, or terminal employees. Often they represented individual airlines rather than the entire industry. Airlines found this system unsatisfactory. Consumers were not able to gain reliable information about the services of the still-nascent industry and airlines did not have reliable information about reservations for their services.

In USA the Air Traffic Conference (ATC), a division of the airlines' trade group, the Air Transport Association, created a new travel agent accreditation program in 1940. Through a series of agreements, the airlines jointly determined not only the necessary qualifications for travel agents, who would now represent all airlines, but also important details of how they would operate, including the amount the airlines paid for their services. Pursuant to the Civil Aeronautics Act, these agreements were approved by the Civil Aeronautics Board (CAB) and granted immunity from the antitrust laws.

Because of World War II, the ATC did not fully implement the program many aircraft had been turned over to the war effort and commercial traffic was very limited. After the war, airlines were more interested in signing up agents, especially to help them attract travellers away from the then-dominant railroads and steamship lines, and implemented the agency program. Airlines paid agents a commission for their services, based on a percentage of the ticket price.

For many years, airlines limited the number of accredited agents according to a so-called "need" clause. Airlines added agents only if, in their view, there were not enough to meet demand in a particular area. The limitation was part of the airlines' attempt to restrict agents from certain categories of traffic. They viewed agents as promoters of air travel and saw their role as generating new traffic from passengers who would otherwise not fly.

Through various restrictions in the agency agreements, airlines attempted to retain for themselves the non-discretionary sales; i.e., passengers who would otherwise have flown and merely needed ticketing services. But as agents became more prevalent, they not only promoted new discretionary air travel, but increasingly served existing travellers who sought their services.

In 1959, the Civil Aeronautics Board banned the "need" clause, granting unfettered entry into the travel agency industry. The introduction of efficient jet aircraft in the late 1950s meant airlines were charging lower fares, which made flying more affordable. Unsurprisingly, passenger demand boomed, and airlines and the travelling public increasingly turned to agents to advise travellers and write tickets. Relying on a pool of common agents to provide information and dispense tickets was more efficient for airlines than setting up parallel and competitive distribution channels. This was especially true in light of pervasive CAB regulation, under which the agency limited route competition among carriers. A significant amount of air service was provided jointly, with passengers changing not only airplanes but airlines on the way to their ultimate destination. As a result of the limits on route flexibility, plus the near total ban on price competition, a jointly operated distribution system made even more sense. Travel agents had become an important cog in the airline ticket distribution system.

Despite the ban on the "need clause", the CAB continued to permit airlines to regulate agents extensively, in almost all facets of their business. The agreements covered many areas of agency operation, including location, qualification of staff, bonding, and financial responsibility. They not only provided some assurance that customers were receiving accurate information, but also that airline reservations were made and tickets were issued correctly.

Agents also controlled blank ticket stock and validation plates, valuable commodities that require special monitoring and storage. Anyone able to acquire them could write tickets that airlines had to accept for travel. And, because passengers needed that paper ticket in order to travel, the agent became an important vehicle by which airlines delivered tickets to their passengers.

The most important agreement set commission rates to be paid to agents. By the late 1970s, airlines were paying agents base commissions of seven percent, and higher rates for air travel sold as part of tour packages.

Deregulation and the Travel Agent Industry

For several decades, travel agents experienced substantial growth under the ATC agency system. Starting from a total of less than 600 recognized agents in 1941, total locations reached 6,021 by 1968. By 1977, the year before airline deregulation, the figure had more than doubled, to 13,454, the result of an average annual growth of 10 percent during the 1950s But the biggest boom was yet to come, owing to passage of the 1978 Airline Deregulation Act and the introduction of computer reservation systems (CRS).

Deregulation gave travellers a vastly wider range of flight and fare options, and CRSs became the tool that travel agents used to deal with this increased array of travel choices. Under regulation, the CAB determined not only the carriers that could offer interstate air service but also the routes each carrier could serve and the fares they could charge. Therefore, carriers had only a limited ability to establish prices on a route. As a result, passenger fare and flight choices were limited. Even connecting passengers had only a few options and, in any case, under regulation, connecting passengers paid the same fare, regardless of routing or carrier.

With deregulation of pricing and entry, the situation changed radically. Airlines were free to enter and exit domestic routes and to establish their own prices. In order to operate efficiently and gain traffic, airlines restructured linear route systems created under regulation, and began to organize their route systems around hubs. These new networks increased the number of city-pairs served and reduced the time consumers spent in the airport transferring fro m one flight to another. At the same time, new and formerly intrastate carriers, often with substantially lower costs and lower fares than the once-regulated incumbents, began to compete in many markets throughout the country.

However, more choice brought more confusion in deciphering the available options and choosing which option to select. Accordingly, travellers began to look more to travel agents to explain the options and find pricing value. Airlines anxious to take advantage of their new freedom started so many new routes that they had to rely on agents, who had immediate information available in their CRSs, to inform travellers about the rapid changes to their networks. In fact, the well-established travel agent industry now made it easier for airlines to reshape their networks.

The impact of deregulation on travel agent sales was quickly apparent. Travel agents accounted for 38.4 percent of total domestic sales in 1977 but by 1979, the first full year after the Deregulation Act, their share had grown to 53 percent. Thus, travel agents not only benefited fro m the increase in air travel that accompanied the end of government regulation but also from an increase in their share of the business. The law itself did not deal with travel agency commissions. However, the CAB was required to review immunized airline agreements and determine whether antitrust immunity for them continued to be in the public interest. The agreements establishing commission rates were among the first to be re-examined.

The Board removed immunity from the agreement setting international commission rates in 1978 and deregulated domestic commissions in 1980. Soon thereafter, commissions paid to travel agents began increasing, which might have been expected since commissions may have been held below market levels by the airline agreements. The higher payments included both base commission rates and the newly introduced override commissions, in which the agency's compensation depended on its ability to increase an airline's share of its bookings.

Base commissions increased, as airlines matched one another in order to avoid agents shifting traffic to other carriers. As a result, average commission rates on tickets processed through the industry settlement plan went from 8.3 percent in 1978 to 9.6 percent in 1981. Override commissions were paid outside the settlement plan, so actual commission rates for some agencies were even higher. In fact, average commissions grew almost continuously after deregulation and reached a post-deregulation peak of 11.80 percent in 1994.

Characteristics of Computer Reservation Systems

In addition to mounting commission costs, airlines were paying more for the computerized reservation systems (CRS) used by travel agents to handle the booking transaction. Carriers pay for these systems in the form of booking fees, which currently can amount to approximately $11.00 for an average passenger ticket. These fees are in addition to commission expense, and have been controversial for almost 20 years.

When they were introduced in 1976, the airline-owned computer reservation systems included not only their own flight and fare information but that of other carriers, too. Before airline deregulation, passengers often used more than one airline for a single trip. The system of exchanging passengers, called interlining, meant carriers had to store rivals' flight and fare data because each airline acted as agent for other carriers in selling their flights. The availability of data on other airlines enabled CRS vendors to offer comprehensive information on the entire industry, and also gave other airlines free access to the efficiencies of dealing with agents through the CRS, rather than over the telephone.

During the early 1980s, as airlines and vendors encouraged agencies to install new systems, the cost of providing CRS service far exceeded the revenue generated from the systems. In order to offset these costs and to gain assistance in marketing systems in cities where the vendor carrier provided little service, vendors created host programs.

Cohosts received preference in schedule displays and helped to market the systems in their territories. While early airline cohosts paid $0.25 per booking, many carriers continued to pay nothing. The airline owners did not pay fees, but absorbed the losses incurred in offering the systems. They also achieved incremental airline revenues because of schedule display bias and the relationship established with the agent. As CRSs became ubiquitous, and more valuable in distributing information on schedules and fares, vendors increased fees for later cohosts. They also refused to provide service to post-deregulation new entrants until they agreed to pay much higher booking fees than cohosts were paying.

These and other tactics spurred vigorous complaints about anticompetitive behaviour. In response, and as one of its last official acts, in 1984 the CAB imposed regulations on the airlines and the CRSs they owned. Two central elements of the regulations were the requirements that all airline-owned CRSs offer unbiased displays and charge non-discriminatory booking fees.

In response to the new rules, vendors established per-segment booking fees of $1.75 or more for all airlines. These new booking fees represented a dramatic increase for many carriers that had been paying little or nothing. Non-CRS-owning airlines regarded the payments as not only an increase in distribution cost but also a subsidy to rivals. Since the original charges were set, fees have increased to approximately $4.25 per segment. That means an average of almost $11 for an average passenger ticket. Airlines testified that the booking fees have increased by 7 percent per year, when information technology was driving costs down in other businesses. Vendors respond that fees are higher because their systems have many more sophisticated functions, and computer programming costs have risen substantially. But airlines remain unpersuaded.

Indeed, carriers believe that they are the unwilling participants in a transfer of income to the distribution system in the form of both commissions and booking fees, particularly because vendors transfer a portion of the booking fees they receive from airlines to travel agents in the form of marketing incentives. Because the competition among CRSs for placement of their systems in agencies is so intense, the systems actually pay travel agents that can produce substantial booking fee revenue to use their systems. In some cases, this rebate can be $1.00 - $1.50 of the $4.25 paid by the airline. Galileo testified that more than half of its expenses are "commission costs," which include incentive payments to agents.

These increased booking fees have had direct and important consequences for travel agents. As each additional CRS booking adds little to the vendor's operating cost, signing up an additional travel agent subscriber is quite profitable. The $4.25 segment fee, even after the travel agent rebate, far outweighs any added cost. Thus, developments in the CRS industry did more than increase travel agent productivity. For many agents they also generated an added source of revenue, as rival CRS vendors offered them attractive financial inducements to use their systems.

Agents do undertake obligations in connection with these financial packages. The contract terms offered by the CRS vendors are weighted heavily in favour of the vendor, and often have the effect of locking the agency into a relationship that can become unfavourable but inescapable. Typical CRS contracts impose a financial penalty on the agency when its CRS bookings fall below a specified threshold. An agency attempting to reduce its reliance on air sales faces a similar problem.

Impact of Internet on Travel Agents

Three factors fuelled travel agent revenues:

(1) increased air travel,

(2) increased share of tickets written, and

(3) higher commission rates.

Although there is no consistent data on travel agent profitability, it can be safely assumed that it increased substantially after deregulation. Indeed, because there were no impediments to establishing new agencies or expanding existing ones, the number of travel agent locations increased considerably. Agency growth flattened out in the early 1990s as the airline industry suffered financial hardship. But agencies resumed their growth after the 1990-92 recession. By 1996, the number of retail agent locations reached its peak.

In a deregulated environment, agency services were useful to both business and leisure travellers. As the needs of the two segments diverged, agencies began specializing in one segment or the other. Throughout the 1980s, agents increased their penetration of the corporate travel market. Corporations used their services not only to handle the booking transaction but also to obtain special fares from carriers and provide reports on employee travel that enabled companies to monitor travel expense. The increasing complexity of fares, and the constant changes of routes and carriers, enhanced the value of agents to both the corporate and leisure markets. The combination of higher commissions and deeper penetration resulted in a substantial increase in the proportion of airline revenue that went to travel agents.

By the mid-1990s, the major airlines began to experience new economic pressures. Major carriers suffered from a combination of higher costs and lower yields, the result of increased competition from one another and from low-cost airlines. They were competing with carriers that had much lower costs and could operate profitably at lower prices. They incurred substantial distribution costs that the low-cost carriers avoided. They felt captive to high booking fees and commission expenses, as well as travel agents'control of 85 percent of industry revenue. With the development of technology, they sought new ways to solve these problems.

Their solutions—commission cuts, direct sales over the Internet, electronic ticketing, disinvestment in some CRSs, and other actions to reduce the influence of traditional travel agencies—transferred much of the problem of distribution costs from the airline to the agency. Now the travel agents are suffering.

Financial Declining of Travel Agents

During ealry 2000, the travel agencies' financial condition has deteriorated to such an extent that some agencies are consolidating, and others are being forced out of business altogether. In USA, by June 2002, there were 31 percent fewer agencies and 21 percent fewer agency locations than there had been in 1994, the year before the first commission reductions. If agents had continued to be as profitable as they were in the mid-1990s, there would be no reason to expect the precipitous decline in the number of industry participants. The accelerated decline during 2001-2002, when economic conditions have been particularly bad and domestic base commissions have been eliminated entirely, leads to an inescapable conclusion: the travel agency industry is in distress.

The number of agencies peaked in 1994, at 23,937. In 1995, airlines implemented the first in a series of commission reductions. There after, the industry experienced a gradual decline through 2000. By year-end 2001, an accelerated decline reduced the number of agencies to 18,425. The agents' share of sales eventually declined, too, but the reduction occurred later and at a different rate. Total sales kept growing during the late 1990s, to a peak of $83.5 billion in 2000. But 12 months later, by year end 2001, total agency sales had plummeted more than 16 percent to $69.9 billion.

By year end 2001, base commissions per agency location were sinking to 1988 levels. The downward trend in both agencies and sales continued into 2002. In the first six months, the number of agencies had dropped 10.6 percent to 16,470. Airline sales through ARC were 17.0 percent lower in the first eight months of 2002 compared with the same 2001 period and domestic airline sales decreased even more, by 23 percent.

During that same period, there were 1,988 voluntary deletions, or closings of agency offices, up 32 percent from the same period in 2001. Several factors contributed to this decline in the financial fortunes of the agents:

— Airlines have cut commissions
— The Internet has impacted how people purchase travel
— The economy has had an adverse impact on travel agencies
— Airlines are attempting to bypass travel agents

Cut of Commissions

By the early 1990s, travel agent base commission levels had settled at 10 percent of the ticket value, more than 40 percent higher than they had been prior to deregulation of commissions. Agents deduct these commissions before remitting ticket revenue to the ARC Area Settlement Plan. At the same time, airlines paid separate, override commissions to agencies that met carrier-established targets for market share or growth. However, it must be remembered that many smaller agencies did not receive overrides. These incentives were reserved for the larger agents that airlines hoped could increase their share of traffic in a particular market.

In February, 1995, the airlines began to implement what became a series of commission reductions that continued into 2002. The first action capped domestic base payments at $50. The $50 cap meant that agents would continue to earn the standard commission, but only for tickets with a value up to $500. Tickets with higher values produced the same $50 commission, sharply reducing the agent's income from such sales.

Most agents were unprepared for the alteration to a pay structure unchanged for 15 years. Agents were continually frustrated as airlines made major changes to their businesses with no advance notice. However, agents did not respond in the marketplace to alter airline actions. Delta was the first carrier to announce the new commission level, but did not suffer any loss of travel agent business.

The agents' failure to make a significant impact on market share, coupled with cost pressures on the airlines, provided the incentive for carriers to continue cutting commissions. Throughout the process, airlines continued to pay incentive commissions to high-volume leisure and corporate agents. Overrides have increased since base commissions were cut to zero. Unfortunately, unless they are members of travel agency consortia, smaller agencies are less likely to receive override commissions. To offset the loss of commissions, agents had to develop new sources of income. The most readily available was service, or transaction, fees. Agents also turned to sales of other, non-airline products to supplement income.That strategy required more development time, however, and fees remained the primary tool. According to ASTA, fewer than 2.8 percent of agents were charging such fees before 1995. By 2002, it was projected that 95 percent of agencies would be imposing service fees on some or most airline transactions. For leisure agents, any fee increases are too small to compensate for the loss of base commissions.

Smaller agents are reluctant to test the waters and risk losing clients by boosting charges. If that reluctance continues, more agents will fail to cover their costs and will be forced out of industry. There were relatively little demand elasticity for service fees up to $25, but feared that fees of $40 for leisure travel tickets would meet substantial resistance. Service fees also put agents at a disadvantage. When airlines sell directly to passengers, whether offline or online, they do not add a separate fee to cover their own distribution costs, as many agents feel they should. Therefore, an airline-direct fare for the same seat for the same journey is lower than a comparable ticket offered by an agent charging a fee. That provides an incentive for the customer to deal directly with the airline, and reduces the agents' share of the distribution pie.

To remedy this, some agents want air fares to be offered on a net, or "wholesale," basis irrespective of the distribution channel. Then each channel could add a fee to cover its services. Some agents suggested that airlines be required to list fares with two numbers: net fare and distribution fee. Agents believe displaying this information would make them more competitive. However, several witnesses said that requiring airlines to do this would be an unwanted step back toward fare regulation.

Impact on Travel Purchase

The Internet has brought fundamental change to the economy and to how commerce is conducted. Many businesses use the Internet as a way to bypass product and service intermediaries to deal directly with consumers. The airline industry is no exception. In fact, it is a leader in the degree to which it is aggressively using e-commerce.

Airlines had offered information on their own web sites in 1995, and a year later began offering passengers online booking. At first, their booking site development was slower than that of the leading online travel agents, Expedia and Travelocity.

Individual airlines recognized that they could reduce distribution costs by combining their already well-established national networks and brand awareness with direct Internet sales. Travelers responded, knowing they could obtain direct access to information and handle their own bookings. To encourage people to book online, airlines offered numerous incentives. They attracted customers to their sites with exclusive web fares, undercutting the prices offered via CRSs and travel agents. They offered mileage bonuses to already-existing frequent fliers, and signing bonuses for travelers joining their loyalty programs. They sent their frequent fliers weekly e-mails, offering special fares not available through travel agencies. They broadened the range of online services and information, and made their sites more user-friendly by reducing the number of keystrokes necessary to search and book.

As a result, online bookings increased. So did the depth of data airlines were able to collect about customers. Such information gives the collector an invaluable marketing advantage in boosting direct relationships with consumers. Airlines wanted to recapture that advantage from agents who, using their CRSs, were the primary data collectors. The low cost of Internet marketing also enabled airlines to contact consumers more frequently and less expensively than through the mail. Now, all major carriers have powerful web sites where passengers can make reservations, review their frequent flyer accounts and confirm the on-time status of flights. These sites have become the airlines' most effective tool to encourage direct dealings with their customers.

Carriers are now obtaining a substantial part of their revenue from Internet sales, either from their web sites or those of online travel agencies. For example, Delta testified that it sold $1.1 billion worth of tickets on its own web site in 2001, a 45 percent increase over the prior year. Delta.com sales in 2002 are 30 percent higher than in 2001, amounting to 12 percent of all Delta tickets. Sabre testified that approximately 15 percent of all airline tickets are sold through the Internet. Of these, 57 percent are sold directly by airline web sites, and 43 percent through online agencies. The low-cost carriers, with whom the majors must compete, are leading the parade to the Internet and will continue to do so. While Southwest's web site produces 46 percent of passenger revenue, travel agents account for only 20 percent. AirTran's online revenue is estimated to be half its total. Two-year-old JetBlue, which painted its web site address on the fuselage of its aircraft fleet, reports that during the first half of the year, its web site generated 63 percent of total revenues, traditional agents ten percent.

In parallel with airline web site development, online travel agencies -including Sabre's Travelocity, Microsoft's Expedia and smaller firms -were investing large sums to create their Internet presence. In their early years, the two big online agencies catered almost exclusively to leisure travelers. Their high-profile, expensive marketing campaigns, combined with airline efforts, pushed the idea that the lowest air fares available were on the Internet—and only on the Internet.

One essential element in the development of the Internet as a medium for the sale of air transportation was the advent in 1995 of electronic ticketing. Passengers could now board the airplane without obtaining a paper ticket. Without this innovation, the Internet transaction would be much more cumbersome: tickets would have to be mailed to consumers, or issued to them at airports. Passengers would have had to book flights far enough ahead to have paper tickets delivered, or arrive at the airport earlier in order to process the paper transaction. The growth of Internet ticket sales would have been far less rapid and saved the consumer less money.

Since 1995, a number of online booking and fare search sites have appeared. Almost unlimited information on any possible destination has sparked even more interest in travel. As a result, travel is the most successful commercial sector on the Internet. Two-thirds of all adults have access to the Internet; 66 percent use it to get travel information, and 42 percent actually buy or make a reservation for travel. As the Internet's asier-cheaper'reputation grows, distribution channel shares are changing markedly.

These trends point to three conclusions:

— the Internet increasingly will become the distribution channel of choice for airlines, whether through their own sites or online agents;

— airlines prefer and are pushing sales on their own sites, and

— traditional agents will lose sales -not only to airline sites but also to online agencies.

Economic Impacts

Another factor adversely affecting travel agents has been the poor economy of the last two years. During the 1990s, even as carriers cut commissions, travel agent sales continued to grow with the buoyant economy.

But because of commission cuts, agents' total commission pay peaked earlier, at $6.64 billion, in 1997. The number of agencies declined gradually from 1995, the date of the first commission cuts, to 1998, but then moved steadily downward. Complete details on the travel agent industry since 1995, including breakdowns of travel agent sales by small agencies. By 2001, the recession was in full swing. Travel decreased and passengers became increasingly price-sensitive. The September 11th terrorist attacks were particularly devastating to air travel, making an already weak travel market worse. In the immediate aftermath of 9/11, concern over the safety of travel was a major factor. That eased eventually, only to be replaced by concern over the increased inconvenience of travel caused by new security measures. Short-haul trips, which involved a greater percentage of time spent going to and from and waiting at the airport, were the most affected. As a result, agency sales plummeted dramatically.

Airline traffic declined for the first several months of 2002, as did average fares. For the first eight months of the year, domestic fares decreased 11.6 percent, and international fares 4.8 percent, compared with the same period in 2001. Passenger enplanements for the same 2002 period were 11.1 percent below the comparable period of 2001. Unavoidably, such substantial reductions have had an adverse impact on travel agents. The number of ARC agencies declined from 18,425 in 2001 to 16,470 in the first half of 2002. There is reason to believe in light of all the factors discussed in this report, and regardless of the future performance of the economy -that the number of travel agencies will continue to decline.

Airline Ticketing and Travel Agents

Travel agents have also been confronted by a strategy of many major airlines of diverting business away from agents and dealing directly with the passenger. The industry calls this disintermediation, but we find 'pass' a simpler term. The benefits to airlines of bypassing agents are twofold -reduced distribution costs and increased control over passengers.

While the airlines publicly acknowledge only one reason for bypass -cost reduction -the control issue is equally, if not more, important. For generations, airlines have tried to encourage the sort of passenger loyalty that would inhibit their customers from using an alternative carrier. Airline clubs and frequent flyer programs were some of the mechanisms developed to meet this goal. But travel agents have always been impediments to such relationships because they could offer the passenger independent advice about schedules and fares, undermining an airline's ability to bind consumers to a particular carrier.

The Internet became the airlines' vehicle for breaking the agents' hegemony over the distribution of information and sales of air travel. If carriers could attract passengers to web sites they controlled, they would achieve their long-term goal of dealing directly with consumers and deterring them from comparison shopping.

The airline bypass strategy has had two major elements -development of each carrier's own web site, and creation of a jointly owned online agency that would compete with Expedia and Travelocity, the two largest on-line agencies.

Airline websites

Airlines lagged behind the major online agencies in building their online presence, though now they actually sell more online travel through their own sites than through online agents. Sale of travel over their web sites has not only reduced CRS booking fee and commission costs; it has also attracted passengers who previously might have used travel agents. The discovery of the sometimes sizable differences between promotional web site fares and fares offered through travel agents has attracted many people who at least shop, if not always book online. Agent witnesses complained that these differences often amount to hundreds of dollars, and that passengers who find such differences are lost to the agency for future purchases. Agents testified that these differences in fares, plus the fees they are charging to compensate for lost commissions, put them at a competitive disadvantage. They also recognize the right of airlines to deal directly with consumers, and have not proposed any regulatory intervention to restrict such sales.

Orbitz -Orbitz is an online agency owned by the five largest U.S. carriers: American, Continental, Delta, Northwest and United. Orbitz has another 37 airline partners who do not hold equity, but who have signed the same marketing agreements as the owners. Together, the 42 airlines are called charter associates. The company began taking reservations in June 2001 amid a cloud of controversy that continues to this day. The Orbitz contracts include two controversial clauses that agents claim prevent them from gaining access to airline web fares. The socalled most-favoured-nation (MFN) clause requires charter associates to provide Orbitz with any fares posted on their own or third-party web sites. The second clause requires participants to provide Orbitz with marketing support, including advertising and publicity, in relation to their sales on the site. This support may take the form of exclusive web fares. The clauses do not specifically preclude carriers from giving web fares to Orbitz'competitors. However, agents contend they have that effect because the agreement gives Orbitz the right to match any web deals its owners may offer to other agencies.

From its initial announcement in November, 1999, Orbitz and its owners have said that it had two missions. One was to drive down CRS costs. The other mission was to provide competition to online agents Expedia and Travelocity, which had attained a dominant position in third-party Internet sales. Both agencies had the potential to supplant traditional travel agents as intermediaries controlling the flow of information from airlines to consumers, particularly because each had the financial strength of major corporations behind them. Airline participants in Orbitz did not want the Internet to establish online agencies as powerful intermediaries in travel distribution.

Online competitors, traditional travel agents, and CRSs have filed voluminous testimony critical of Orbitz and its airline owners. They complain that airlines have adopted a policy of sharing their low web fares only with the online agency that they own, and that this gives Orbitz an unfair competitive advantage. For their part, several travel agent witnesses cited numerous instances where they had quoted clients a CRS fare, only to lose the sale because the customer had found a fare as much as hundreds of dollars less on the Internet. Orbitz'critics propose various regulatory solutions to eliminate this advantage: require airlines to provide web fares to all agencies if they give them to any; eliminate certain contract clauses that require or encourage carriers to provide all their web fares to Orbitz; some would even require airlines to divest their ownership of Orbitz.

Orbitz and its airline owners argue that airlines choose to provide web fares to Orbitz because other methods of distribution would require airlines to pay both exorbitant booking fees, averaging almost $11 per ticket and, until recently, agency commissions. However, critics argue that the cost reduction from avoidance of booking fees does not justify what can be a far wider differential between web fares and those off e red through CRSs. If the fares were based on cost differences, the difference should be equal to the amount of the booking fee. Therefore, they conclude, the fares must be designed for another purpose-to divert traffic from traditional agencies. The difference between web fares and other prices cannot be justified solely on the basis of booking fees, and that the fare differentials serve the strategic goal of bypassing travel agents.

Airlines do incur costs when they receive an Orbitz reservation. Orbitz charges a transaction fee of $6.44 per transaction -and a carrier also pays the Worldspan CRS booking fee of approximately $3.89 per segment. Then

Worldspan rebates to Orbitz, and Orbitz rebates to airlines perhaps a third of the booking fee. Thus, at present, the cost of a Worldspan/Orbitz booking may be approximately $13.00, more than $2.00 above the cost of booking through a CRS. Of course, some bookings through a CRS may result in the payment of override commissions.

However, airlines project that the cost differential between Orbitz and CRSs will change, since the agreement between Orbitz and the carriers gradually reduces the Orbitz transaction fee over the next several years. Moreover, Orbitz has developed software to link its site directly with airline inventory and thereby avoid booking fees altogether. "Supplier Link" has already been announced for American, and other carriers will be added in the future. Since Orbitz will charge $4.00 per ticket for this technology, the total cost may be lower than CRS booking fees, but not by much.

The debate over the relationship of air fares to CRS costs overlooks the broader issue of how airlines price tickets. In the short term, air fares are not based on cost but rather on demand. Since airlines want to attract passengers to the web, fare differentials are designed to stimulate increases in traffic to the web, not to reflect cost differences. Airlines undoubtedly want to avoid booking fees, but the determining factor in establishing the price of a web ticket is whether it will generate incremental revenue for the carrier. In the long run, the carrier bypass strategy may force CRS vendors to reduce fees. In the meantime, it has a negative impact on the ability of traditional agents to compete and to serve their customers.

Orbitz' second mission was to provide competition for online agents Expedia and Travelocity, and it has done so in dramatic fashion. Within a few months of its launch, Orbitz' share of travel volume, mostly through airline bookings, had vaulted it to third among online travel agencies. Expedia, Travelocity and other witnesses complained that the most-favoured-nation and marketing clauses in the Orbitz contracts are unfair and cause them harm in the marketplace. They allege that the most-favoured-nation clause precludes Orbitz participants from offering exclusive deals to other agents, which reduces the likelihood they can underprice Orbitz. Moreover, the marketing agreement makes it illogical for Orbitz charter associates to spend money on advertising and publicity for Orbitz while simultaneously giving the same fares to its competitors.

Agents complain hat the airlines are even increasing their cost to use the distribution system, and that this places increased economic pressure on small agencies. Some of these costs, imposed by airlines through the Airlines Reporting Corp., may seem insignificant to outside observers. But a $1,000 cost increase is a major one for agencies that are very small businesses. Agents interpret some of these increases as a deliberate attempt by carriers to make their operations more costly, or more difficult.

In 1999, ARC initiated the Certified ARC Specialist (CAS) program. At new agencies and at agencies experiencing a 30 percent ownership change, at least one person must take the CAS examination. The CAS training course costs from $275 to $395 and the examination costs from $145 to $175. ARC says the program is designed to increase agency efficiency in performing several business functions -including ticketing, refunds, exchanges and settlement -and that it was created in response to concerns expressed by agents about finding experienced personnel. Agents also cite higher costs for paper tickets, even though fewer are being issued. In a recent month, 69 percent of total travel agency volume was recorded on e-tickets. Still, some passengers will want paper tickets, even if the airlines impose a separate paper ticket fee. And ARC is now requiring better, i.e., more costly, storage equipment for paper tickets than was used previously. Since tickets will increasingly be issued electronically, these paper ticket costs will be incurred for a smaller and smaller proportion of the agents' business.

Debit memos cover charges airlines impose on travel agents to recover deductions taken by agents, or to cover errors in processing tickets. For example, prior to March, 2002, an agency selling a ticket deducted its commission and remitted the balance; if the ticket was then refunded by the airline, the airline claimed the commission back through a debit memo. Another example: reservations ticketed at the wrong fare, such as one issued at a discount fare for which the passenger does not qualify. The airline may issue a debit memo to reclaim the difference between the ticketed price and the full coach fare, even if the passenger would have qualified for another discount.

Apparently, some airlines have become particularly arbitrary in issuing debit memos, and the time required to respond to them has risen considerably. For example, agents were incensed at American debit memos issued after 9/11. Agents handled refunds for passengers on cancelled flights through the Area Settlement Plan, but American claimed that such refunds should have been forwarded only to its revenue accounting department. Agents responded that American employees had told them to handle the refunds through ARC. For each refund processed through ARC by the agent, American issued a debit memo of $200, even though the passenger was entitled to the refund. Agents criticize airlines for refusing to help them operate efficiently. For example, they want ARC to provide a place on tickets to record their service fee. That would eliminate the need to process the fare and the fee separately. And, agents say, it would produce a re cognizable link on credit cards and other billing statements between the fee the customer pays and the ticket he or she is buying. Agents say they would pay the portion of the credit card charge related to their fee. But the change would require approval by the International Air Transport Association, which requires unanimous consent to changes by its almost 270 member carriers. One airline told ASTA that it would not approve any such change. Airlines currently receive the entire ticket revenue processed by ARC for domestic air transportation.

The credit card fee can amount to two-to-three percent of the entire ticket price. When commissions were paid, this would have been 20-30 percent of the agent's entire revenue. With no commission, it would be patently impossible for the agent to absorb this amount, and unreasonable as well, since the agent is merely acting as an agent for the airline principal. These cost increases are minor, compared to the other major changes that have impacted agents, but they are burdensome for small businesses. Particularly with respect to debit memos, there is room for improvement in airline procedures that would reduce the burden placed on agencies.

Effects of Changes in Travel Agent Industry

The world population is quick to adopt, and adapt to, the revolution in technology. A Harris Interactive telephone survey shows that, as of February-March 2002, 74 percent of adults are using a personal computer in US. That compares with 50 percent in 1995, when the U.S. population was already well on its way to computer literacy. This means that slightly over one-quarter of the U.S. population is still not using a personal computer. But, Harris found, in the same period the Internet grew much more quickly. In 1995, nine percent of adults were using the Internet, while the February-March, 2002 survey period puts that use at 66 percent, which translates to 137 million people. The growth in online use is expected to continue, though at a slower pace.

The same survey indicates the profile of Internet users tends towards more affluent, better-educated consumers. When analysed according to age, however, the profile look(s) more like a cross-section of all adults up to but not including those over 65. Those over 65 comprise 16 percent of all adults but only 5 percent of Internet users. The conclusion was that the majority of people who will use the Internet for travel research and bookings already have the ability to do so. A poll taken during the last quarter of 2001 by Pew Internet & American Life Project Surveys found that two-thirds of those contacted who have Internet access go online to obtain travel information. A Plog survey of interactive travellers earlier in 2001 found that 78 percent of respondents had used the Internet not just to research trips but to buy travel, compared with 27 percent three years earlier.

According to a demographic study in 2001 by the Travel Industry Association, Internet users are younger, better-educated and more affluent than non-users. For users, average age was 40 compared with 52 for non-users. Education of users was higher, too, with 69 percent having some college education versus 29 percent for non-users. Users with full-time jobs comprised 66 percent of respondents, compared with 33 percent for non-users. Mean household income of those using the Internet was more than double that for non-users, $67,400 versus $29,300.

Consumers are purchasing an increasing amount of travel online. A Com-Score Networks survey in the first quarter of 2002 showed they spent $7 billion at domestic travel sites, up 87 percent from the same period in 2001. Second-quarter travel sales totaled $7.8 billion, up 46 percent fro m the same period in 2001. Such volumes make travel the leading sector in e-commerce sales, with more than 40 percent of the total. A survey of travellers with e-mail addresses shows large increases in the use of all types of Internet booking sites.

Table 1. Typical Booking Method for Leisure Travel

Booking Method	2000	2001
Travel agent	36%	32%
Book directly	61	59
Travel club (AAA)	4	5
Corporate/Internet	1	3
Internet (Net)	27	49
Internet travel site (Travelocity, etc.)	11	24
Specific Internet site (Airlines, hotel, etc.)	15	29
Travel agent Internet site	3	2
Other method	6	4

Total adds to more than 100% because of multiple responses. According to a Forrester Research survey of consumers using the Internet for research and purchasing travel during 2001, the major reason for booking more travel online is price. The survey separates consumers into two categories: those who had researched but not bought travel online, and those who had made travel purchases.

Of those booking online, 68 percent said they did so because they thought prices were lower, 67 percent because they were assured prices were lowest there, 56 percent because information was more complete and 55 percent because agents were charging higher fees. A PhoCusWright survey produces a similar result. Of three types of distributors — traditional agents, travel suppliers and online travel agents — consumers perceive online travel agents as having the best price.

Table 2. Who offers the Best Practices

Traditional agents	17%
Suppliers	18
Online travel agent	44
Don't know	21

However, most consumers tap several sources before they commit to buying. One poll shows a steady increase in the use of each category of information source, although increases were greater in the use of Internet sites and e-mail as sources.

Table 3. Top information sources (Leisure travel) for online air travellers

Source of info	1999	2000	2001
Travel agent	48%	56%	55%
Toll-free number	45	62	65
Online/WWW	57	66	93
Corporate travel department	4	5	30
Airline schedules/timetables	27	31	41
E-mail notification	23	29	48
Friends/relatives	25	22	34

The companion survey of the general population, which was done only in 2000, shows that 31 percent of adults used travel agents, while 56 percent of online users contacted agencies. The Department of Transportation says that consumers on average visit at least three sites while planning travel. Another 2001 survey indicates that consumers not only use multiple sites, but are shifting their use of certain online sources. Visits to supplier and online agency web sites increased, while use of search engines declined.

Table 4. Types of Internet Sites used for Travel Planning
(Among 64.5 million Online Travellers who used the Internet to make travel plans)

	2000	2001
Search engine sites	77%	69%
Company sites	63	67
Online agency sites	52	63
Destination sites	63	63
Special interest sites	30	23

Travel guide sites	14	17
Newspaper/magazine sites	16	12
Community sites	15	7

The Forrester survey also shows an increase in multi-site shopping. Its research indicates that 41 percent of consumers researching travel and 33 percent of travel purchasers had a favourite web site, which they visited first but not exclusively. Consumers with a favourite site chose it, first, for ease of use and, second, because of a previous good experience.

The use of multiple sites suggests that travel consumers are not yet convinced they should trust Internet information to the exclusion of other information. Indeed, both travel planners and purchasers said they trusted information from friends and family more than any other source. Nonetheless, for those consumers with Internet access, online travel purchases are increasing markedly, showing a 50 percent increase from 2000 to 2001.

Table 5. Online Travel Purchases

Year	Percentage of Respondents Making an Online Travel Purchase
2001	78
2000	51
1999	37
1998	27

The cost of computer hardware, software and Internet connections is coming down, making home computing and surfing more affordable. Web sites will become easier to use and intelligent profiling will create travel offers based on prior experience and preferences. The perception that the lowest prices can be found on the Internet remains, and the consumer trend to online purchasing will continue.

Consumer Benefits

The changes in the travel agency industry have not had a material effect on consumers, but that, on balance, their position has improved. Even though they may now have to pay for advice from a travel agency, they have gained fro m the ease of accessing the vast amount of information available on the Internet. They can either rely on their own ability to make choices, or call on agents for independent advice and assistance in the reservation transaction.

For complex purchases, such as tours or cruises, consumers may continue to prefer travel agents. Those with simpler requirements, such as roundtrip flights, can either go it alone or use an agency. While we noted above that one of the airline goals is to gain control over consumers so that they rely only on a preferred carrier, the choice remains the consumer?.

Consumers who continue to avail themselves of travel agents , and must now invariably pay a separate fee for their services, may seem to be worse off for the change. However, all passengers paid for the cost of these free services in the price of their ticket. The move to a fee-based system for travel agent services may ultimately be fairer and more equitable because those using the service will pay for it. Because passengers now bear much of the cost of utilizing travel agency services, they are increasingly searching out lower-cost alternatives.

Although the number of agents providing service to leisure passengers will continue to decline, and consumers will pay for their services, there is reason to believe that a sufficient number of agencies will remain to provide consumers a wide array of choices and competitive prices. Some agencies will become more specialized and geographic coverage may become less ubiquitous. However, because paper tickets a re no longer necessary, consumers do not need geographic proximity. Consumers have benefited from the changes in the distribution system, that there will not be significant impact on consumers in the future, and that the current condition of the travel agent industry will not have an adverse effect on consumers.

Consumers now have the best of both worlds —they can book for themselves on the Internet or they can use the services of travel agents. It is not clear, however, that the Internet always provides a better solution than using a travel agency. Because of the expertise of travel agents, those who pay to use them may achieve savings and services that would offset the added cost of service charges.

Agents have superior knowledge of the industry and are aware of various alternatives that can offer lower fares. They are far more likely than consumers to know enough to check alternative airports, or times of departures. Moreover, they can easily search the Internet as well as their CRSs for low fares. Since they are making reservation transactions throughout the day, and also have specialized web search tools, they can make such searches more efficiently than consumers. Once a booking is made, travel agents often continue to manage the client' travel, serving as an alert system, trouble shooter, and advocate with the travel supplier.

Once airlines have attracted travellers to their sites, travellers are less likely to search for alternatives. Consequently, some witnesses testified, consumers may pay more for web fares than they might have had they used a travel agent because web sites generally limit the menu of fare and schedule requests off e red to travellers. As always, there are exceptions. Some airline sites do allow consumers more manipulation of data during their search; some third - party sites are also better than others.

There is a real possibility that consumers may pay higher fares on the Internet than they would if they used an agent. He cited the example of his roundtrip to Washington to testify at our hearing. First, he searched the Internet. The Internet fare, using the same outbound and in-bound airports, was higher than expected. A travel agent suggested using a different airport for the return trip, producing a significantly lower fare.

It seems clear that major corporations that negotiate their own deals with airlines for corporate fares achieve prices that are the same as or lower than web fares for comparable service. Since corporate clients often have specially negotiated air fares that are available via CRS, use of web-only fares would not produce any great advantage. This is particularly true because the deepest discount web fares are highly restricted and non-refundable and, therefore, not suitable for much business travel. Indeed, a recently completed study by Topaz, a corporate travel agent auditor, found the fares provided by corporate agencies were fully competitive with web fares.

At the request of corporate clients, Topaz compared 19,000 fares booked on CRSs between January and June 2002 with fares found on comparable airline and online agency web sites. Topaz then attempted to replicate the booking on the Internet by searching the web sites specified by the company. The comparisons took place within two hours of the actual bookings, used the same itineraries as booked, and checked the airline or online agent web sites designated by the requesting corporation for the market. Topaz' results showed that Internet fares were lower eight percent of the time; and that 77 percent of the time corporate agencies found lower fares for the same itinerary than they would have on the directed Internet search. Corporate agents matched or beat the prices on similar airlines on the Internet 92 percent of the time. Topaz results notwithstanding, and despite corporate managers' attempts to crack down on deviations from policy, individual employees do use the Internet to compare and even book. As the economic downturn continues, these travellers remain concerned about their individual travel budgets. However, individual corporate employees who find lower fares on their own would not qualify for the more flexible contract terms airlines allow them under managed fare policies.

Impediments to Agency use of Web Fares

Impediment is defined by the dictionaries as hindrance or an obstacleor that which hinders progress, motion, activity or effect. Using this broad definition, the method in which fare information is distributed on the Internet clearly creates some impediments to the way participants in the industry do business. However, there are no actual impediments for the vast majority of consumers—they have numerous sources for all the information they might desire about fares and schedules. Far from creating impediments, the Internet has made available a wide range of information to which consumers never before had direct access. Consumers benefit for having a multitude of traditional agencies, online agents and airline web sites competing for their business. Never before have they had such easy access to complete information that will enable them to make travel decisions.

Some may argue that consumers would be even better off if all the fare information were the same on every web site and in travel agencies. However, the benefits of uniformity could be more than offset by the loss of competition, which forces suppliers to improve service and limit fees. For consumers, any confusion due to the proliferation of channels is no more in evidence than when they shop online or in person for other goods and services, such as refrigerators, stoves, cars, medical information, and tax information. The growth of Internet sales, and the fact that travel is the industry with the largest volume of Internet sales, suggest that consumers appear satisfied with what they see and with their shopping experience.

The refusal of airlines to make some web fares available to agents through their CRSs, and therefore not efficiently accessible by agents, is an impediment to the operation of travel agencies and corporate travel departments. While travel agents can gain access to most web fares, the real problem is the inefficiency of such searches, compared to the CRS single-source system. Agents must undertake substantial additional effort to integrate searching for and booking web fares with their normal methods of conducting business. The ways in which web fares are now distributed, therefore, pose an indisputable impediment to efficient travel agent operations. Businesses continually modify their procedures to adjust to new circumstances, however, and agents can be expected to make such changes.

There are several software and Internet programs that search the web for fares, and also permit agents to book online. New tools are available to even the smallest individual agent at what the vendors contend is a price these small agents can afford if analyzed on a cost-benefit basis. Some vendors license their software, others charge by the transaction. All of the tools search many web sites. They may also connect with back-office accounting systems that offer agents customer tracking and billing services. All CRSs are developing programs to enable agents to search web fares through their own CRS equipment. The rate of development and the business models differ from one CRS to another, but all CRSs want to offer corporate and leisure agents access to web fares.

Third-party software allows agents to access a significant amount of online travel information, even though such information can be obtained only by using these additional software tools outside their CRSs. Some online agents and airlines were attempting to block the ability of these tools to search their online fares. American Airlines has threatened litigation against third-party search engines that search its web site, and has filed a complaint requesting an injunction against one such company.

Peoples resistance to permitting third-party delivery of web fares to travel agencies is part of a strategic design to transfer its CRS costs to agencies, and, failing that, to induce consumers to book on its own web site. If the efforts to foreclose use of third-party search software succeed, they will not only delay progress in the evolution of Internet sales, but also undermine consumers' ability to obtain important fare benefits. If consumers cannot use tools that search multiple sites concurrently, they will be relegated to time-consuming consecutive searches. If airlines publish fares beyond their own individual sites, they should be available to consumers through modern technology, so long as it does not impose undue burdens on carrier systems. Technological innovators and airlines are, of course, free to reach agreements on access to individual carrier web sites. These software tools will require agents to change their way of doing business, forcing them to invest in the new software or Internet services. Even then, their operations will be less efficient than previously, when they handled the entire reservation transaction in their CRS.

Several aspects of selling web fares impose changes on current agency procedures:

— Agents may not control the passenger record as they do with CRS transactions. This makes changes to a reservation record more difficult.

— Agents cannot consolidate invoices with other client financial records accumulated by the CRS system.

Some web systems do have the ability to integrate records into some back-office accounting packages.

— Agents receive no CRS booking credit for web bookings. Most CRS contracts with agents have a productivity clause in them. When a booking is made using the CRS, it reduces the potential subscriber fee that the agent will owe the CRS.

— Passenger profiles and other information may have to be created and updated on multiple web sites.

The lack of integrated information imposes costs on agents, both for separate search equipment and in the extra time required to perform the searches. These costs will ultimately be reflected in service charges to consumers.

Corporate Travel Departments

Corporate travel departments also view the current distribution of web fares as an impediment to efficient operations. The typical travel department contracts with agencies to procure a wide range of services related to transportation. The agency not only handles the reservation transaction and provides extensive accounting information, but also ensures that the booking complies with corporate policy.

When individual travelers act as their own travel agents and search for web fares, these departments contend, many of the benefits of the corporate structure are lost. The employees are wasting time, and usually fail to achieve significant savings over the corporate rates that the travel department has already negotiated with airlines. The contracts with airlines often require the company to meet minimum market share or volume thresholds. Fares booked on the Internet do not count against these thresholds.

Employees who use web fares create other problems for corporate travel departments: standard records can be kept for employees flying on web tickets, and it becomes difficult to track compliance with company policies and practices. The September 11th terrorist attacks demonstrated the importance of this concern. Many corporate managers whose employees were travelling on web fares that day had substantial difficulty finding and contacting the web ticket purchasers. Undoubtedly, web fares complicate the work of corporate travel managers. But if web fares provide significant savings, they will force corporate procedures to accommodate them. On the other hand, many corporate travel departments discourage employees from using web fares at all, believing the small potential savings are not worth the trouble.

Many online travel agencies claim that airlines are creating barriers by using Orbitz as the only significant online site to distribute web fares. They say this gives Orbitz a competitive advantage. Currently however, travel agencies such as Expedia and Travelocity continue to succeed in the marketplace. For example, Expedia and Travelocity may not be able to offer web fares from all Orbitz charter associates, but they have already obtained, and could in the future obtain more, web fares from those airlines. Both Orbitz rivals have preferential marketing agreements with various airlines which include incentive fees to boost volume. These agreements, however, may require the online agents to take inventory risk, i.e., block out or buy seats for which they are responsible.

Even if Expedia and Travelocity do not provide all fares for all people, they continue to innovate and expand into new markets. For example, Expedia operates as a merchant for hotel rooms and tours, assuming inventory risk and reselling that inventory at a price it establishes. Since the launch of Orbitz, both have declared profits, despite the travel downturn. Expedia earned $19.1 million on total revenue of $145 million in the second quarter of 2002. Most of its sales now come from its merchant operations, and it acquired a major Hawaii tour operator in March, 2002. Travelocity has been operating successfully as a public company, with first and second quarter revenue of $82 and $76 million. In April, 2002, it was re - acquired in its entirety by Sabre. Consumer Reports, which has conducted two in-depth studies of web fares, concluded that none of the three biggest online agency rivals always offered all the best fares. They also found that none of the six online agents tested always offered fares equal to or lower than the fares offered by the CRSs. They found that particularly curious, since all of the sites are powered by CRSs. In fact, Consumer Reports rated Expedia and Travelocity as the two best sites.

Expedia beats its competitors in providing the greatest numbers of lowest fares; Travelocity offered the best array of low fares coupled with viable flight choices; Travelocity had the best booking tools; Expedia and Travelocity offered the best customer service; and Expedia and Travelocity had the tightest privacy and security policies. Orbitz, which is owned by five major airlines, performed well at providing lowest fares and viable flights, but it was edged out on most tests by either Expedia or Travelocity.

Consumers search several different web sites before booking travel. An airline should be allowed to distribute its products as it sees fit. The marketplace tends to resolve such problems through competition, as is now occurring.

10

AGENT-BASED TRAVEL SUPPORT SYSTEM

The fact that tourism-related services have emerged as a leading product category to be promoted and distributed to consumer markets through the Internet is hardly surprising considering the high suitability of the tourist product for e-commerce and the industry's great traditions in the IT-sector. Consumers are likely to derive many advantages, including price reductions, from the commercial opportunities offered by the Internet. There are, however, many hindrances to a mass-market adoption of online shopping solutions even in the highly e-suitable travel industry. Making self-bookings on the Web may prove to be too difficult and time-consuming for most consumers as travel arrangements, especially complex ones, tend to consist of a number of problematic elements that inexperienced travelers may not consider. Consequently, many industry representatives believe that even educated customers are no threat to the future livelihood of the travel agency community.

Agent technology has been suggested as a potential way to reduce or eliminate the most obvious impediments to consumer self-bookings in travel. Today, there are many practical hindrances to designing an optimal Web agent solution to serve the needs and purposes of prospective travelers. However, although agent applications are unlikely to be able to compete with the convenience and security offered by human agents in travel bookings, they may still offer consumers savings in time and money, and can certainly reduce their uncertainty as to whether the price of the journey is reasonable or not. Moreover, software agent solutions may offer prospective travelers a much greater choice of travel service providers than traditional or Web-based travel agencies can offer. This research highlights the need for agent assistance in Internet bookings, presenting the structure, behavior and the operating environment of a multi-channel software agent application, FareTracer, which has been designed to assist consumers in making their travel arrangements on the Web.

The concept of intelligent or software agents has been around in the IS world for some time, indicating that the field of agents is rich and diverse. Most agent researchers would find themselves in broad agreement with the following key principles in the definition of software agents and agent-based systems: Software agents are computational programs or entities situated in a computing environment and assisting users with computer-based tasks. They act to accomplish specialized tasks on behalf of users and act towards reaching certain user-specified or automatically generated goals with a certain degree of autonomy and flexibility. Agent-based systems refer to systems in which the key abstraction used, either in conceptualisation, design, or implementation, is that of an agent.

The future of computing will be 100% driven by delegating to, rather than manipulating computers. A fruitful application area for software agents is in e-commerce, where potential buyers can easily be overwhelmed by the flood of information that is available, thus potentially making less than optimal purchasing decisions. The heterogeneous presence of information and the exponential growth of the Web is a factor that has impeded the progress and proliferation of e-commerce, and that agent-based e-commerce can solve these problems. Intuitively, the advantages of agent solutions seem especially appropriate in the information-intensive travel industry: as vacation choices are high-involvement decisions, travelers tend to engage in active information gathering.

Much work has been done on software agents in the recent years, but only a few studies concentrate on agent applications for the travel industry. Also in this area of agent-related research, the dominating approaches have been agent framework proposals or descriptions of agent prototypes. Using the ZEUS collaborative agent-building toolkit, Ndumu et al. developed an agent-based travel assistant demonstrator providing integrated travel assistance based on combining services from disparate sources.

The most work has been done in the area of automated reservation assistants that interactively learn about travelers' preferences in a problem-solving process aimed at suggesting services fitting the users' special needs. Völksen et al. describe an agent application for integrating several distributed travel-oriented services such as hotel and flight reservation systems, restaurant information systems, motorway and local traffic information systems, and parking management systems. A somewhat similar approach for electronic travel planning is presented by Camacho et al., whereas Merlat investigates the use of mobile agents to perform multiservice negotiations on the behalf of the consumer, using the travel agency application as a test scenario.

The consumer benefits of e-commerce have been widely cited in the academic literature and the popular press. Potential advantages for travelers who plan and book their journeys on the Internet include: greater convenience; greater amounts of multimedia destination information and real-time information on price and availability (e.g. last-minute deals); increased opportunities for comparison shopping and price comparison; and personalization benefits (where personalized relationships between suppliers and customers can be achieved through customer profiling). Additional suggested consumer benefits, which are particularly relevant for the e-travel industry and this study, are:

(i) time savings resulting from the rapidity of the entire purchasing process;

(ii) price reductions resulting from increased competition as more suppliers are able to compete in an electronically open marketplace, as a result of reduced selling prices due to a reduction in operational costs, and manufacturers internalizing activities traditionally performed by intermediaries;

(iii) ease of transaction, e.g. ease of bookings as the travel reservation-making process can be automated by EC technology; and

(iv) a wider selection of products/vendors (e.g. travel service providers).

These four benefits certainly deserve some special attention due to their contradictory, and partly interrelated nature. Although these consumer benefits certainly may be derived even in the travel industry, we nevertheless present the suggested benefits as four myths in order to highlight some important issues.

1. *Time Savings:* Although some travel industry representatives and authors have suggested that direct bookings are creating tremendous savings in time as travelers no longer need to spend much time on the phone talking with travel agents, the results of studies

done by Anckar and Walden indicate that self-bookings in travel tend to be highly time-consuming - irrespective of the complexity of the journey. There are multiple reasons for this: First, finding service providers (i.e. locating Web sites offering the services needed) might take time and perseverance, especially as it is often not possible to book travel directly online or to buy the separate parts of a trip through the same supplier. Second, many travel sites do not even allow consumers to check prices and availability unless they have completed the time-consuming registration procedures, which often include profiling information. Likewise, the availability check (and the booking process) usually involves entering (and re-entering) many search parameters (dates, destinations, etc.), which can be a lengthy procedure. Fourth, although the potential for making price comparisons often has been mentioned as a great consumer benefit of e-commerce, it is no doubt a time-consuming task.

Comparing prices from site to site could certainly ensure the lowest expenditure for the consumer, but the cost in time and effort might not be worthwhile. Still, most travelers, exhibiting normal consumer behavior, are likely to tirelessly make price comparisons prior to making an Internet booking.

2. *Price Reductions*: Although the suggested consumer benefit of lower prices on electronic markets may seem intuitively realistic, it is becoming increasingly evident that getting a good travel deal on the Internet is no easy task. Research by Anckar and Walden indicated great variations in price of offered online fares, and showed that even experienced Internet users are unlikely to be able to compete on price with physical travel agents, who offer experience, knowledge and intuition that cannot be found in an online service.

The traditional, intermediary approach may still be the cheaper than booking online since:

(i) most consumers do not know where to find low-fare Internet service providers, and also lack the basic knowledge about and the pricing principles of the travel industry and the strategies travel agents use to get a low fare;

(ii) special fares with restrictions are not always advertised on the online travel sites;

(iii) travel agencies have ways around airline reservation systems that are technically "sold out";

(iv) consumer do not have access to travel agent negotiated rates; and

(v) multilegged journeys typically carry outrageously high prices on the Web, since online fare finders tend to assemble these trips by piecing together one-way tickets, which are always more expensive than round-trip faresconsumer benefits.

At the very least, the effort to get a fair deal is likely to be time-consuming. It should, however, be pointed out that consumers perceive costs of search activities as resource expenditures - the time and money required to undertake search - as well as the cognitive effort required to process the information required, meaning that the indirect search costs should be taken into consideration when assessing the total costs of a journey.

3. *Ease of bookings:* Although there certainly is a potential for automating the travel reservation-making process with EC technology, it has turned out to be a very complex software problem to give consumers online tools to shop for travel, particularly in the insanely volatile fare marketplace. Many industry representatives feel that the complexity of international

flights and GDSs (global distribution systems, also known as computerized reservation systems, CRSs), with many confusing explanations of terms, will render consumer online reservation systems impractical for all but the most sophisticated users. According to Chircu and Kauffman, many companies using online reservation systems have documented great knowledge barriers in the case of complicated travel arrangements, as making reservations in international markets is very complicated. Hence, Turban et al. suggest that complex trips, which require specialized knowledge and arrangements, must be made by travel agents. It should be noted, though, that some studies indicate that even experienced Internet users tend to fail to make even low complexity travel arrangements on the Web.

A journey consists of many problematic elements that an inexperienced traveler may not consider. As a result of the feeling of uncertainty associated with self-bookings, many people want to interface with human travel agents, patronizing them to lower the risks involved in travel and to take advantage of the convenience that an agency has traditionally provided. Although the online booking approach has been seen as a highly convenient way to make travel reservations, it should nevertheless be stressed that contacting a human travel agent by phone or e-mail in most cases remains the most convenient way to make one's travel reservations.

4. *A Wider Selection of Service Providers:* With the boundaries of e-commerce not being defined by geography or national borders, Internet users could benefit from a large, global choice of travel service providers. Three facts, however, inhibit consumers from deriving these advantages in full:

First, small and medium-sized tourism enterprises (SMTEs) remain underrepresented in most large, established GDSs. The vast majority of tourism enterprises around the globe can, in fact, be classified as SMTEs, which means that a great many tourist service providers' services are unavailable to e-bookers, especially since most SMTEs cannot afford a Web presence of their own. As a result of this limitation of the GDSs, not only the SMTEs that are outside this infrastructure are at a disadvantage, but also the prospective tourists, whose choice of service providers is heavily restricted.

Second, online booking travel sites on the Internet offer, as a rule, a Web interface to the one GDS to which they subscribe. Consequently, their selection of service providers is limited to the ones that are represented in that particular GDS, meaning that potential travelers will have to locate and browse numerous Web sites, all connected to competing GDSs, in order to obtain the largest possible choice of service providers, fares and itineraries.

Third, although the Web does offer an enormous selection of service providers that are not represented in the GDSs, but nevertheless can be reached through the Web sites they operate, this approach may, in practice, be too time-consuming for most e-bookers. Nevertheless, providers using the Web as their primary tool to reach the global tourist market are likely to represent the most attractive target for bargain seekers, as they have eliminated the intermediaries in their distribution channel.

Travel Service Providers on Web

As an arena for travel service providers, and as the operating environment of the FareTracer, the Web is full of nuances, offering a wide range of suppliers and intermediaries with business models that are not always obvious to the customer.

Web-Based Travel Agents

Within the academic literature, the hypothesized disintermediation effect in the travel industry, i.e. the bypassing of intermediaries as a result of e-commerce, has received much attention. Up to this point, however, Internet self-bookings have rarely been characterized by a complete disintermediation, as individual travelers do not have direct access to the GDSs, but have to use eintermediaries, i.e. third-party online agencies as gateways to these immense systems, through which reservations can be made for flights, hotels, cars, etc. The travel agencies operating on the Web are either virtual extensions of physical travel agents or virtual start-ups. The former generally accept inquiries and submit offers by e-mail, whereas the latter as a rule offer automated online booking services.

Web-services of Individual Travel Service Providers

Airlines and hotel chains, many of which offer online booking services on their Web sites, would like to sell tickets and rooms directly to the customers via their own Web sites to eliminate commissions and maintain control over customer relationships. From the customer's point of view, however, this is a time-consuming task in comparison to the one-stop-shop services offered by Web-based travel agencies. Moreover, the benefits are questionable as airline Web sites have been criticized for not posting special deals that are not accessible through GDS-connected Web-based travel agencies. Nevertheless, when looking for inclusive (charter) tours, the Web sites of individual tour operators tend to be the only channel for online bookings.

Web Reservation System Alliances

In response to the dramatic growth of online travel sites such as Travelocity and Expedia, airlines have recently banded together to create new reservations sites on the Web. Examples include the Orbitz project by a large number of American air carriers, and a corresponding venture between 11 dominant European carriers - including many fierce rivals. The aim of these high-stake efforts is to give air carriers a more direct line to the consumers, disintermediating e-intermediaries, of which some have grown to the point where their market position is getting dangerously strong.

Within the hotel industry, corresponding online reservation consortia have been accessible by individual customers already for quite some time. For consumers, online travel consortia may offer opportunities for complete disintermediation, with no commissions being paid to middlemen. Moreover, the airlines backing the sites have announced that special deals that are not available through any travel agencies will be offered through the systems. GDS-external Web reservation systems may especially benefit the numerous small hospitality organizations, which otherwise lack resources for a Web presence, as well as prospective tourists, whose choice of service providers becomes significantly increased.

AGENT ENVIRONMENT

Travelers tend to show little or no brand loyalty, but instead require a travel product at the lowest price and of the highest quality - consistent with their own value judgments and preferences. The Web has unleashed a torrent of customers who are increasingly fleeting and irreverent towards brands: If there is a better deal on somebody else's Web site, they go for it. Bearing this fact in mind, it can be assumed - as a general rule - that customers have no distinct preferences for travel service providers or middlemen. If we rule out frequent flyer programmes (FFPs) and other regular customer discounts, the primary priority of travelers is likely to be (i) the price of the journey, and (ii) the convenience of the itinerary.

The traveler will choose the journey that best satisfies his travel needs and preferences, irrespective of whether the transaction is characterized by a complete disintermediation or not. Hence, he certainly has an interest in searching through all the options available, meaning that travel software agents should operate within a broad environment, scanning a large number of sources within each of the actor categories presented above. The FareTracer is an autonomous multichannel software application, which has been planned and implemented as a cooperative effort between a university and a software company.

The agent is a pure Java2 application that will run on any platform with a Java Virtual Machine (JVM) that conforms to the Java2 specification. The application can use any SQL database that offers a JDBC driver. The user interface is implemented with Java Servlet technology and runs on any Web server with a Servlet-runner that conforms to the Servlet 2.2 standard. The application uses threads to handle the user requests and utilizes multiprocessor systems.

The key to finding a journey that satisfies the traveler's requests is in the agent search parameters that are specified by the user. The tourist product is a composite product, meaning that a specification of a large number of parameters may be necessary even in low-complexity bookings in order to coordinate the components of the journey and to obtain a journey that meets the user's personal travel preferences. The agent search parameters can be classified according to their

(i) nature; journey-dependent (non-static) or journey-independent (static), and

(ii) importance (primary or secondary). Primary importance parameters are customer travel demands that by necessity must be satisfied, whereas secondary importance parameters do not necessarily have to be satisfied in the journey/itinerary, although this would be desirable from the user's point of view.

With this categorization, 4 different parameter levels can be identified (Table 1), which essentially form the basis of the search logic and the ranking of search results of the FareTracer It should, however, be noted that this parameter classification is in no way depicted in the user interface. The level-1 input, which is required by the user, includes the most essential information needed by the agent, e.g. the departure and return dates, point of departure, destination(s), the number and age of travelers, etc. The level-2 input is likewise of primary importance, although required only in queries placed through a mobile device.

However, the specifications are intrinsically static, and hence included in the user profile, which is designed to make the parameter specification process faster. The level-3 input (secondary importance) encompasses optional parameters that override the static basic preferences if the user wishes to deviate from his saved profile for a certain journey. The level-4 specifications are included in the customer profile, where the user has ranked these parameters as low in importance. Hence, FareTracer user can define - according to his individual preferences - the importance of a certain parameter. The search criteria set as high in importance in the user profile are interpreted as level-2 input by the agent.

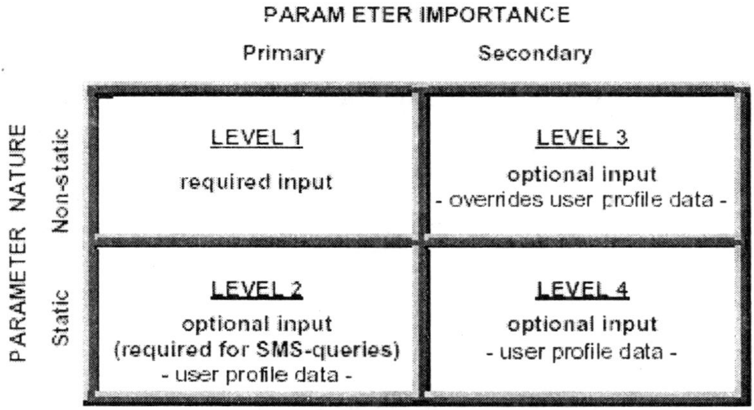

Figure 1. The Four Levels of Agent Search Parameters

Agent Structure and Behavior

The FareTracer consists of five building blocks (Figure 2):

(i) the user interface;

(ii) the knowledge base;

(iii) the user profiles;

(iv) the data sources; and

(v) the agent itself.

The building blocks of the FareTracer agent are the same as they would be for any kind of information collecting agent application The responsibilities of the different building blocks are described below.

The user interface (UI) controller monitors the UI and analyses all the input and output between the agent and the user. The UI is the only connection between the user and the agent. When the user wants to consult the FareTracer for travel assistance, he needs to activate the interface and enter the required search parameters in an input form. The information in the different fields of the form is then used to populate a predefined XML document, which is actually where the user profile is defined. The same XML document is used to store the information retrieved by the agent.

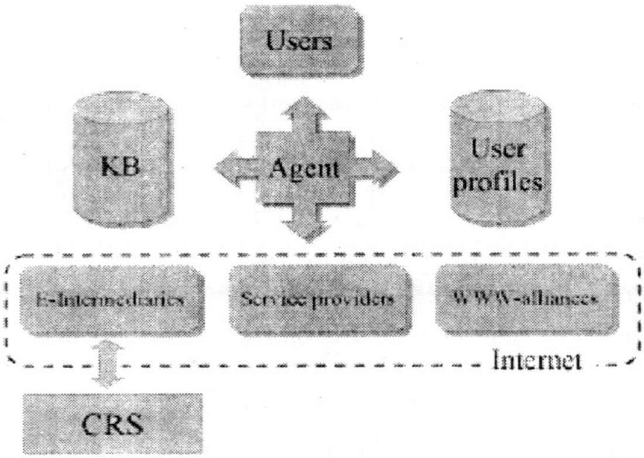

Figure 2. The FareTracer building blocks and the agent environment.

The FareTracer is a hybrid application that can process queries placed through Web interfaces as well as through mobile devices (WAP, SMS). A prerequisite for placing SMS-queries is, however, that the user has completed his user profile (level-2 input) prior to the search in order to limit the number of alternatives to be retrieved.

The FareTracer stores its knowledge of the environment in the knowledge base (KB), which contains information about airlines, hotels and airports, etc. (Figure 3). The information in the KB is entered by the agent (automatic retrieval) or manually. The information in the KB is used to compare the information in the user profile with the information collected from the different data sources. The agent uses the information in the KB to select journey components that best match the specified parameters and the user profile.

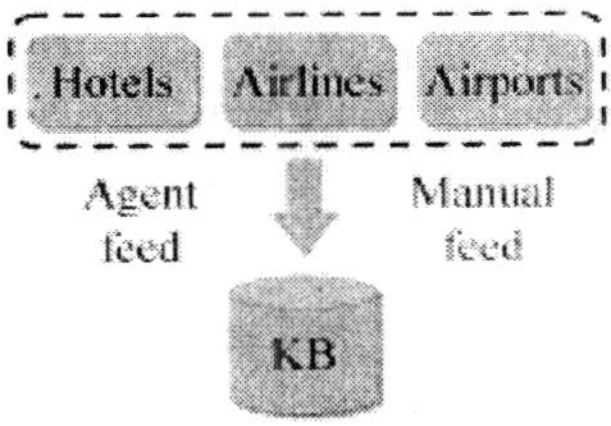

Figure 3. The KB information content

The user profiles consist of information stored about the user's standard preferences. A login process allows the agent to identify the user, after which it fetches his personalized user profile. The user enters these preferences when he registers with the FareTracer application. In accordance with the search parameter classification, the agent can handle profiles that are incomplete by skipping the blanks and using only the available preferences. The user can enhance his profile and add information at any time. The user profile is, in fact, defined by the same XML document that is used to define searches.

Since the format of the profile is identical to the input form, a user can easily update his profile just by saving the information contained in the input form when conducting a query. The information stored in the user's profile is also used to populate the input form when the user has logged in. The last building block of the FareTracer consists of the data sources that the agent scans for information. This is the most challenging part. The look-and-feel of the data sources can differ quite a bit, and the services that they provide may range from the company logo with static information to advanced interactive travel planners. Some of the prices offered may be real-time prices with discounts, whereas other prices may be valid only under certain conditions, or the availability may be unknown.

The agent needs to be very intelligent to extract the right information from all the different types of data sources. The best way to solve this problem is to divide and conquer. The FareTracer has different modules for the different data sources from which it collects information. This allows the agent to, through the modules, know where the important information is located in the data source, and also how it can be collected.

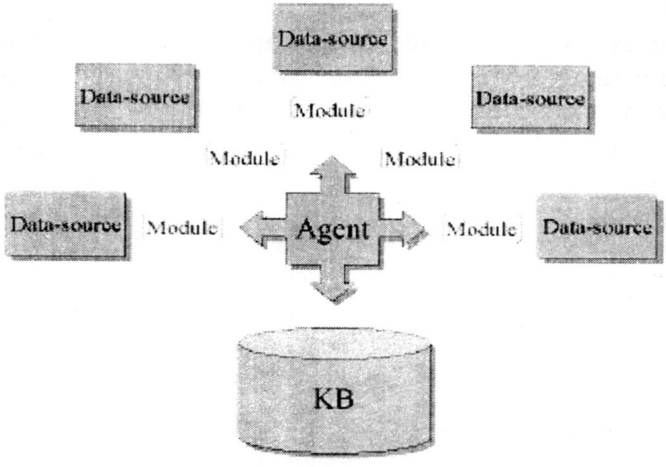

Figure 4. The FareTracer Information Retrieval Process

The advantage of using a one-by-one mapping of data sources and modules is significant compared to the generic approach with one module for all data sources. By using specific modules for every site it is possible to collect exactly the needed information, and nothing else. The modules can be instructed to collect prices and other important information that is needed in the KB. The agent can insert the information into the KB, since it understands the content of the information that it has collected. A generic module that collects information from different data sources can only, at best, guess that the data that it collected is a price for a one-way flight. There is one major drawback with using source-specific modules instead of a generic one:

The modules must be updated whenever the data source is restructured. As soon as one important part changes there is a high possibility that the agent fails to retrieve information from the data source. This is, however, the price that has to be paid since this is the only way, in practice, to make the agent fully understand the collected information, and hence pick out only the essential parts. The retrieved information is temporarily stored until the agent has scanned all the data sources.

When the retrieved information has passed the first filter (the user profile), it is sorted according to the price of the journey (the default primary priority) or the profile fit (the preferences of the user). The information extracted by the modules is stored in the same predefined XML format that is used in the input form and the user profile. As a result, the information collected by the agent and the parameters specified by the user have an identical format, meaning that it is easy for the agent to compare the retrieved information with the user's profile and rank the alternatives based on the weights assigned to the different parameters.

The 'best' alternatives are listed on top, whereas the poorest alternatives are dropped. The user can specify the amount of hits the agent should show. Due to differences in the search engines and the range of information provided on different Web sites, some modules are unable to conduct searches based on all the parameters specified in the user profile. This fact is, however, taken into account when comparing the alternatives as to their profile fit, and presenting the search results to the user, which is done in different ways depending on the medium/technology used. If the user wants to proceed with a booking, the

FareTracer, which can be characterized as a semi-booking agent, repeats the search in the module that retrieved the chosen itinerary, after which the user completes the booking manually with the agent's assistance.

Benefits of Agent-based Travel Assistance

Although many practical obstacles, e.g. the strong position of the GDSs on the Web, make the implementation of an ideal personal travel assistant impossible, the FareTracer agent application offers prospective travelers a number of significant benefits by turning the proposed four mythical consumer advantages of e-bookings into reality:

First, any human user is unable to compete with the rapidity of the FareTracer, which scans all the data sources simultaneously, retrieving the best fares/itineraries to any destination in a matter of seconds/minutes. Hence, using the FareTracer, the time-consuming price comparison process is totally eliminated from the elooking/ booking process. This is no doubt a significant benefit especially as the agent is not restricted to certain or a few Web sites, but can work through an unlimited number of data sources. Furthermore, the agent works autonomously and can repeat the search at any given intervals to get the current situation (prices and availability), and alert the user of updates by e-mail or SMS. This is an important feature for time-critical or limited availability travel arrangements such as last-minute deals. Second, the consumer is likely to can obtain better prices with the FareTracer. It is a fact that for any particular journey, there are a multitude of ticket prices. Different Web sites house different search software and access different GDSs, and hence they do not always come up with the same fare even for the same flight.

Moreover, the FareTracer scans Web sites of individual service providers as well as Web reservation system alliances in order to find GDS-external deals matching the specified criteria. As a result, not only the price comparison, but also the selection of service providers and itineraries is much broader than that of any other travel agent, physical or Web-based. Moreover, one should bear in mind that the time to be invested on each booking is highly limited for human travel agents, which means that the price offered or the terms provided are not always the most competitive, especially as most travel agencies do not use the Web to search for service providers for their client due to the time-consuming nature of this task.

DESIGNING AGENT-BASED TRAVEL SUPPORT SYSTEM

In the two decades there have been numerous attempts to apply the software agent paradigm to travel services and the pervasive problem of information overload. The analogy of software agents to travel agents makes the analogy between real world travel agencies and online agent platforms seem trivial, yet the majority of the proposed systems never left the drawing board. The few active experiments in travel-related agent architectures we have discovered have either been limited in scope or abandoned.

The CRUMPET project is a typical example of what happens with projects aiming at applying agents in travel support systems. CRUMPET was funded by the EU FP5 umbrella between 1999 and 2003, but as of April 2005 it is almost impossible to assess its achievements, because its WWW site no longer exists and information about the project itself is spread across a few auxiliary sites and conference papers that resulted from it.

Since 1999-2001 a large number of researchers that were originally interested in agent-based systems have moved on to more fashionable ventures such as the Semantic Web or Ambient Computing, leaving behind a trail of papers and unfinished, only partially implemented designs. We have also been trying to develop such a system since 2001, so we can easily understand why these groups have moved on rather then complete a working prototype. Working with existing agent systems is a struggle with cutting edge, constantly evolving and highly unreliable technologies. The design of a system that seems to be quite reasonable one day may become infeasible and/or obsolete sometime before the initial implementation is completed. For instance, we have run into this problem when experimenting with data indexing and the ebXML Registry Repository.

After many futile attempts we were forced to acknowledge that the existing implementation of the repository was unreliable and incapable of handling "real size" load and had to abandon it, after nine moths of work invested in making the repository a centerpiece of our design.

The current system stores semantically demarcated data in a central repository. While the majority of today's Internet-based travel services focus on transportation and lodging, with an emphasis on transactions, our system is designed to deliver an extended travel itinerary, including the standard transportation and accommodation choices as well as restaurants, movie theaters, national parks, historical sites and other points of interest, any of which may be selected by the user from an array of options composed specifically for him/her. The system is accessible via Internet-enabled devices, ranging from standard PC-based browsers to palmtops and WAP-conversant phones etc., and even non-human entities.

System Architecture

The overall architecture of the proposed system is depicted in Figure 5. Before proceeding, let us make two comments:

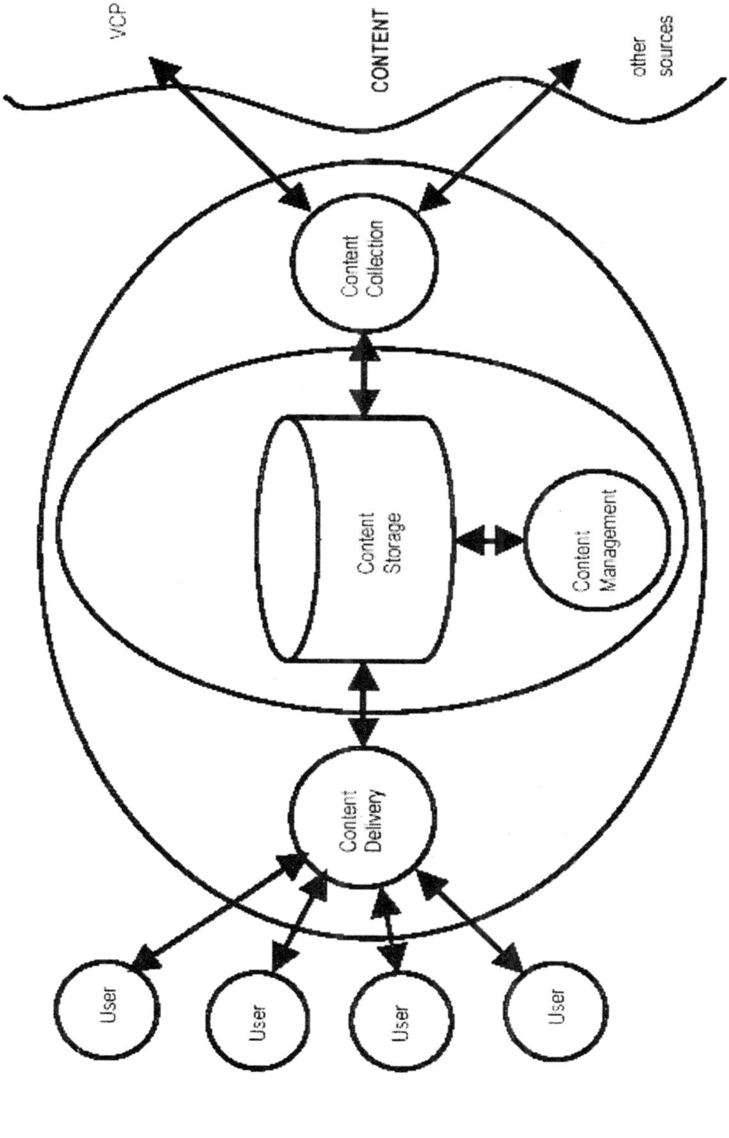

Figure 5. Infrastructure for the travel support system

(1) The proposed system belongs to the class of infomediaries and therefore its development will proceed within the framework presented in;

(2) The general system structure is a modification of the skeleton of the general e-commerce system presented in.

Here, instead of dividing the complete system into two subsystem-spheres: supply and delivery, connected through a communication channel, we are introducing three sub-areas: content collection, content management and content delivery, with the content management subsystem together with the central data repository becoming the centerpiece of the system.

Verified Content Providers (VCP)

Today, a very large number of web sites provide some form of travel-related information. However, as pointed out in, there exist a few serious potential problems arising from the dynamic nature of content on the Internet.

Information relevant to travel is stored in a large number of small, independently operated Web sites (consider all restaurants, bars and independently owned hotels that have their own private websites). Since many of these sites are hosted by small local ISP's that may not be able to provide sufficient quality of service, these sites may migrate and, as a result, change their URL's. In this case information that was once available (its location was known) cannot be found easily. The second situation involves progress in Web site design. Due to technological change (e.g. switching from plain HTML to PHP) or overall change in what is perceived to be state of the art in website design, the layout of a given site may change completely, such that agents that were collecting information from that site are no longer able to access it without errors. To deal with this problem and the more general issues of accuracy and relevancy we utilize the concept of Verified Content Providers.

Conceptually, a Verified Content Provider (VCP) is a site that is known to provide reliable and consistently available information. We assume that VCPs do not randomly appear and disappear from the Internet. Furthermore, VCP's are expected to maintain the same site interface for extended periods of time. It can be even assumed that in the case of a commercial travel support system, VCPs will be providers with whom a contract is signed and thus if the interface changes "we" will be informed about it beforehand. Finally, VCPs are sites that constantly provide reliable information and thus can be trusted. While the category of VCPs is used to mark "the best of breed" information sources, the remaining sources available on the Internet can be assigned varying levels of trust and that level of trust can dynamically change over time.

VCPs can be divided into two groups:

(i) pushing sources - those that provide content for our system in a standard form (such as RSS feeds), and

(ii) static - sites that require agents to collect pages periodically and extract the necessary information.

It is important to stress that at this stage of development of the Internet, existence of any form of VCPs containing travel-related semantically demarcated content.

Other Sources

There exists a number of problems related to dealing with unverified, unstructured Internet-based information:

(a) its amount, which makes an exhaustive search practically impossible,

(b) the unreliability of data, and

(c) contradicting sources that require application of sophisticated data deconfliction techniques.

While we hope that the approach of relying primarily on trusted data providers (VCPs) will alleviate most of these problems, we still should not discard additional information available on the Internet and we will utilize it whenever possible. This approach will become even more important when the idea of the Semantic Web will start to take hold and semantically demarcated information available in small-independent sites will be much easier to process automatically.

Content Collection Subsystem (CCS)

In the proposed approach, the information provided by or collected from the Verified Content Providers and from other Internet sources is stored in a semantically demarcated form. We have selected RDF as the ontology tagging "language." For storing RDF triples we have decided to use the Hewlett-Packard Jena system. The Content Collection System (CCS) stores sets of RDF triples that in aggregation represent travel objects. Travel object tokens may originate either from a direct feed from VCPs or from an agent subsystem that collects data from the Internet and are stored in the central repository.

Content Management Subsystem (CMS)

This subsystem includes all functions related to the data stored in the central repository. Observe that at least two cases of possibility of data inadequacy have to be taken into account. First, we have to deal with incomplete data items. For instance, an object to be stored in the repository may contain triples for the name, address and web site of a restaurant, but not the phone number. In this case such an object is incomplete and we must attempt to find the missing information. The second case involves data that is stored in the system and that is in some way time sensitive, e.g. cinema programs change on Fridays, and thus they have to be updated. Obviously, even information that is not explicitly time-sensitive has to be re-checked in some unspecified time intervals.

Content Delivery Subsystem (CDS)

Here the data stored in the central repository is manipulated for delivery to end users. The agents in this subsystem obtain a query from the user and work with the CMS to find information matching the user's personal preferences. Data presented to the user may be acquired from the repository, or result form additional Internet searches.

Users

The system will be accessed via Internet-enabled devices, ranging from standard PC-based browsers to palmtops and WAP-conversant phones etc., and even non-human entities (such as other agents).

Content Collection Subsystem

The structure of the content management subsystem is presented in Figure 6. Recall that the central repository of our system stores RDF triples - semantically demarcated data tokens. Because currently there is very little RDF-demarcated data natively available on the Internet, we must extract HTML content from existing web sites into RDF triples "manually." Our Content Collection subsystem uses Wrapper Agents (WA) that interface with various WWW sites, mapping XML- or HTML-demarcated data into RDF triples describing travel objects (according to an appropriate ontology used in our system). Sets of triples gathered by Wrapper Agents, and assembled into travel tokens, are sent to a Coordinator Agent (CA), which schedules Wrapper Agents and relays the resulting triples to the Jena database.

Earlier we suggested that some of the VCPs may, sooner or later, contain and/or start delivering RDF demarcated content directly to the system. In this situation all we have to do is to adjust some of the WAs to be able to handle these particular inputs, while the remaining parts of the CCS remain the same. An interesting question arises when ontologies available on the Internet do not match our custom ontologies.

In general we assume a collection of WAs capable of interfacing with an assortment of data sources and delivering to the CA RDF demarcated tokens describing various travel resources. Communication between WAs and the CA occurs through exchange of ACL messages. All incoming information is received by the CA. Its primary role is to act as a large priority queue, where all data objects will be temporarily stored. Obviously, having only one CA may become a bottleneck and in this case having additional CAs may alleviate the problem.

The CA prioritizes the data in the queue. This is done based on the answer to the questions: why is given data taken brought to the system and when it will be needed? If the data token is a result of web crawling, it will be assigned "basic" priority. If the token is a result of time-oriented trigger event (for instance that the theater program is changing) then it will be assigned an "elevated" priority (it is quite possible that someone will soon request this information and thus it has to be inserted into the system as soon as possible). Finally, tokens resulting from the "user queries" will be assigned "highest" priority. Here the assumption is that user is still online and necessary information has to be delivered as soon as possible.

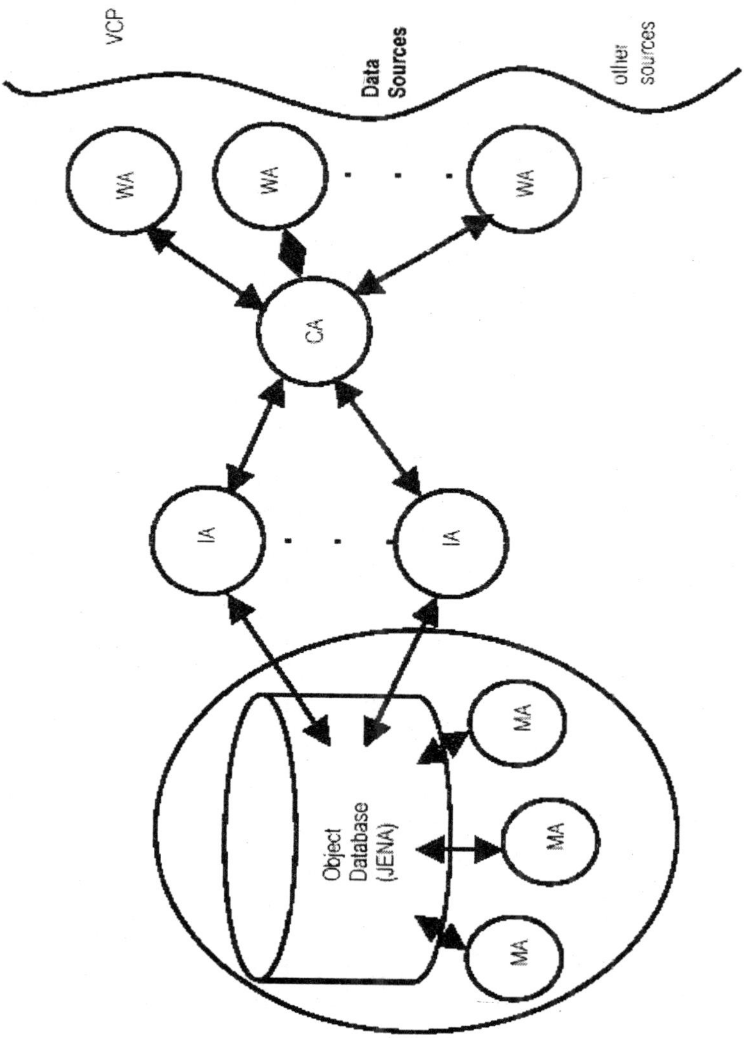

Figure 6. Content management subsystem

Information is inserted into the repository by a pool of Indexing Agents (IA). These agents request from the CA (via an ACL message) the next data token to work on and obtain it wrapped in an ACL message. IAs check the completeness of data. There are many situations when the data tokens may be deficient (e.g. hotel info misses information about available amenities). In this case, before insertion into the repository, data tokens are marked as incomplete. However, they may still be used by the content delivery subsystem to deliver response to the user. Finally, in the case of a token replacing another token and the two tokens containing conflicting information, both tokens are left in the system and marked accordingly for deconfliction to take place.

Content Management Subsystem

Content management involves all the agents that operate on data stored within the repository. In this way we separate these agents and functions form the rest of the system, with which the communication occurs only via ACL messages. Thus far we have indicated three possible functions to be performed by the CMS agents. The first is related to the completeness of tokens. Incomplete tokens will be marked as such by the IA. CMS agents will traverse the repository to find incomplete tokens. They will then formulate queries to be answered and request (via an ACL message) from the CA that appropriate WA be released to search for the missing information. The second situation involves tokens containing conflicting information. They are marked as such by the IA and left for the deconflicting agents to deal with. Deconfliction may involve additional queries to the Internet as well as consideration of factors such as, the freshness of the older data, reliability of the sources etc. The third situation deals with time-sensitive data.

There is a large amount of travel-related information on the Internet that changes in regular intervals (e.g. programs of operas, theaters, cinemas, etc.). It is possible, for each of these situations, to establish proper time to find updated information. We assume here that the database will generate triggers that will result in agents involved in management of time-sensitive data to communicate with the CA to request an update of a given token. However, we also must recognize that all of data available in the system is time sensitive. Even content that seems to be relatively "stable," like the restaurant menu or ZOO opening times change from time to time. Therefore each data item will have a "time stamp" describing when it was created.

After a specified time (different for different travel objects), the database will generate a trigger that will start the update function. Here one of the adaptation mechanisms available in the system will take place. When the update request does not result in any changes, the time length before the next update will be increased, while the request resulting in change will cause the update time to be shortened. Obviously, there may exist other data management functions involving data in the central repository. The clear advantage of the agent system is that in such a case the only required function is to add new agent type that will perform the required functions.

Content Delivery Subsystem

The content delivery subsystem is responsible for answering user queries. Here the primary challenge is communication between clients and agents in our system. While in theory this should be relatively straightforward, in our earlier work we discovered that this is not the case. Specifically, the absence of agent platforms to host agents on client devices limits the reach of the agent platform to protocols supported by the client, and those only to the extent that the agent system may be adapted to them. Thus we make only a minimal set of assumptions about expected capabilities of the device (like that it will be able to communicate with the Internet using the HTTP protocol).

Furthermore, all the computational power and support for communication has to be on the server side. Our initial attempt to solve the problem employed the Mozilla XUL and XUP languages for platformindependent user interfaces. Recently we changed our approach to this problem, and our current design will be described detail in the next Section. Here we will proceed with the assumption that the user has submitted a query through an Internet enabled device to his Personal Agent (PA) (Figure 7). This message has been translated from its original form by the Proxy Agent (PrA) residing on the "gateway HTTP server." Regardless of the form of the original query the "query content" is extracted and wrapped into an ACL message and in this way send to the PA. The PA forwards the message to two locations.

First, to the group of agents responsible for content personalization. This message is stored in the user behavior database, where information about all interactions between the user and the system is logged. More precisely, all user queries sent to the system and all system responses are logged for future mining. Based on the queries and responses and user responses to the queries it is possible to establish a profile that can be used by the PA to filter and personalize content delivered to the user.

Second, the query is send to the DB Agent (DBA). The DBA is the interface of the system to the Jena database. The DBA translates the user query into the RDQL language (the database language used by Jena to query the entire set of RDF triples).

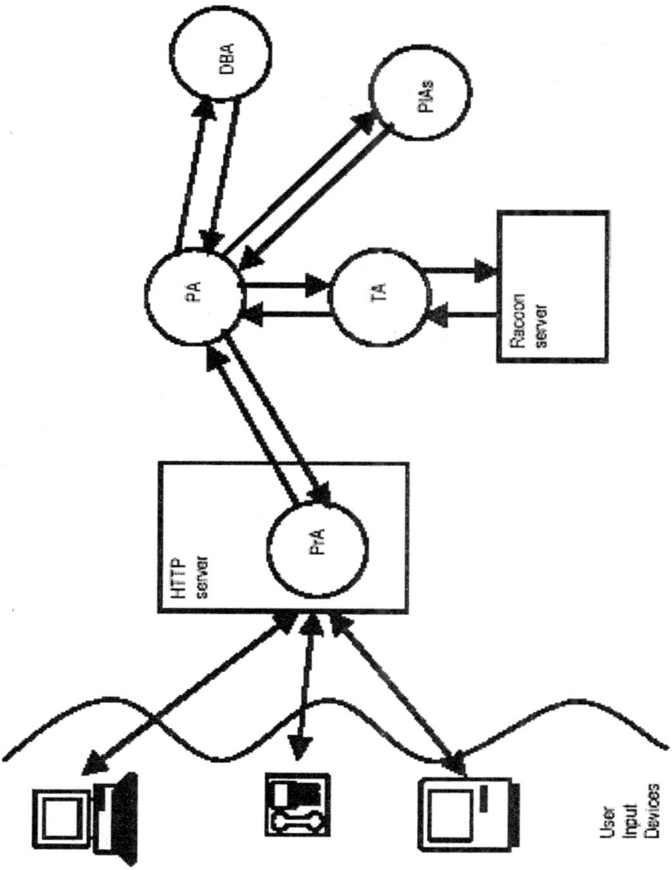

Figure 7. Content delivery subsystem

The DBA executes the query and as a result obtains a set of tokens describing one or more travel objects. These RDF demarcated tokens are then sent to the personalization infrastructure. The personalization infrastructure consists of a number of "RDF Agents." These are simplistic agents. Each represents one of more of simple rules of the type "Szechuan food is also Chinese food" or "Romantic Comedy is also a Comedy." These rules are applied to the set of RDF triples returned by an RDQL query. Rule applications may involve querying the repository and expand the result set. The personalization infrastructure agents operate as a team passing the result set, wrapped in an ACL message from one to the next and their role is to maximize the set of responses to be delivered to the user.

The maximal set of responses is sent back to the PA. The PA utilizes the user profile filter the answer set. For instance, the DBA and the PIA agents may not know that the user never stays in Howard Johnson hotels and never visits Braum's restaurants. Thus RDF triples representing these two chains will be included in the expanded answer set. However, the PA will remove them form the set. The answer set is send to the Transformation agent (TA) that utilizes a Racoon server to render the response to be displayed on user device.

11

Price Dispersion in Online Travel

Online travel agents (OTAs) provide a point of contact via the World Wide Web (WWW) to enable customers to search for appropriate flights and fares and make a selection, which is then booked and ticketed by the OTA. There are dozens of OTAs representing on-line travel agents, airlines, traditional travel agents, and computerized reservation systems, although the top two agents accounted for 60% of all traffic in 2001.

The operational process of an OTA is straightforward. It collects information from the customer, principally departure and arrival cities (airports) and preferred flight times. The OTA then takes this request and some additional parameters set by the OTA and submits these to a computerized reservation system (CRS), which searches for relevant flights from the collection of offerings from all airlines. The agent then takes the collection of flights returned by the CRS, selects one or more flights for presentation to the customer and sorts the final output.

When the customer chooses to purchase a ticket, the OTA processes the booking with the CRS and receives a commission from the airline in return. An important feature of this process is that OTAs have to pay the CRS a fee for each request, but only collect revenue if the customer books a flight. Since only 1-5% of "browsers" actually make a reservation, targeting segments of customers to increase purchase probability is crucial to maximizing profits.

Competing OTAs have to take into account the search behavior of their customers. Greater market transparency in electronic markets would lead to greater price competition. With vanishing search costs, competing firms offering undifferentiated products have to charge the same competitive price. Undoubtedly, electronic markets on the Internet have made it far easier for consumers to search for services from various OTAs.

However, initial evidence suggests that this does not hold for nearcommodity products like books, CDs, and software. While we cannot determine whether all costs associated with online search have disappeared, we can certainly observe if market participants behave as if search costs were zero, by utilizing results from well-established economic models.

In addition, the OTA environment has several unique competitive characteristics. First, OTAs can only select tickets from the (possibly large) available set offered from the airlines -they do not have the ability to alter prices or other product features. OTAs compete for consumers by striving to select the best available tickets according to their preferences, attempting on the consumers' behalf to offset non-competitive pricing by airlines.

However, serving potential customers is not without costs for OTAs. Exhaustive search through computer reservation systems may prove to be too costly, hence, OTAs may choose to specialize and serve a limited number of segments. Any systematic variation in ticket selection would imply a horizontal form of differentiation among OTAs.

Second, because we are considering a good with multiple characteristics and heterogeneous consumer preferences over these characteristics, all comparisons must be made relative to one or more specifications of preferences. While there can be a wide range of consumer preferences for airline tickets, we follow industry practice of considering two specific groups: price-sensitive leisure travelers and time-sensitive business travelers. By offering multiple choices for a given request, OTAs can attempt to serve multiple customer groups simultaneously.

The central question we analyze in this chapter is whether OTAs, given the same request, provide the same ticket recommendations. To the extent that this is not true, we further try to distinguish between two alternative explanations:

1) that differing ticket selection is due to systematic attempts at product differentiation, and
2) that differing ticket selection represents errors on the part of the OTAs.

The economic theory of search suggests that when customers are well informed about available prices and face few barriers to searching multiple providers, equilibrium prices will converge to marginal cost, eliminating price dispersion, even in markets where goods are horizontally differentiated.

Travel is an important online market and the product is complex, yet fully describable, enabling products of differing qualities to be objectively and accurately compared.

This chapter describes the results of a study which examined the presence of price dispersion and product differentiation using data on the airline ticket offerings of online travel agents (OTAs). The study shows that different OTAs offer tickets with substantially different prices and characteristics when given the same customer request.

Some of this variation appears to be due to product differentiation — different OTAs specialize by systematically offering different tradeoffs between ticket price and ticket quality.

Using software agents, the study team made over 900 ticket requests (drawn from actual travel patterns at a traditional travel agent) identically and simultaneously to five online travel agents - four popular publicly available OTAs and one proprietary system. They then examined the characteristics of the ticket recommendations they provided in response to the requests. The study data indicate that OTAs systematically provide ticket recommendations with different prices and qualities, and with average price s varying as much as 28% across OTAs for the same ticket requests. When the study team accounted for variation in prices due to differences in quality using a hedonic price model, the price variation drops to about 18% across OTAs, suggesting some effects of product differentiation. This is further supported by the observation that OTAs, given the same ticket request, return a ticket unambiguously inferior to one offered by another OTA between 2.2% and 28% of the time, depending on which two OTAs are compared. The results of the study suggest that this industry is characterized by both product differentiation and random error in product selection.

Attributes of Airline Tickets

Airline tickets are complex but unambiguously describable. A ticket for a direct flight can be fully described by specifying the airline, departure and arrival airport, departure and arrival time, price, class of service, and fare restrictions. Tickets for connecting flights have additional information related to each segment, but the salient features can be summarized by the number of connections, the total connection time, and the total duration of the trip.

The principal concern of the stduy was isolating the relevant ticket attributes that can vary across the selections of various OTAs. Of the list of possible attributes, some are held constant across OTAs by study design, others are fixed due to technological constraints, and some can vary based on design choices by the OTA. In the ticket requests to the OTAs the study team specified departure and arrival airport, service class (all tickets are coach class), and travel dates and times, eliminating variations across OTAs from these sources. Technological limitations of the OTAs or legal restrictions on their behavior eliminate variations due to fare restrictions and airline.

The software agents made simultaneous reservations on all OTAs, eliminating variations in fare structure over time or time to departure. Thus, of the universe of ticket characteristics described above, the principal ticket characteristics that can vary by OTA in the study are:

— *Timeliness*: an inquiry for a specific flight includes the desired departure time for both legs of the flight. An OTA is not bound to report only flights that meet the time requirements specified by the traveler, but can also select other flights, which might be less expensive.

— *Number of connections:* connections often permit more options to be considered, which may make a flight less expensive, and may sometimes be necessary to ensure the timeliness of the flight.

— *Length of connections*: an OTA has to make the decision about the duration of a connection that is acceptable for the customer, given his or her priorities for time and price.

— *Flight Duration*: although principally a function of connections and connection time, an OTA can choose a more complex, longer routing in an attempt to save cost.

— *Price*: OTAs can select tickets with different characteristics even on the same routing which leads to differences in fares.

This list represents the exhaustive list of dimensions upon which tickets can vary by OTA and will form the basis for a set of comparisons that attempts to determine whether OTAs offer optimal or inferior flight offerings when provided the same request. It should also be noted that this list includes all available preferences that can currently be expressed by the consumer to the OTA as well as preferences that the OTAs can express to the CRS to guide ticket selection.

The study started with a data set of actual tickets written by a major corporate travel agent in the U.S. for five corporate clients in the month of April 1997. By using a base of actual tickets for the analysis the study team were able to make comparisons among OTAs under a scenario that closely matches how they would be used by a group of travelers. To ensure that all systems could process these tickets, the study team applied a number of screening rules to eliminate problematic tickets. The five online travel agents to be studied were selected based on recommendation of market participants and represent relatively large OTAs. Three of the five OTAs provided users with the option to indicate a preference for either price or time. The study team treated each OTA that offer the ability to choose between time preference and price preference as two separate OTAs, which results in studying eight OTAs.

Using this screened sample of tickets, the reservations were then replicated on each of the OTAs using intelligent agents. This ensures high data quality and allows simultaneous data collection across all agents, virtually eliminating the chance of fare changes influencing the results. The set of flight alternatives offered by OTAs are stored in a database. Based on the input of market participants, the study team applied two different decision rules to select a single flight from the set of alternative flights offered. In the first decision rule, the study team emulated the preferences of business travelers by making timeliness the top priority.

Of all flights offered, the study team selected those flights that depart in the time window of one hour before or after the specified departure time for the departure and return flight. A ticket that meets the time window constraint in one leg is preferred to a ticket that does not meet the time window constraint at all. If a ticket meets the time window in only one leg, the tickets where the time window is met in the departure leg was given preference. In case of a tie, the cheaper ticket is given preference. The second decision rule reflects the consumer preferences of price sensitive leisure travelers. Hence, price is the top priority, with timeliness as the tiebreaker. For discussion purposes, the study team labelled these the time-priority and price-priority data sets. They also collected other data, such as the difference of the desired and actual departure time as well as the length of the connections.

The study team sent thier intelligent agents for four consecutive days for 24 hours. Each day, the set of intelligent agents made reservations for flights that were originally made on that weekday with the same number of days to departure, seeking to replicate travel attributes such as trip duration and departure times. On average, each of agents made between 300 and 500 reservation requests per day. The total number of reservation requests that the intelligent software agents made depended highly on the availability of the OTAs and the response time of the slowest OTA. In order to obtain a consistent data set, the study team discarded all reservations where one or more OTA made no recommendation. This reduced the data set to 939 unique tickets for which the study team have reservation recommendations from all eight OTAs.

Overall, the study team have a total of 7512 tickets with an average price of $557 in the time priority data set and $515 in the price priority data set. The tickets otherwise show similar characteristics between the two data sets except for the percentage of flights meeting the time window. The price priority data set contains more than twice as many tickets that violate the time window. There is large variation across the sample in prices, primarily due to route differences.

The results of the study shows that different OTAs offer different types of tickets and that they do so at substantially different prices. OTAs achieve product differentiation through parameterization of their requests to the CRS. Each OTA uses a specific set of decision rules to identify which tickets will or will not be considered in the search process - altering these criteria causes different tickets to be offered. Interviews with a system designer suggest that the key parameters relate to: permitted deviation from requested departure or return time, minimum savings required to justify a connection, maximum duration of a connection, and minimum distance before a connection is considered.

Overall, there is a wide variation in the effects of connections and satisfaction of time window requirements across OTAs. The high variation in the coefficients for the interaction terms of OTA and ticket characteristics reflects the differences in the set of parameters that an OTA has chosen.

Given that agents are representatives of the airlines and not the consumer, it is possible that agents offer higher price tickets in an effort to increase their own revenue.

While a fully efficient market would cause consumers to avoid agents that offer unnecessarily expensive tickets, limited search, advertising, brand loyalty, or other market imperfections may allow this behavior.

The results of the study suggest that even in a market with a potentially low degree of search costs and strong incentives for consumer search, there exists persistent price dispersion across service providers. One possible explanation is that search costs prevalent in traditional markets are replaced by new types of costs. The results also show that service differentiation is a key strategic component of online sellers that offer access to heterogeneous goods. While this may appear unusual for markets that should theoretically have greater information transparency, it mirrors behavior in non-electronic markets: by exploiting consumers' heterogeneity in tastes and uncertainty of vendor quality, vendors can ease price competition by segmenting the market. Moreover, with a product with little cost of differentiation, new strategies may emerge; for example, creating "Sister OTAs" strategically to capture different customer segments and utilizing user interface quality to segment the market.

12

TRAVEL AGENTS AND AIR FARES

Travel agents provide their customers with information and advice, make reservations, provide tickets, and other ancillary services. Their services include making reservations on airlines, hotels, car rentals, cruises, tours and other events. Travel agents make approximately 70% of all airline reservations. Airline fares often confuse and frustrate customers and travel agents. The price for a seat paid by one individual may be ten times more than that paid by the person next to him. This is primarily the result of two factors:

— Airline seats are extremely perishable; when the aircraft door closes, an empty seat is lost forever. Any revenue the airline receives for what would be an empty seat, that offsets the direct cost of carrying an additional passenger, will add to profitability. When empty seats are expected on a future flight, as determined by their revenue management system, an airline may price them very low.

— Airlines sell a commodity product in the coach cabin of the aircraft. Pricing is based on the price sensitivities of different types of prospective passengers. The differentiation is given form by governing rules, such as an advance purchase and duration of stay requirements. Airline fares were deregulated in 1983 and airlines have been able to charge whatever price they wanted since then. The procedure has been to provide the global distribution systems (GDSs)with fares that would be sold to the public. Negotiated fares, for consolidators, corporations and tour operators would be distributed privately. In 1996, web fares were made available. Individuals who signed up with an airline were emailed information on deeply discounted fares would be announced weekly. These fares were designed to unload seats on routes that had low load factors. Over time, carriers also began offering reservations capability on the Internet and offered lower fares or other inducements such as bonus frequent flyer miles in order to get passengers to book online. When a passenger books online, there are no travel agent commissions or CRS fees.

In order to service their customers travel agents need access to information on airline schedules, the availability of seats at various fare levels and the fares and rules that apply. Since the late 1970's travel agents in the US have relied on the GDSs. The GDSs show the "published" fares, which are available to the public, on virtually every airline in the world.

However, the GDS's:

— Do not show, as part of their normal offering, the fares that airlines have made available at their own websites for visitors to those sites.

— Do not show fares that airlines have given to consolidators, tour operators and other intermediaries for resale.

— Do contain fares negotiated with corporations, governments, and other organizations. However, these negotiated fares are visible only to the travel agents and employees of the organization who has negotiated them. Only members of that organization may use them. The issue that frustrates travel agents, business travelers and personal consumers is the difference between the fares shown in the GDS and those available on the web. The web fares are often lower than the published fares available on the GDSs. While these fares are not necessarily the lowest fares offered they are visible which makes them desirable.

Travel agents are frequently frustrated when trying access fares directly from a website, for the following reasons:

— To complete a transaction a credit card needs to be used. This creates a potential cost to the agent when they have to use their own credit card for payment.

— The web fares that would be lower than those in a GDS are highly restricted in their use and non-refundable. This creates a problem when working with business customers.

— They do not have control of the passenger record as they do with GDS transactions.

— As compared with working in GDSs, working on the Internet is time consuming. Web displays typically take longer to sort through and use.

— Invoices may not be consolidated with other client financial records accumulated by the GDS system.

— The nature of the process creates a poor impression of the travel agent and their capabilities.

— There is no CRS booking credit received for web bookings.

— Passenger profiles and other information may need to be created on multiple web sites.

Corporate travelers are frustrated when they are told to save money in what they do and then prohibited by corporate policy from booking lower web fares when available.

Individual travelers are irritated when they purchase a ticket through a travel agent and then find they could have bought a cheaper ticket online.

Travel Agents Access to GDSs

Travel agents have relied on the GDSs since the end of the 1970's. In 1976 both American and United installed versions of their internal airline reservations systems in a few travel agents offices. Both agents and the airlines found the installation gave them significant benefits. Airlines noticed that sales from these travel agents increased dramatically, because of the bias each airline had in its own reservation system towards its own flights. The agents accepted the bias since the availability of the information in the reservation system gave them the ability to get real time information and to confirm seats to a passenger on the initial call.This gave the travel agent parity with the airline that provided the system. It also increased their productivity.

Prior to automation the agent had to call the airline to book space and did not know if was available until the airline had confirmed it. This booking process could take hours and even days. Installation of an automated system gave American, United and the agents using their systems a competitive advantage. As other major airlines realized what was happening they began installing their reservations systems with travel agents. Each airline installed their system in the markets in which they had their greatest concentration of activity. If an airline dominated a city it was judicious for an agent to be in that airlines system since the majority of sales would be made on that airline. As a large sales outlet for the airline, the agent would get better service for special requests such as overbookings, upgrades and waitlist clearance. As a result, the airlines that had the largest market share in a city tended to dominate the automation in that city.

While the reservations system contained accurate information on the owner's flights it contained less accurate - or no information - on other airlines. This situation did not satisfy the other airlines or travel agents. The airline reservations system owners began expanding the collection of data from other airlines. They began charging booking fees to those suppliers who wanted to have their schedules shown. The process is known as co-hosting.

As their automation business grew, the airlines needed to provide servicing to the travel agents. They established organizations to meet their needs and branded them for recognition. These organizations were American's Sabre, United's Apollo (now known as Galileo International), Eastern's SystemOne (which is now part of Amadeus), US Air's PACER, TWA's PARS and Delta's DATAS. The latter two have combined into Worldspan.

Over the years, the systems added functionality and participants. The system provided the agent with centralized statistics and the ability to do their own back office accounting. The improved functionality allowed easier usage of the systems and better connectivity between the GDS and airline. This improved connectivity allows real time access too many airlines and improves the quality of the information. The number of participating suppliers, airlines, hotels and car rental agencies increased offering greater sales opportunities. This enhanced the travel agents usefulness and ability to sell air travel.

The booking fee schedule used by the airlines for co-hosting was arbitrary. New entrant airlines paid more than the established carriers did. This and other perceived problems led to complaints to the Civil Aeronautics Board. The Board established a series of rules that required booking fees be the same for all carriers using a system. They also prohibited much of the bias in the systems that favored their owners. These rules, established in 1984 and subsequent ones issued in 1992, eliminated most of the advantage the airline owners had in providing a system. As this advantage disappeared so did the reasons for an airline to own the system.

With the advent of airline deregulation beginning in 1978 airlines could change their fares and schedules frequently. There was an explosion of information that required automation. Automation by a GDS became the only way a travel agent could do business. The GDS systems gave travel agents the ability to become the purveyors of all the information available regarding airlines.

The GDSs and the travel agents became mutually dependent. Until the late 1990s, the two groups were almost totally dependent on each other. The GDSs by establishing consumer web sites such as Travelocity have moved into the broader Internet market. At this time there are four GDSs operating in the country. Sabre, established by American, is now a publicly owned company. Apollo, also known as Galileo International, was founded by United and is now owned by Cendant Corporation. Delta, Northwest and American own Worldspan. Air France, Lufthansa and Iberia effectively control Amadeus, which is headquartered in Spain. It is moving towards becoming a public company.

Travel agents sell approximately 70% of airline seats, which is down from over 80% a few years ago. GDS collect a fee of about $4.30 on average from the airline for each segment sold.These segment fees are the primary source of revenue for the GDSs.

Types of Travel Agents

Travel agents are differentiated by the type of market they cater to and by size.

— The largest agents in terms of volume focus on corporate travel. They cater to large organizations and assist them in a number of ways such as developing travel policies and supplier agreements; summarizing travel information by individual, department and in total; and providing other reports. They provide 24-hour service for travelers with problems. The largest of these companies have their own IT development and processing organizations that provide services that extend beyond what the GDSs offer.

— Medium size agents are often service a blend of corporate and personal business. Small agents tend to be leisure oriented. These agents occupy niches such as ethnic groups, tours, cruises, or focus on destinations that give them a value in the market place. Their specialty makes them more or less dependent on having the most accurate and up-to-date fares.

GDS Information Services

GDSs have contracts with both service providers, such as airlines, known as participating carrier agreements. They also have contracts with travel agents known as subscriber agreements. Since the adoption of the CRS Rules in 1984, the GDSs have been neutral repositories of information feed to them by suppliers on schedules, availability and fares. They rely on information exchanges with the airline reservations system for availability. They transmit the sales made by travel agents to the airline systems and keep a record of those sales so that each travel agent can access what he has done. A substantial part of their utility to the travel agent was the fact that they provided almost all the agent needed to service his customers in a single resource.

In order to provide current and consistent information procedures have been established which govern how airlines provide information to the GDSs.Airlines provide schedule information to the Official Airline Guide (OAG) and some airlines send directly to the GDSs. The GDS draw schedule information from the OAG several times a week. They provide published and negotiated fare information to the Airline Tariff Publishing Corporation (ATPCO). The GDSs download new information from them as often as five times a day. On a typical day there will be more than two million fare changes made. The GDSs contain more than four billion basic and constructed fares in their files.

Airlines send availability status messages (AVS) to the GDSs and partner airlines. The status message will indicate when a particular fare type is open or closed for sale.There are different methods and formats of communicating this information. The largest airlines use what is almost a real time exchange of information for the last several seats available. At the other extreme, an airline may only send a single message telling the GDS not to sell any more seats on an individual flight. GDSs retain that information and use it as the basis for not allowing any additional sales on that flight. Since most agents exclude a closed fare class when searching for an available seat this information has a significant impact on the fares displayed. Lack of synchronization in closed fare classes is one of the major reasons that different web sites and GDSs will have different availability for a fare type.

A few airlines, most notably Southwest, do not file their fare information with ATPCO. Southwest files their schedules only with Sabre and they are visible only to Sabre GDS users or at their own Web site. Other airlines file their fares with ATPCO but do not allow everyone to use them.

A key element of a participating carrier agreement between an airline and a GDS is the level of connectivity. The level of connectivity determines how the GDS and the airline reservations system communicate with each other. At the highest levels of connectivity, there is effectively real-time communication between the airline and the GDS. At the lowest level, an event, such as the closing of a fare class, will trigger a closing message communication to the GDS. The flight will be closed in the GDS even if it remains open in the airline system. The higher the level of connectivity there is between the systems, the greater the level of accuracy of the information. The greater the accuracy the more reliable are the reservations made. GDSs charge more for bookings made at the higher levels of connectivity.

Travel Agents Access to Webfares

Airline fares shown on the web come through different channels. Most of the fares shown will be the same as fares found by travel agents in the GDSs. However, airlines also sell fares directly at their web sites that they do not give to the GDSs. These fares are the most contentious since they are only available at the airline site or at Orbitz. There are also fares that airlines have provided to consolidators who market directly to consumers or through travel agents. The agents get these fares from web sites or by phone; these sites are often not available to the public.

Many types of suppliers offer airline information on the Internet. The major types, showing an example of a site, are:

— GDSs (Worldspan.com)

— Airline web sites (aa.com)

— Online travel agencies (Expedia.com)

— Search engines that examine web sites (Sidestep.com)

— Consolidators (airlineconsolidator.com)

— Travel agents with online capabilities (rainbowtvl.com)

— Bid based sites (Priceline.com)

— Portals (travel.yahoo.com/)

There are hundreds of web sites providing airline information. Only those recognized as providing a significant tool are discussed.

Website Characteristics

Each type of supplier has features that distinguish them and the way they operate. This section describes the characteristics that differentiate web sites. These characteristics will be discussed individually by web site. The characteristics are:

— Ownership-Airlines or other parties own the sites. Airline sites attract direct bookings thereby eliminating the need for the airlines to pay travel agency commissions, CRS fees and other expenses. Non-airline sites make money by taking a percentage of the transactions cost, advertising, service fees or markups taken on the products sold.

— Information requirements. All sites require the input of travel dates and origin and destination. Most will ask if price or schedule is the most important factor in your selection. Before making a reservation all sites require credit card information. Some sites allow the input of information on passenger preferences for seating and meals and a frequent flyer identification number. Some sites offer to check alternative dates and airports for lower fares.

— Method of operation -the search engines that are described below operate by screen scraping, through an application program interface (API) and in some cases through and electronic data interchange (EDI). In screen scraping the user receives a picture of what was 'on the screen' when it was visited by the search engine. With API and EDI you are working with structured data and if the target system changes their processing you have the option of accepting or requesting a change to your API to include the new data elements or you can continue your business activity with no disruption. If you are screen scraping and the target system makes a change, you have to make a change in your scraping program or your whole capture could be trash. The biggest advantage offered by an API over screen scraping is end user independence.

— Business model - the distribution of airline information on the Internet uses traditional and new business models. While most sites operate on conventional business, models there are a few who are unique such as Priceline. The models used typically involve brokerage services, advertising, and merchant or manufacturer models. Often there is a combination of models used in the generation of revenue.

— The functionality provided to the user - there are differences in the underlying applications and how that affects the collection of data and in terms of the ability provided to the user.

— Sources of information - most rely on airline web sites or GDS systems. There are variations such as including the use of consolidators.

— The level of transparency in the information provided to the customer about the supplier, departure time or fare rules prior to purchase.

GDSs communicate with travel agents through their own communications networks as well as through leased ones. The GDSs also allow agents to access to the Internet. The GDSs do not have the airline web fares or consolidator fares as part of their standard offering. They are in the process of assisting agents find lower fares on the web by developing their own software applications or by using third party software to do this.

Functions of Companies having Access to webfares

Amadeus: Amadeus is introducing the ability to display book fares not stored in the Amadeus Central System through corporate and agency channels. This will be done through the integration of third party web search tools within our corporate booking engine (e- Travel Aergo) and through our agency portal product (AgentNet). Such facility will be charged by Amadeus to the channel customer (agency or corporate).

Bookings will be performed within the airline web sites or online travel agents selected by the third party web search tool. In order to avoid any interference or confusion by end-users with Amadeus own booking, pricing and ticketing rules, such bookings will not be copied or mirrored within the Amadeus PNR (passenger name record - the generic record containing passenger itineraries) nor within the Amadeus Interface Record (AIR - used to transfer data to third party systems like agency back-office, corporate ERP).As a result, no booking fee will be charged to the airlines, and the agency will not receive booking credits (incentives)

Apollo/Galileo; Galileo is conducting tests to determine whether it should integrate one or more of the third party Internet software products into its GDS service for travel agents. They are currently in pilot tests with two such providers. The hardware will be the agents' current GDS hardware. These pilots will be evaluated for another 30-60 days. If modifications are found to be necessary they would be made and beta tested. Implementation would occur after that was finished. The training session for one of these software products is estimated to be a one and one-half hour training module on the web. Galileo has not finalized its policy regarding booking credits. Galileo has not finalized its policy regarding charges to agents using third party software.

Sabre: Sabre is currently testing a web application that they expect to have available in the third quarter of 2002. Sabre agents will be using a web based application and will input the origin and destination information, preferred date and time, class of service and the airlines to search in a Web based input screen (similar to any airline web site) to initiate a search. Training requirements will be minimal. The response (including both Sabre host and web fares) is formatted in HTML and displayed to the user in his/her browser. The presentation is handled by eVoya (Sabre's web based application) The web fares will be queried through a service (called an aggregator) that goes out and searches the airlines websites for information on the search parameters requested by the agent. The results will then be displayed along with the fares from the Sabre system in one page. The agency will not get credit for the booking made on the airline web site.

Sabre is planning to charge a fee for booking made on airline web sites, the amount of the charge is still being determined. On July 18 Sabre announced its new Corporate Connect pricing program for agents and corporations. Agents who choose this program will forgo booking fee incentives on the airline(s) they designate. The airline gets a 50% lower booking fee for bookings made through Sabre's GetThere tool by the corporations that agent serves.

Worldspan: Web fares are currently available through a proprietary product that allows an agent to view information from multiple web sites. They estimate that about 25% of available web fares can be found. Familiar entries are used to access this information. Web-based fares are returned along with an indication of their source. They are working with airlines to have them file fares with

ATPCO so that they can be incorporated into all responses.Standard entries will be used when this is available.

Existing hardware and communications are all that is necessary now or when fares are made available through ATPCO. Both current and future products are intuitive and do not require additional training. They currently access fares directly from the airlines' websites. If airlines file their fares with ATPCO Worldspan picks them up in the normal ATPCO downloads. Worldspan gives booking credits only when they receive a booking fee from the airline. There is no fee being paid now. Currently the service is free to the agents. Worldspan's policy is under review and they may charge in the future.

Airline Websites

All major airlines have their own web sites. All sites ask for the city-pair and dates of travel and class of service desired. Most sites allow one-way and open-jaw trips to be constructed. The airline sites allow the selection of classes of service and offer the same types of fares with the same rules offered by a travel agent using a GDS. They will also have their own special web fares that have not been filed with ATPCO for use in the GDSs. All sites require credit card information to complete a sale.

The cost of a web sale is lower than sales by their own reservations agents and travel agents using a GDS. The cost saving averages about \$10 as compared with a sale at an online agency and is a few dollars lower per sale than an internal reservations call center. All have the ability to display their inventory and fares and most offer the ability to redeem frequent flyer reward miles, get upgrades, seat selection, lounge entry and some offer automated check-in and wireless notification of changes in flight status. Their functionality is richer as it relates to their own operations than any other site. Several offer weekly specials by email to people who have subscribed online. Information provided -is very transparent, most show code share flights, and some show other airline schedules and fares as well as their own.

Online Travel Agencies

Online travel agents operate on the Internet without a brick-andmortar location. They aim towards the leisure traveler but this is changing.

Travelocity

— *Owner* -Sabre

— *Method of operation* - a robust site offering all types of travel arrangements, last minute deals, travel information. Passenger enters travel plans and Travelocity shows available options in time or price order based on passenger preference. Offer ways to find lower fares by using alternative airports and dates. Allows a reservation to be 'held' for 24 hours.Have special travel deals and 'last minute' deals. Allows ticketing through a Sabre travel agency.

— *Business model* -a buy/sell brokerage service. Uses merchant modeling, collects promotional fees, commissions from some suppliers and advertising. Negotiates for special fares that will be available only at its site.

— *Significant functional abilities* - will monitor specific routes a customer has listed and will advise of special fares offered. Has a good deal of destination and other supplementary information.

— *Sources of information* - Sabre GDS, other suppliers.

— *Information provided* -transparent except for items sold using the merchant model.

Expedia

— *Owner* - USA Networks

— *Method of operation* - Lots of features and information, similar to Travelocity, does not have the 'reservations hold' feature.

— *Business model* - a buy/sell fulfillment broker. Makes extensive use of merchant model, moving into corporate market, collects commissions and promotional advertising fees.

— *Significant functional abilities* - has capitalized on the merchant model by negotiating deals that allow air/car/hotel packages to be put together with significant cost savings for customers and large markups for Expedia.

— *Sources of information* - Worldspan is primary source, special deals signed with airlines and other suppliers.

— *Information provided* - transparent except for merchant packages.

— *Other information* - Expedia has become the largest of the online agencies. It has recently acquired a large commercially oriented travel agency in order to enter the corporate travel market.

Orbitz

— *Owner* - Owned by five airlinesit has 38 airline associates that participate and offer their web fares.

— *Method of operation* - they query airline Web sites and use Worldspan is used as a backup system. Orbitz has indicated they will move to direct connections with suppliers reducing or eliminating the need to have a GDS backup.

— *Business model* - brokerage using a marketplace exchange. Orbitz receives a booking fee from airlines and charges a $5 fee for making a reservation on their founding charter airlines and $10 on other airlines and for multi-legged flights. Some promotional advertising is an additional source of revenue.

— *Significant functional abilities* - They allow a user the option of selecting airports within 100 miles of origin and destination as a means of finding lower fares. The user can also request the system to look beyond the dates requested by using the "bonus days" option. This looks at days before and after the requested date to see if lower fares are available. Orbitz uses software from ITA Associates to find and display fare information which is the first item shown on their response screen. The passenger sees prices ranked from lowest to highest and the number of stops on the flights they refer too. The passenger then selects a non-stop, one-stop or multi-stop/connection services and may view a price and schedule options for each selection.

  Orbitz has also announced an Orbitz for Business that will search web sites. In addition to providing the airline web fares, the site will allow corporations with negotiated rates to access them as well. It also allows a third party to work as a "travel arranger."

— *Sources of information* - owner and associate airline reservations systems/web sites with a fall back to Worldspan for both availability and pricing. Orbitz has announced that they are looking to become the fifth CRS with a direct connection - which would bypass the older GDSs - to airline reservations systems as the basis for their information.

— *Information provided* -shows fares of all carriers except Southwest. Shows JetBlue fares but booking must be made with the airline.

— *Other items of interest* - Orbitz has announced that it has signed an agreement with AQUA Software Productsto offer direct booking access to Orbitz' Web-based search engine and inventory of low fares. The AQUA product, which has not yet been produced, will allow travel agents to link to Orbitz' database in order to conduct a search. The agent will be able to make the booking on Orbitz without being required to log on separately to the Orbitz site. Orbitz will consolidate the data with the GDS bookings. Many analysts consider the Orbitz method of displaying fares and schedules as the most effective and user friendly.

Search Engines

Sidestep

— *Owner* - privately owned

— *Method of operation* - passenger requests city pair, system searches airline web sites for schedules and fares. When passenger selects it delivers them to that Web site to make the booking. The site often offers bonus frequent flyer miles as an incentive for use.

— *Business model* - searches websites for price and availability. Delivers the requester to the site where they may directly book trips. Receives a fee for bookings made.

— *Significant functional abilities* -allows user to download their fare comparison system. Sidestep will then operate in tandem (on a separate screen panel) with the other system the user has chosen for a web-fare search. It will provide its responses shortly after the other system has finished. Requires that user be very liberal in what they will accept on their PC in the way of cookies and ActiveX applications.

— *Sources of information* -searches 130 airline and other supplier web sites.
— *Information provided* -transparent except from some consolidators

FareChase

— *Owner* - Privately owned
— *Business model* - Search agent and booking engine. Licenses its software to other portals such as Orbitz, Sabre and Outtask so users do not have to switch portals to conduct Internet searches. It also provides information to publications.
— *Significant functional abilities* - Licensees can integrate FareChase's software into their system to provide customers with the ability to book Web-based flights, hotels and car rental inventory while still allowing for full customer retention and support by integrating transaction data into existing GDS and back office systems.
— *Sources of information* - airline and other supplier web sites.
— *Information provided* - for requested city-pairs provides availability and fare displays, processes booking at web site. Can keep track of fares searched for future reference.

AgentWare

— *Owner* - AgentWare, Inc. is a privately held software company headed by Mr. Les Ottolenghi.
— *Method of operation* - Searches 29 web sites for price and availability. Links directly to the booking page of a web site when a customer is ready to book, and can link into the back office systems for billing or tracking purposes.

— *Business model* - Search agent and booking engine. Charges users a monthly license fee; it also gets a fee from some suppliers when a booking takes place. The company has agreements with ASTA and Galileo as a preferred provider.

— *Significant functional abilities* - a Web-based tool for travel agents that searches airline and consolidator Web sites in real time. Use of a consolidator Web site allows the travel agent to mark up the price before advising the consumer of the final price. In international markets this can be a significant advantage. Allows integration of data into some important back office systems. Creates a passive booking in the agents CRS for record keeping.

— *Sources of information* - web sites

— *Information provided* -what is available on Web sites that are selected

QIXO

— *Owner* - privately owned, founded by Daniel Ko.

— *Business model* -. Search agent and booking engine which makes the reservation. Charges consumer $5-25 for each reservation.

— *Significant functional abilities* -agents can access customer information about bookings made on QIXO, can establish their own service fees which are built into the record, can export PNR and billing info to some back office systems such as TRAMS.

— *Sources of information* - Web sites.

— *Information provided* - anything available on the site.

TRX

— *Owner* - privately owned

— *Business model* - Search agent and booking engine designed for use by travel agents. Yearly contract with a fee per hit.

— *Significant functional abilities* - automatically launches with low fare searches in a GDS, integrated with GDS, creates a passive booking in GDS for record keeping, integrated with their own back office system.

— *Sources of information* - currently searches ten airline and related web sites. Appears to use an API interface.

— *Other* - the site is still in beta testing, customers expected to come online in August 2002.

Consolidators

— *Owner* - privately owned businesses

— *Business model* - operate as brokers or merchants. Contract with airlines for seats at steeply discounted prices and resell with their own markup to agent or passenger. Agents can mark up to what the market will bear.

— *Significant functional abilities* -basic reservations capabilities

— *Sources of information* - has obtained inventory directly from a limited number of airlines. Some will supplement what they have with inventory from a GDS.

— *Information provided* - will often not provide airline name until booking has been made although they will hint at it.

— *Types of fares sold* -mostly discounted international economy class fares. Some airlines do offer first and business class as well.

Bid based Systems

Hotwire

— *Owner* - Hotwire is owned by six airlinesand the Texas Pacific Group
— *Method of operation* - passenger indicates days and citypair, willingness to take a "redeye" or multi-stop or connection. Hotwire then makes an offer without providing departure time or airline. The passenger has an hour to buy it. All purchases on Hotwire are final and cannot be changed for any reason. This site uses visible Web fares of the partners and affiliates and even lower fares that have been offered and are not shown elsewhere. The severe limitations put on the purchase of tickets make this site unreliable for most travel agents.
— *Business model* - An auction broker. They receive a fee for each booking; some promotional advertising is an additional source of revenue.
— *Significant functional abilities* - offers some of the lowest fares available.
— *Sources of information* - internal reservations systems; Worldspan for non-participating airlines.
— *Information provided* - an airline, departure time and final price.
— *Types of fares sold* - distressed merchandise. No refunds or exchanges. Airlines do not provide information until user makes reservation and pays for ticket.

Priceline

— *Owner* - privately owned
— *Method of operation* - Priceline is a 'submit a bid' site where prospective passengers submit a bid for a

round-trip reservation between a pair of cities, on specific dates, with the ability to indicate how many stops they are willing to make, how much they are willing to pay for a flight, exclusive of taxes and charges. If an airline accepts a bid, they charge the passenger's credit card and issue only non-refundable tickets. Neither the departure time nor airline is disclosed until after the purchase is finalized. Priceline either has inventory or routes its requests to the participating airlines who determine at what level they are willing to accept bids. As with Hotwire, this site is unreliable for most travel agents.

— *Business model* - A unique, patented, "name your price" brokerage system. They add a fee to bids that the customers make. Will keep any difference between prices it has obtained from a supplier and what buyers say they are willing to pay.
— *Sources of information* - airlines reservations systems.
— *Information provided* - after a sale, the airline provide flight number and price.

Travel agents with online capabilities

Often referred to as "click and brick" these sites are owned by retail travel agents who use them to extend the marketing of their business. They include sites from the largest agents like American Express to small local agents. These agencies are usually supported by their GDS and offer the same services as the GDS. Many of them are now specialist in destinations. They offer little or no advantage to other travel agents.

Portals

Portals serve as a point of entry to the web. They usually have a search engine, forums, instant messaging, email and shopping malls. They are among the most widely known and frequently visited sites on the web and include Yahoo, Lycos and AltaVista. Most portals have an agreement with a GDS or online agency to provide their booking services. The portals get a share of any fees collected for a booking but primarily make their money from advertising. They are not a basic source of low fare booking information.

Alternatives to GDS Systems

For travel agents, using web fares will not be as efficient as using their GDS. Problems will arise in a number of areas and the process will be more time consuming. If an agent decides to use a web fare, he or she has the ability to search each airline web site individually, which is not practical, or use one of the existing online travel agents or search engines. This will take more time than it would to process a normal CRS booking.

- When at the web site the agent must log on as if he were the passenger, entering name, credit card, frequent flyer and other information. This information is on file in the GDSs and is easy to for repetitive use in the GDS.
- One of the main concerns is keeping track of a passenger's record. The agent will not be working in his GDS but to keep track of a reservation made on a web site they may make a passive booking in their GDS for recording keeping purposes.o Selecting a web fare will require both training and more time to process.
- Changing a web fare when possible will be very time consuming.
- Keeping track of unused web fares will be difficult and subject to potential economic losses for the customer.

Almost all agents using a GDS have the ability to connect to the Internet using their existing terminals. The problems some will encounter relate to their communications connections and the capabilities of their computer terminals and screens. If their existing equipment cannot support an Internet connection, they will need to have a separate computer terminal that can. These terminals will have response time problems if they are not using a broadband modem.

Travel agents settle their accounts with the airlines through the Airline Reporting Corporation. They also need to keep track of their transactions for corporate clients. Most agents have a back office system, either provided by the GDS, or acquired separately by the agency. These systems record all the reservations made, and the associated charges made with them. Records that are not automatically integrated will need to be manually updated- a time consuming and expensive and potentially inaccurate process.

There are a number of strong economic forces in conflict with each other. It is unlikely that any of them will prevail in the near future. Customers, including business customers, are looking for less expensive travel arrangements. They know low airfares are available with conditions. Recent public statements by major agencies indicate that more than 40% of their clients are booking non-refundable fares. They will continue to put pressure on their agents to get the best deals. This will mean searching more intensively for low web fares.

Airlines are suffering severe economic losses. They will continue to seek ways to reduce their cost. Their CRS fees to cost them two or three hundreds of millions of dollars annually. They will continue to try to bypass the CRSs and travel agents to the extent they can since this is one of the few controllable cost areas.

GDSs will seek to provide the agents with total availability of low web fares. They need the travel agents to survive if they are to maintain their major source of revenue. They will develop ways they can allow agents to seek out web fares from within the present systems. They will apply covert and overt pressure on the airlines to provide their web fares through ATPCO that can be booked as any other fare is booked. The reasonable outcome would be to have the airlines offer their web fares at two levels: their site price and their marked up price, depending on the channel of distribution. This would allow them to avoid the costs of the GDSs and it will give them broader market exposure. Their marked up price could include other charges such as credit card fees. Their pricing structure should be made public so that it is understandable to all.

Bibliography

Mann, Mark for Tourism Concern, "The Good Alternative Travel Guide: Exciting Holidays for Responsible Travellers", Earthscan, London, 2002.

Mann, Mark, "The Community Tourism Guide: Exciting Holidays for Responsible Travellers", *Earthscan*, London, in association with Tourism Concern, 2000,

Mann, Mark with Ibrahim, Zainem, "The Good Alternative Travel Guide", *Earthscan*, London, for Tourism Concern, 2002.

Manning, T., "Indicators of tourism sustainability", *Tourism Management*, 1999.

McCarthy, John, "Are Sweet Dreams made of this *Tourism in Bali and East Indonesia*", IRIP, 1995.

Middleton, Victor T.C. & Hawkins, Rebecca, "Sustainable Tourism: a marketing perspective", Butterworth Heinemann, Oxford, 1998.

Neale, Greg, "The Green Travel Guide", *Second Edition*, Earthscan in association with The Sunday Telegraph, British Airways & WWF-UK, April, 1999.

Newson, Carey, "Tourism without traffic: a good practice guide", Transport 2000, London. Oversize G155, 2001.

Pendleton, Tom, "Young People and Bicycle Touring", Velo City '01 Conference, Edinburgh, Glasgow, September 2001.

Pizam, Abraham & Mansfield, Yoel, "Consumer Behavior in Travel and Tourism", The Haworth Hospitality Press, Binghampton, New York, 1999.

Prideaux, B., "The role of the transport system in destination development", (Elsevier) *Journal of Tourism Management* 21 (1), December, 1999.

Taylor, Gordon D, "Tourism and Sustainability - Impossible Dream or essential objective?", *Travel and Tourism Research Assocation*, Canada, 1991.

WTTC, World Tourism Organisation (WTO) & Earth Council, "Agenda 21 for the Travel and Tourism Industry: Towards environmentally sustainable tourism", *WTO*, Madrid, 1996.

INDEX